MARJORIE'S

VINE

A compilation of newspaper articles
Written by Columnist
Marjorie McGuire McConnell

Compiled/Edited by her daughter
Rosemary Reed

Cover by: Rosemary Reed & Morris Publishing
ISBN: 978-0-9820985-0-9
First Printing October 2008

Additional copies of this book are available by mail. Please see
the order form on the last page of this book.

Published by Rosemary Reed
roseyblooms@live.com

Printed in the U.S.A
by Morris Publishing
3212 East Highway 30
Kearney, NE 68847
800-650-7888

SPECIAL THANKS TO:

Community Newspaper Holdings, Inc. for the publishing rights to Marjorie's articles.

Becky Maxwell and Dan Ehl, the Centerville Daily Iowegian.

The wonderful Staff at the Drake Public Library, Centerville, Iowa and the use of the microfiche.

Morris Publishing Company, Kearney, NE.

Sara, for her reviews, proofreading and gentle critiques.

The family of Mary Robinson Klum for the use of her two poems.

Ron, for the jump-start; Kerri, for the "Lynch" book; and Darleen, for her optimism.

My sister Nancy, for her saved newspaper clippings.

And my daughter, Marsena, for her expertise and advice.

CONTENTS

INTRODUCTION

Marjorie McGuire McConnell was Society Editor and later a newspaper columnist for a small town newspaper, the Centerville Daily Iowegian, Centerville, Iowa (population around 7,000). Marjorie was born in 1917 in Kansas City, Kansas, one of two daughters of David and Pearl McGuire. When Marjorie was quite young her father passed away unexpectedly. She, her little sister and mother moved to Centerville, Iowa, to live with her grandparents.

In 1936, at the age of 19 she was hired by the Iowegian as the Society Editor, attending several social events, and writing the daily "Society & Clubs." Four years later she married and put her career aside to care for her husband and five children. The Iowegian contacted her in 1967 to work in the composition room as a proofreader and to write feature stories. Later she had her own column "Talk, Travel & Tidbits" and worked from home.

They say you know a writer by their writings. Mom was well known in the community as happy, quick witted, very loving in her expressions and a wonderful Mother. Her personality was neither pompous nor comedic but rather gentle and genteel. Sometimes, like most humorous writers, she was inclined to add a little spice to her writings but didn't make up stories that didn't actually happen.

This is a compilation of some of her articles, feature stories and tidbits - all were published in the Centerville Iowegian.

The first chapter briefly touches on the late 1930's. The remaining chapters cover a 14 year period from 1967 through 1981 which she wrote primarily during her 50's.

In compiling, condensing and editing her articles, no attempt was made to re-write or to improve upon them. Her writing style, along with some old English usage and her use of single quotes, etc., have been left intact.

The articles have been categorized according to subject matter and are not in chronological order. A very few of her articles from different years were paired together into one article. Rarely was a word changed and then only to clarify.

This book is a tribute to her works and is dedicated to her grandchildren and their children that they might know her.

Rosemary Reed, Compiler/Editor

MARGES' VINE

In the last days of August,
As school begins
There's a vine on my porch that blooms again.
Its' tender green foliage, a joy to behold,
The last blooms of summer before the winters' cold.

The fast growing tendrils intertwine
Like loving hands reaching out to all mankind.
It blooms so profusely and grows so fast
You wish its beauty would always last.
The bees swarm over the blooms of the flower
Savoring the nectar of the lacey white flowers.

Marge used to say you could tell the times
Of the seasons by this blooming vine.
There's a botanical name I don't recall
But every year in the early fall
I enjoy this awesome beauty of the late summertime
And in memory of a friend of mine
I re-name it, Marges' Vine.

by Mary Robinson Klum 1981
(*Poem to the Iowegian*)

Chapter 1

MISS MARJORIE MCGUIRE, SOCIETY EDITOR

In the late 1930's when I first worked for the Iowegian the late publisher, John R. Needham and J.M. Beck were super strong on having a local news column (and a daily one at that). I recall that it was part of my job to circle the town square business houses every day and gather items about who went where. Any less than 20 such items per day appearing in the newspaper would call down the wrath of John Needham. So I pounded the pavement until I got 'em.

Marjorie's Writing Style - 1937

Jill Edwards Captured Imagination of Audience Here as She Addressed H.S. Students and Women's Club.

To see some eight hundred wriggling parcels of humanity suddenly subside into an absorbed audience is a rather amazing transformation. That they should continue for an hour to be absorbed in a talk on Personality is a testimonial for the speaker and for the intelligence of the youth of today.

The moment Jill Edwards walked onto the platform yesterday, clad in a chic black velvet gown, she captured the imagination of her audience. She was charming in person, voice, and manner.

With a slight gesture of head, hand or shoulder, she occasionally conserved her words and drove home her thought.

Jill knows the language of modern youth and she clothes her excellent advice in an attractive garb. The body, she said, is personality's best tool. Take care of it, make it a magnet. Cultivate a pleasant voice – it will form a bridge across which a friend may reach you. An athlete learns that training is a day-by-day job. So is developing a personality. The story of the Great Stone Face by Nathaniel Hawthorne sought to teach what pursuing an idea may mean to body and character. Determine to have a constant turnover in new ideas. Make each hour in the day, each person you meet, count in developing your personality. Cultivate the acquaintance of older people; draw from your teachers all the inspiration they can give you. Know something, it gives you power. Know more about some subject than anyone else in your room. A girl of 13 knew about birds, read, observed – became an authority on the subject. She was no longer just a girl … she stood out from the crowd.

Among your habits cultivate the Light Touch. Bring into your contacts any gift for mimicry, anecdotes or other talent. It assures you a welcome. Cultivate gracious ways with others. Respect their rights. Steam-roller methods may get by sometimes but they develop animosities and come back at you. Create an ever-widening circle of influence. Learn to control your emotions.

It was a rare tribute to Jill's skill that she could recite "Millay's Lament" to an all but breathless audience. Look for beauty and appreciate it every day. Learn to take what life brings you "on the chin". Religion plays a vital part in your personality. There is a deep human need for a greater power without. Scientists are reverent men. Jill believes one can cultivate a contact with the Creative Force – call it God or by some other name – and find there a source of strength in any emergency.

Following the prolonged applause at the close of her talk, Jill returned to the stage, thanked her audience for paying such close attention and recited a story in Chinese.

It seems a pity that every thinking man and woman in the community could not hear this remarkable address.

Millay's Lament

LISTEN, children:
Your father is dead.
From his old coats
I'll make you little jackets;
I'll make you little trousers
From his old pants.
There'll be in his pockets
Things he used to put there,
Keys and pennies
Covered with tobacco;

13

Dan shall have the pennies
To save in his bank;
Anne shall have the keys
To make a pretty noise with.
Life must go on,
And the dead be forgotten;
Life must go on,
Though good men die;
Anne, eat your breakfast;
Dan, take your medicine;
Life must go on;
I forget just why.
By Edna St. Vincent Millay (1892-1950)

1938, Wienies on Wednesday

Before an enthusiastic audience which completely filled the auditorium of the Central school and left but little standing room, the Drama department of the Centerville Women's Club presented an excellent and enjoyable program Wednesday evening. The central feature of the evening's entertainment was a clever one-act play entitled "Wienies on Wednesday," which proved to be one of the best of its kind.

Miss Oda Hall, English teacher at the local high school, added just the right touch to the program by giving an interesting and fitting paper on the one-act play. She brought out that a dramatization in one act must appeal almost entirely to the emotions, making the choosing of a cast most important. "As there is no fixed length for one act plays" Mrs. Hall told the group, "those attending the play must be given a definite idea of the plot from the very beginning." The speaker also pointed out that a single well sustained theme is necessary, and most important, every work or joke uttered by each character must have gotten over to the audience.

Just as naturally as though they were true members of an everyday Centerville family in the throes of economizing, the cast of "Wienies on Wednesday" proceeded without a noticeable hitch through to the end of the presentation, drawing many laughs from the audience.

Dealing with a family of four in the midst of uncertainty, a noted opera singer for breakfast, lively action and humorous dialogue predominated through to the end. What with the daughter of the house in constant worry and fear that everything, including the rest of the family, will not please their distinguished visitor, the play rides to the point where, to the distraction of all but the carefree son, it is learned that common wienies are to be served for breakfast, simply because, according to the mother, their purchase price is lower than that of eggs and because it is Wednesday. The head of the house, who is pointedly bored with the whole affair, proceeds to have a hectic morning until time to catch the 8:20.

The arrival of the operatic star upon the scene, which by the way is a kitchen in white, changes the theme as she is found to be less than ordinary in her tastes. The comedy skit comes to a laughable close as the singer informs the wide-eyed family that one of her tastes is … "Wienies on Wednesday."

1938, Star Hall Tonight

Every one of the two hundred fifty persons who attended the "Star Hall Tonight" entertainment Monday evening in Centerville left the Masonic Temple bearing an honest to goodness 'ear-to-ear' smile. There was good reason for the happy countenances and excited approving comments as the curtain closed on the program of fun. And this reason was that the Masonic and Order of Eastern Star bodies last night offered to local people one of the most hilarious and definitely successful programs ever given in this city.

Mrs. B. F. Tade provided a musical interlude as she sang two current and lovely melodies "Once in a While" and "One Rose" playing her own accompaniment. Mrs. Tade has a really beautiful voice and rendered her numbers in a charming manner.

Anyone who could sit through the next part of the program without holding his sides, either wasn't capable of laughing or was unconscious. Claude Eggert unfolded the strange tale of the Magic Pill. He brought out, in due seriousness, the fact that one of his famous magic pills could completely change a life. And after the first few minutes of his experiments on human patients, not a soul in the large audience doubted that this indeed was a scientific wonder. For before their eyes black cats changed into white cats, an old maid into a year old babe, a homely girl became a modern flapper, and even a hot dog ring became the tiniest puppy.

Something in the way of old fashioned "mellerdrammers" was announced as the next part of the varied program. "Belle and Bill," or the "Reward of Virtue," was an exact replica of the

16

silent performances of days gone by, and brought down the house with its fast moving plot ... which was, incidentally, as perhaps you have guessed, the tale of the pretty blonde belle, her honest boy friend, the villain, a mortgage, and of course the luring vamp. Each character in this melodrama was well suited to his or her individual role and the talent represented furnished many laughs.

"Harbor Lights" and "I Double Dare You" were sung by a trio of young ladies.

Probably the funniest and most enjoyable part of the evening was the climax of "Star Hall Tonight" in the form of a rollicking baby show. Opening with a soothing lullaby, the curtain swung back revealing eight of the most lovable men (pardon us, we meant babies) in dainty pin, blue and white gowns, and wearing the latest thing in baby bonnets, one, we might mention revealing a shiny bald head. In case you are still in doubt, we will explain that the eight babies with rattles, balloons, etc, were none other than the same number of Masons. Watching their precious offspring were the proud mothers. To say that what followed when the judge of the contest appeared on the scene was a scream, would be putting it mildly. After the prize was awarded, a climax worth the whole show was in order when the "fathers of the children" and two policemen ended the show.

1940 Wedding Bells

Sunday morning, December 29th at 8 o'clock at the Methodist parsonage, Miss Marjorie McGuire, daughter of Mrs. Pearl McGuire of Centerville became the bride of Mr. Lowell

McConnell, son of Mr. and Mrs. Ira McConnell of Centerville.

The ceremony was read in the presence of the immediate families.

The bride was lovely, gowned in a vagabond blue dress with which she wore black accessories. Her shoulder corsage was of Talisman roses and baby's breath. Miss Wauneita McConnell, sister of the bridegroom, was the bride's attendant. She wore a dusty rose dress with a shoulder corsage of tea roses and baby's breath.

The bride is a graduate of Centerville high school with the class of 1935 and for the last four years has been an employee at the Centerville Daily Iowegian, being the former society editor.

The bridegroom is also a graduate of the Centerville high school with the class of '34. For the past six years he has been employed by Gamble Stores. He was recently transferred to the Gamble store in Lawrence, Kansas, where the young couple will make their home. *Society, Centerville Iowegian*

Looking Back

The Iowegian Printing Company building on North Main is a busy place. It takes a staff of 28 people, each doing his or her particular job, to turn out a credible finished product like your daily newspaper.

And a newspaper plant is also a noisy place. Three open telephone lines ring almost constantly, typewriters click steadily in the newsroom, a copying machine plunks out advertising proofs in the ad room, and in the composition room skilled typists and ad setters handle an array of machinery eight hours a day.

The circulation department has an addressograph machine that plunks out addresses on metal plates and mail pouch racks that clank. And you should hear the big press rolling out thousands of newspapers and the mingling of the carriers when they come to get their newspapers for the routes.

But there is one part of the office that is strangely and forlornly silent. That's the upstairs back room. Once the center and hub of the newspaper in years gone by, that back room sort of reminds you of a ghost town. Only sound now is the occasional flapping of a window shade.

Four linotypes once shuttled upstairs, but now they are silent - ever since the plant went to offset several years ago. They were old and outmoded and their usefulness was over. So were the typesetter jobs.

One linotype (17-tons) is being dismantled and its parts will be sold. That was Oscar Hobart's machine which he operated for many loyal years. The other three will be taken apart and before the year is over the last vestige of the upstairs newspapers vital organs will be gone.

But not the memories. Oscar was the longest employee of the Iowegian. As a typesetter, in his heyday, he was unequalled for the number of words he set over the years. Oscar was also the main fixer-upper of all the linotypes, and as he always said, "When you've got machinery, you've got problems."

Oscar paid the Iowegian a visit, and when he saw that "his" machine had been stripped down to the floor, he shook his head.

19

"A million memories come back," he said, "Newspaper work was my business. There was never a dull day."

His son, James, worked as a typesetter alongside him back in the late 30's. James had one crippled hand, but set type with a flourish anyway. On the third machine at that time was a bouncy lady named Lydia Butz. Lydia never had much to say, but when she said something it paid you to listen. If she complained about the copy you were sending back, you felt obligated to meet her specifications the next day. She got along with the other typesetters because she tended to business ... mostly her own.

Now on the fourth machine was Lizzie Malaney, a pleasingly plump lady who put a green eyeshade visor over her black hair before starting up her linotype.

Everybody liked Lizzie and she was staunchly proud of her boys, Paul and Tom, and her family. She was said to be the fastest of the four typesetters as far as galleys of lead slugs went. Lizzie was a staunch Democrat, but she rarely turned a conversation to politics in the office full of Republicans. It didn't pay anyone else to either, since Lizzie never wavered nor backed away from a good political argument. She and Claude Breese, pressman (just as staunch a Republican), used to keep the back room lively with their "issues" but everybody knew that Lizzie had the advantage – she kept her back to her opponent and kept right on setting type, shouting above the clatter of metal.

Another outstanding linotype operator was Glacyl Harvey. Glacyl was an expert grammarian and speller. She also had great respect for her linotype machine. She always called it "Sir" ... well, almost always unless it spit out hot metal on her or kept the line slugs from dropping correctly into pan. Then she would get up, kick the side of the iron monster and yell: "Now you so-and-so (Sir), straighten up or I'll throw you out (Sir)." Monster and Glacyl must have had pretty good rapport, because he usually tended to business after a sharp kick in the side and a few choice words.

There were others who were dedicated and colorful employees and kept the presses rolling, but none were more colorful than John R. Needham, co-owner of the Iowegian back in those days. John R. never met a stranger. He was as flamboyant as the huge diamond ring he wore on his finger, but he had a hearty way about him and you could depend on his word.

I always liked J.M. Beck, editor and publisher, probably because he hired me in 1936 when I was 19 and it was my first steady job. He was mostly all business and his writings were equally serious. Mr. Beck was a good man and a fair man. Some employees found him unapproachable, perhaps, but I found him to be surprisingly understanding and helpful to a novice writer. In the days when hobos wandered through town, some would come up to the editor's office and ask for a handout. He never turned one away, yet he never gave them money either. Instead Mr. Beck would send the hobo over to Lute Dawkins' hamburger shop across the street with a note saying "feed this man two hamburgers and a cup of coffee." Lute put it down on his tab.

Another person, one who didn't work at the Iowegian but who came up to the office every now and then was Mrs. Edna Beck.

She was as welcome as the flowers in May. Her good spirits were infectious and soon everyone was sharing her laughter. She never missed a person, going into the back room and asking each person about his family, giving each a smile showing genuine interest. Certainly she could have interviewed and written "people stories" as well as anyone had she wanted to.

The years pass, and working staffs change. New offset equipment and new people are on the staff. It's the people who have newspaper ink in their blood that make it so and the carry-on tradition. A good newspaper is no better than the people who put it together.   *February 1977*

Chapter 2

UNNAMED COLUMN

"Watch for the Iowegian's new feature column beginning in our Wednesday, April 12th issue" wrote the news editor in last Friday's paper. "It will be full of local news for and about Centerville people" he continued optimistically.

Well, today is the day you were alerted to watch for, Wednesday, April 12th. We're sorry you had to go completely through the pages four times with a magnifying glass before you found anything that faintly resembled a news column. But that's no fault of yours.

The kindest thing to say so far is that we're off to a slow start. Actually, we're hardly off to any start at all. For an opener, the column doesn't even have a head over it that is eye-catching, brilliant, intriguing or witty. A column without a head. That's bad!

But it gets worse. My telephone hasn't rung once. Not one sweet soul called in any news. When I realized finally that things weren't going so well with the news gathering, and that the deadline was galloping along, I began calling people I knew who were always on the go. They were all home, for once, and furthermore not a one had any intention of leaving town this week.

I tried to talk a few of them into going to Florida for the moon blast-off or to Hot Springs to take some thermal baths so I could have the news, but they would rather stay home and clean house. And neighbor Betty Vandike, good friend that she has always been, adamantly refused to leave town even if it meant a special favor to me.

The deadline day dawned, I arose earlier than usual to bake a pie, put a stew on to simmer and whip the laundry through the fast cycle, all this before 8 a.m. so I would not be tied down with trivial family stuff when all the news calls started coming in. They didn't.

The only thing left to do was call Mary and Joyce who always have company over the weekends. Their homes are Grand Central Stations for visiting relatives, but no, they had spent a blessed quiet weekend (for once) and enjoyed hiding and relaxing. And no - they weren't looking for company next weekend either and would hold me personally responsible if any showed up.

It's a horrible feeling to have a new news column that is supposed to mirror what the readers have been asking for and not have much to put in it. It's a little like going to our Lake Rathbun with no fishing pole, no sunglasses, no lounging chair, no picnic basket and no boat. You get a sinking feeling.

So I'm asking you Centerville people (no, I'm begging) to call in some news items any weekday morning Monday through

Saturday or bring them by the home. You can even send them on a postcard or by carrier pigeon. Many of you have been requesting just such a spot for hometown news, so this is your chance to have your own column just like the other towns do.

If you'd like to try your hand at naming the column head, we'll consider any suggestions except "What A Mess".

April 1972

&&&

Centerville is a great town. There's a lot of heart here. After my frantic and I hoped heartrending appeal for local news last Wednesday, the phone started ringing and I almost needed a stand in just to leave the room. Not only did the callers have items I could use, but sixteen persons came up with super suggestions for the "Unnamed" column head. Still others called just to encourage me to "hang in there".

Anyway, the response was so great that the column might not hold all its good fortune this week. The typewriter runneth over. There was everything from poetry to a human interest tale of an old gray goose who thinks it owns a home and yard. Think I won't make a story out of that one?

It was difficult to choose a permanent head for this column. We finally decided on *(Centerville's)* Avis Kimberlin's "Talk, Travel, Tidbits" just because it seemed to hit the spot. We also liked "You, Me, and Somebody Else," "Timely Thoughts and Things," "Marge's Meanderings," and "Moments with Marge." We thank everyone for putting on their thinking caps. I did not give a hoot, however, for "Gossip, Corn and Bull" a smirky

25

smarty suggestion which came from my own family.

&&&

I like the name Iowegian. It's a distinctive masthead for our south-central hometown newspaper. Sort of fits the area it serves. I prefer Iowegian to Gazette, Courier, Post, Chronicle, Register or Times.

&&&

Half the reward of writing a newspaper column is getting more letters in your mailbox. Some of them are from people you don't even know but feel that you do after you read them. With so many interesting people in Iowegian territory I know you could pick, at random, almost any one of them and come up with a good story. Most of us have never done anything spectacular or earthshaking, but that doesn't mean that we haven't contributed something to our towns.

&&&

Ethel Lira, one of the busiest (and nicest) people I know, still takes time to write notes of encouragement to others. She has raised my spirits many times. Ethel's not only busy at her job but writes about Numa people for the Iowegian. Hers is not just a somebody-ate-dinner at somebody's house column, she really writes the news.

J.M. Beck used to call such stringer village columns the "bread and butter" of a newspaper. "People like to read hometown news," he'd say. However, I well remember one lady correspondent years ago who had to be told by the boss not to make her columns so "newsy". That certain ambitious correspondent was apt to write about whose dogs killed whose chickens; whose wife locked whose husband out of the house one Saturday night; whose black eye wasn't from walking into a door.

Needless to say, those small town items certainly had high readership. *March 1981*

&&&

My grandma always said that there is a bright spot in every day and mine came last Friday when the florist from the Flower Center brought a beautiful basket of yellow and white feather-fringed mums. It was an anniversary gift from that loyal group of Iowegian composition room friends.

I probably will never forget the first day I came to work in the composition department. Since I had worked only in the news department in my previous stints with the Iowegian, how the newspaper was "put together" was all new to me.

I reported that first day for work, punched the time clock and suddenly realized that I was old enough to be everybody's mother.

Since Publisher Robert Beck had hired me to be part-time proofreader, the young composition people had no choice except to let me in.

Nobody said much, but I could tell that the crew was thinking: 1) She won't fit in with us. 2) There goes our fun. 3) She won't like our music. 4) She's old enough to be our mother.

27

The boss didn't help much when he came in one day and asked openly, "Well, Marge how are you managing in here with this motley composition crew?"

He should have asked THEM how they were putting up with me!!

Weeks went by and we began to know each other. I hoped I was "fitting in" and being accepted. When six people and six huge electronic machines take up all the space in a small room, you are either compatible ... or else.

I always liked newspaper work and I liked proofreading. I noted that the other five employees knew their jobs and showed expertise in getting them done against a strict time schedule and amidst fun and good humor. Stuffing-insert time wasn't dull because we had word games. For an example one time we took turns naming songs with colors in the titles, like "Yellow Rose of Texas". See what I mean?

I guess it was when the young folks decided that I respected them as individuals and didn't run to the boss with every little annoyance that the rapport began. So my thanks to my fellow workers for caring and making me feel welcome.

&&&

Marjorie McConnell or McConville, that is the question.

People who call me (some of them) say "Is this Mrs. McConville?" I say, "McConnell". That's who they meant.

Other callers ask for Marjorie McConville (she's a great person) and I don't know what to say. They usually mean me, but I can't take a chance on that.

Not often, but once in awhile, the phone rings in the night and someone who sounds very ill asks for Dr. McConville. (I'm pleased to say that I don't become upset when this happens.)

But I'll bet on one thing, I don't get nearly as many wrong calls as do the McConville families. The other morning a lady called and said she had called three McConvilles' before she got me to give me a news item.

Anyway, if my name has to be mixed up with someone's, I'm glad it's McConville. They're all nice people!!

Signed, Marjorie McConnell.

Chapter 3

MARJORIE'S SCHOOL DAZE

Old Lincoln School Days

When the Lincoln School bell rang this August morning, little boys and girls excitedly skipped down the street. I watched, as I always do, and remembered how it was when we North Ward children attended Lincoln school back in the 1920's.

Lincoln is still Lincoln, standing on the same spot of ground, its red brick form looking not much older than it ever did. Once you've gone to Lincoln school, you never quite forget the sounds of it, the feel of it, nor the blackboard scent of it.

For Lincoln school was always a proud building. Its bell tower seemed to reach up into the sky and the south playground sloped down to a running creek and on up a hill on the other side. No other school had scenery like this; no other had its own place to bring sleds in the winter.

The rushing stream had its own uses for the big kids who wanted to get rid of the lower grade 'pests' who always ran to get the ball during a baseball game and wouldn't throw it back fast enough. They were told that there were snakes (genuine poisonous water moccasins) down by the water. It worked almost every time and the little kids went to the swings and slides on the north side of the building where they belonged in the first place.

There were no elementary school buses and everybody went home for dinner. There was plenty of time – more than an hour and school kept until 4 p.m.

Miss Spooner was principal and you knew what "principal" meant as her tall, impressive figure stood at the top of the cement steps regimenting all of us into two straight lines to enter the building after the last bell rang. Until we quieted down we couldn't go in to classes even if it was 10 below zero.

Habitual offenders at Lincoln were sent to the bell room where they usually sweat it out looking at the big paddle hanging on the wall. (Many wished there was some way to slide down the inch-wide rope that clanged the bell.)

There was a paddle in every room in those days and teachers were not only allowed to use it – they knew how. The only consolation about being at Lincoln was that you might have been at Central school instead and everybody knew that Miss Carrie Treon was principal there and she had a fierce reputation for getting things her way.

The first grade teacher back then was Miss Madge Severs – a real pro! Hers was a soft voiced approach to learning, but she was rated as the best teacher of reading in the business. Although we were only five when we were ushered into first grade (no kindergarten), we learned to read and spell and we were taught the rudiments of phonics. I recall we had a few unusual teachers at Lincoln, too.

Fourth grade instructor, Miss Martin, was a great believer in using example and illustrations to prove a point she had made in a lesson. One day, while studying 'heat and cold' she told us that both elements felt the same to the touch and she could prove it. She blindfolded a student and told him she would either touch him with a chip of ice or a match that had been lighted and blown out. She used the ice of course but he yelped and shrieked that he had been burned practically to death.

At one time there were iron rails alongside the sidewalk entrances used to scrape mud off shoes and galoshes. They were more dangerous than the cinders under playground equipment. The acrobats used them as turning bars and many a head was skinned. One schoolmate actually lost the membrane coating on his tongue and lips when he put his mouth on the iron in sub-zero temperatures.

Yes, memories of all kinds seemed to re-appear as school bells ring in the fall. It's nice to see the little kindergarten boys in permanent pressed slacks and bright shirts and the tiny girls in fashion plate dresses. We were clean too, of course, but our dresses were cheap and we wore cotton stockings. Most of us had a new pair of shoes (after going barefoot all summer) and they had to last all school year else when the soles wore out, they were replaced by new innersoles cut out of a cracker box.

So, down through the years, Lincoln school has been a staunch house of learning. Many an illustrious citizen of our town passed through its doors and a few who have held national prestige.

It was built in 1884, I believe, and will be torn down someday. The old creek bed will be bulldozed in, perhaps. May it be replaced by an edifice of education just as sturdy.

October 1969

P.T.A Record Book of 1920

I was once a skinny, chirpy little blue bird with flapping crepe paper wings and a long yellow beak; Lloyd Finks was once a rather shy little boy who gave a humorous reading entitled "After School," Kathleen Craig (Washburn) once sat primly on a piano stool which was almost as tall as she was and urged her nervous fingers across the keyboard.

Ah yes, these program numbers once took place in the upstairs room of Lincoln School before a group of beaming P.T.A. mothers. These gems and many more were gleaned from an old Lincoln School record book loaned to me.

This yellowed but very legible book was started in 1920, the year the Parent-Teachers Association was formed at Lincoln.

From 1920 on, the teachers and parents, especially the mothers, pulled together in the interest of the children. Their main objectives were: (1) good education, (2) good health and (3) good morals. They didn't have much money to work with in those days, but somehow there were always good books on the shelves, an adequate recreational program and enough chalk, erasers, and ink for the ink wells in each desk. There was always enough coal to fire up the huge furnace when the weather got cold. It was an occasion, though, when a new softball or bat could be purchased. We learned to take care of the ones we had and to bind an old ball up with string if we had to. The minutes of one meeting in the early 1920's listed the frugal expenditure of $2.05 for a quantity of 50 small plates to use in serving refreshments. Speaking of refreshments, in one place it stated that mothers who didn't furnish sandwiches could leave a nickel or a dime to cover the cost of coffee and cream. It's a wonder they had any refreshments to go with their coffee!

Many of the school's little extra goodies were bought by the P.T.A. To finance the purchase of extra equipment or slide projector, they had popcorn and candy sales. But the biggest money-maker of the day was the paper sale. Remember those? Each room tried to win the contest (I don't remember what the reward was) and neat bundles of papers and magazines were stacked in the halls and around the rooms for a number of weeks. Competition grew so fierce that every Iowegian was spoken for in advance and every Saturday Evening Post was grabbed out from under father's nose. Many a catalogue was spirited out of wherever it was because catalogues 'weighed in good.' If memory serves correctly, we strived for a ton of paper and Gavronsky and Son paid top price for a carload.

According to the record book, it was the program every six weeks that drew out the mothers to P.T.A. One of them went something like this: "Topic – Child Problems: Cheerfulness, Obedience at Home, and Obedience at School, Indolence at Home, and Indolence at School."

Sometimes the Superintendent spoke and the school nurse gave current health reports including how to take care of a child's cold. Violin playing seemed to predominate and it was written that violin solos were offered. Many a piano student got up before the group.

It was in the year 1925, during the annual Spring Festival as it was called, that my little stint as a blue bird marked my stage debut. It was a heady role, but I was the most jittery blue bird that ever heralded in the spring at Lincoln School, tra la. The day was saved, however, by excellent performances around the Maypole and outdoor pantomimes in crepe paper costumes.

A favorite teacher taught second grade at Lincoln. She was Eva Khyler (White) who lived near the school. In Miss Khyler was the embodiment of all the talents a teacher should have. She was firm, yet wasn't afraid to 'lose face' by laughing out loud at a funny situation. Many a coin went out of her own meager salary for a pair of warm mittens for a needy child. She could hold a wiggly class's interest longer than any other teacher I have ever known.

We can't help but wonder if that old painting "Sir Gallahad" is still around some place. It was the picture that was hung in the classroom with the highest percentage of mothers present at P.T.A. each six weeks.

Like Bob Hope always says "Thanks for the Memories!"

&&&

Valentines Day brings back memories of my Lincoln elementary school days when each room outdid itself to come up with the most elaborate Valentine box in the school.

Those were the days when most valentines were homemade, colored with crayons and trimmed with paper lace doilies. Those were also the days when sweet verses and violets bespoke childish sentiments ... and comic valentines were also on the market. One year everyone in the class was the recipient of an 8 by 10 poster.

Mine had the caricature of a skinny, bowlegged girl with mousy brown hair and freckles. "Who would want THIS for a Valentine?" the verse asked.

We never did find out for sure who sent the "comic" valentines since everyone in the class got one, but we had our suspicions all right! She was the only girl in the class who could have afforded the cash outlay in those days of the depression. She later moved out of state and I've never seen her since. And don't ask me who.

&&&

One of my jobs on Monday washday when I was small was to shred the P&G soap to put in the copper boiler. I really didn't mind that job and like the clean smell of P&G.

However, when the teacher assigned us to carve (sculpture) a dog or something out of a bar of soap that was a different story. A monkey could do a better work of art with a bar of soap than I ever could. All I ended up producing was a pile of soap chips for the next washday. I was the bane of my art teacher's existence. Being artistic is not my forte.

&&&

St. Patrick's Day was always a lot of fun at school. Most of us got into the act and either wore something green or pinned on a big felt shamrock. It wasn't hard for me to get into the spirit of St. Patrick's Day with a name like McGuire, but the real fun came when our Jewish friend wore a sleeveless emerald green sweater over his shirt and our black schoolmate showed up in the widest, greenest tie you ever saw flapping on his overalls. The Croatian kids rarely let us Irish down either.

3 years after the *Lincoln School Days* article ...

I walked over to Lincoln school yard the other day. I knew that my first school house was being torn down and that there would be sentimental lumps in my throat if I watched the workmen methodically take its bell tower off. Yet I had to take a last look at the 1884 building before it became a meaningless collage of rubble.

Then I remembered what my grandmother always said when something unavoidable happened. "Don't cry over spilled milk. You might as well laugh as cry." she'd say. And I guess she would say not to cry over knocked down buildings either. As I stood there I transported my mind back to my first five years of school and that was some transport job – backwards to the 1920's. I tried to remember the happy times we had. I pictured myself again as a shy, freckled, thin, insecure 5-year-old in Miss Severs first grade room. (Yes, I have since outgrown the thinners and a few other things.)

I remember: singing the Cobbler's Song ... some of my classmates ... my first love affair with Claudie Climie because he smiled a lot and was nice to me ... Maypole dances, Christmas programs, walking back and forth four times a day from home to school ... overalls, cotton dresses, crocheted mittens, long wrinkled black and tan cotton socks ... the old interurban trolley shuttling noisily out of the nearby roundhouse and blasting its whistle every block ... the tiny rivulet stream at the bottom of the softball incline ... marble playing and rope jumping ... the bell room discipline ... hiding treasures and notes in old tree hollows ... my first taste of bribery and fear when an older raw-boned girl threatened to "tell teacher" (because I came down the steps too fast) and I preferred to get her a candy bar pay-off ... the beauty and reliability of first school friendships ... the lingering sweetness of a Valentine card from my wonderful second grade teacher, the late Eva Khyler White.

But better than all this, I have the pride in knowing that Lincoln teachers stuck with me until I learned to read and understand what education is all about. They had a job on their hands. The thousands of us who went through Lincoln's doors now know how other folks felt when their schools were torn down.

But as with most things, something good will come of it. Something like new schools, new teachers, advanced courses of study, more creative thinking and, of course, many more fond memories.   *May 1972*

Puppy Love Crushed

Every once in a while you get to feeling pretty good about yourself and your self-esteem runs high. You know what I mean. That's the week that almost everything turns out better than usual ... you lose three pounds, visit shut-ins, clean out a dresser

39

drawer and remember to fill in a check stub. Your ego knows no bounds!

Well, take it from me, your ego can hit a new low just as fast. Something usually comes along to deflate it. Mine got swatted down last week when I received a phone call from someone I hadn't seen in more than forty years.

The conversation went something like this:

"Are you Marjorie McConnell, the one who wrote an article about old Lincoln schooldays?" a pleasant male voice began.

"Yes," I answered, wondering what was wrong with it months later.

"Well, several people clipped copies of it and sent it to me in Detroit because you mentioned in it that you had a puppy love crush on Claudie Climie when you were in Miss Severs first grade.

"Yes, I was sure in love with Claudie when I was five years old."

"I'm Claudie Climie. My wife, Betty, and I are visiting relatives here. I went up to the Iowegian office but you weren't there."

My mind raced in pulsating spins back to 1922 and Miss Sever's first grade room. I could see that cute little boy with the devastating smile sitting at his desk cater-cornered from me. I could see him, clean and neat in his striped overalls, playing marbles in the school yard. It was like yesterday.

"Can you folks come out to the house," I asked, and had the presence of mind to tell him that he probably wouldn't recognize me now because I wasn't skinny and freckled any more.

"It doesn't matter," Claudie said. "I don't remember you anyway. I've tried to place you, but even though we went to school together through the 7th grade until I moved to Cincinnati, I just don't remember you." So he couldn't remember me. What an irresistible chick I must have been to make no impression at all in seven years. Some blue-eyed femme fatale I was. My ego was swatted down like a fly.

And to make matters worse or add insult to injury and turn the knife in the wound, Mr. Climie went on to reminisce that he DID recall several other girls in the class ... Vera Bryant because she was so pretty; Kathryn McConville because she was a 'good kid'; Betty Whicker because she was so ornery; Margaret Vinzant because she lived across from the school and Velma Sager because she made him so darn mad every time she bested him in arithmetic. But Marjorie McGuire he didn't remember.

We didn't get to meet Saturday because they had to leave town that day. He works for Northwestern Bell Telephone in Detroit. He told me that they had called on Miss Severs while vacationing in California and found her to be the same sweet person who started us out in first grade. Ah ha! You see ... he also remembered his teacher of 1922 but he couldn't remember the little girl who had stars in her eyes!

Well, I reckon I'll live. Ah, life can be so cruel!

Have a pleasant week. And you first grade girls. Don't fall for one of those little boys. He'll never remember you.

November 1972

&&&

41

I recently received a get-well card from a former teacher who wrote that she remembered how I used to look when I was a student in her 5th grade class. She recalled that I liked to write "themes."

I am glad her memory is clearer about that than about my arithmetic. When I'd go to the blackboard to do addition or division problems in front of the whole class I'd turn into the biggest dummy in class and if it was fractions or percentages I always had to go to the bathroom. Thanks Esther, for remembering the right things.

&&&

There has been a to-do lately in the papers about people who can write backwards, left-handed, upside down and with both hands at once.

Why, every kid in my old neighborhood could do all those things and do them fast. We learned to write backwards (mirror writing we called it) just for the heck of it and to write notes to each other. We practiced writing with left hands because "what if we broke our right arms?" We wrote upside down, backwards and with both hands. I can still do it, by golly.

We also practiced Pig Latin until we could talk it so fast that parents sitting in porch chairs didn't know we were talking about the cute boy who just went down the street. Or did they?

But then, we didn't have television in those days to occupy our time.

Pride

Sometimes pride can get in the way of common sense.

For example, when I was in my pre-teens in Grammar School back in the late '20s some agency or group inaugurated a free milk program for underprivileged and undernourished children. A half-pint of milk was doled out to each child who qualified.

When the teacher called my name as one of the underprivileged, undernourished minority who was to march up in front of 200 or more other youngsters and get free milk, I refused to go. I was scared to death to defy my teacher, but my pride and self respect had been shattered to bits and I would not drink a drop of it. This episode still stands out in my memories of grammar school. I could write several columns on those two years in 7th and 8th grades. (They were not the high points of my educational career.) Underprivileged, undernourished indeed!

Autograph Books

Well, I found my old 6th grade autograph book and that wasn't easy, especially for a person who can't remember what she did with the Wednesday Iowegian with the grocery coupons in it. I knew it was around someplace and sure enough, there it was, stuffed back in the bookcase behind a book on how smart raccoons are.

Autograph books were all the rage then and you wrote something in each others 5 x 7 booklet at the end of the school year, sort of like writing in the high school yearbooks today, only instead of being original like the kids are today, we wrote little ditties like: "When you are old and cannot see, put on your

43

specks and think of me." Or: "When you get married and live in the flats, don't call on me to take care of your brats." It didn't take much brains to sign an autograph book in 1929.

Here are some others: "When you see a cat running up a tree – pull on its tail and think of me; When you get married and live by the lake, please send me a piece of your wedding cake; As sure as the vine grows around the stump, you are my darling sugar lump; Love many, trust few, and always paddle your own canoe; I know a secret and you'll be sorry if you don't know. I am your friend forever; May God in heaven bless you and keep you from all sin. And when you knock at the Golden Gate may angels let you in; When you are in the kitchen frying meat – remember me and my big feet. Ha, ha." One friend told the truth when she penned: "Roses are red, violets are blue, I found a nut when I found you."

There were pages and pages of such great masterpieces.

Well, you might know. There always are a few sentimental people who save such things as old autograph books. Two of my school friends called me this week to let me know that THEY weren't the only ones who wrote dumb things in autograph books. After I made fun of everyone else's efforts, they tell me I wrote: "If I were a poet I would write something nice. But since I am not I will give you advice – Don't Flirt!" They were kind enough to say, though, that I have improved a little bit since then. I think it is great to keep things that once meant a good deal to you and it's fun to know others have kept autograph books too.

May 1973

44

Palmer Writing Class

If Mr. Palmer of the old Palmer Method writing techniques were alive today, he would throw up his hands in despair at my present-day "chicken tracks."

In 7th grade at Grammar School, Palmer Method reared its ugly head. In the old days (note: I didn't add the word "good" here) Miss Lantz presided over spelling and writing classes. She was a perfectionist.

We had to practice writing the alphabet in capital letters and small letters until they looked EXACTLY like those in the Palmer Method book. We had to make Push-Pulls and Round 'n Rounds until we got them right, or a reasonable facsimile.

Miss Lantz generally carried a foot-long wooden ruler. She said it was for showing us the proper slant of our work, but it often slanted on a few knuckles.

"Heads up, hands over, feet flat on the floor," she'd always order as she'd peer over shoulders at the writing tables.

Passing the annual Palmer Method test was nothing but torture. No matter how much you had practiced on your Big Chief tablet, somehow when you tried the Push-Pulls on the sheets of expensive Palmer Method slick paper, using your wooden pen holder, new pen points, blotter and bottle of dark blue ink, everything went wrong.

Sheet after sheet was ruined. Maybe your circles stayed in the lines but your capital X got fouled up. Miss Lantz and Mr. Palmer wouldn't accept that. I was known to cry at home when a blob of ink dropped on a finished sheet at deadline time.

And what did you get when you finally sent in your work to

be graded? A little blue Palmer Method pin … and the first kind word you'd heard from Miss Lantz all year.

In all fairness to this teacher, however, I will say that I did sharpen up my spelling in her class. She wouldn't settle for less than 100 percent correct spelling list, you see.

She was a perfectionist and tried to have us be.

Ah, Grammar School.

Homemaking Classes In 1928

An enjoyable visit in the local high school Home Economics department the other day made me recall my own Home Economics class (or Homemaking classes as we called them). I say 'made' me recall, because when I recall those days – I recoil!

There has never been any doubt in my mind that it was my initial confrontation with the so-called ladylike subject of homemaking in Grammar school that made me what I am today – a safety pin pinner of ripped seams and a scotch tape taper of loose hems. And because I was forced to shove my sewing paraphernalia into a box before the tardy bell rang, I am also a drawer-stuffer.

From the first time I walked into that drab sewing room on the northeast upper floor of that old yellow brick building at the tender age of 11, my doom was sealed. My school life became utter dire disaster.

To actually understand the whole thing, you would have had to have been identified with the depression years and the sternness of that era. Today's colorful homemaking rooms with flowers on the window shades and facets of home management and child psychology are just not in the same category.

Our instructor was a fearsome figure in white who told us at the very beginning that since we were no longer babies in the elementary grades, we would be expected to behave like little ladies.

Imagine how this ultimatum sounded to skinny tomboys who had spent the summer climbing trees, shinnying up ropes, roller skating and arguing about soft ball rules with the neighborhood boys on the vacant lot!

Indeed, the instructor in white laid down the law and enforced it with a ruler whose numbers had long since been worn off, and which she never seemed to be without. Little did she know that we were so cowed by her unbending stand that she could have waved a feather and we would have fallen over from fright.

As the first two weeks of school droned on, we found out the hard way that the sewing teacher did not take kindly to mistakes - even tiny ones like cutting the notches 'in' instead of 'out'. She frowned on giggling and laughter was out of the question. After the first week, that didn't matter because there wasn't any.

If a girl dared ask a question, open humiliation resulted. No girl in her right mind ever asked a question and the usual result was that things were always done wrong. You'd think that an unbleached muslin tea towel could be sewn up on four sides without the project turning into a Federal case. Wrong. You should have seen the tea towels we scardy cats turned out. They were so tattered, dirty and puckered they couldn't even be used to scrub the floor.

Things grew so bad in the sewing room that we couldn't even

sneak a glance out the window to see what exciting things were going on across the street at the rear of the hospital. One time we were grabbed by the arms with fingers like steel vices because we were entranced with the spectacle of a taxi cab lurching up to the ramp, lots of nurses running out and a woman in the throes of labor right in the taxi.

It was also in this sewing room that adolescent middle fingers were forced into metal coverings destined supposedly to protect them from sharp needles; shaky hands were goaded into thrusting thick thread into tiny needle eyes; devilish paper patterns caused us to cut everything on the bias instead of with the straight of the material.

But it was those horrendous instruments – the sewing machines – that produced more mental anguish that anything else. These four monsters laid in wait at the south side of the room for adolescent girls and delighted in fouling up the thread and sewing the backs and the fronts together. As a final faux pas, the bobbin ran out of thread leaving the complete underside unstitched.

There may be a few girls still around town who will never forget that first pair of pillow slips they made in 7th grade sewing class. Buying the pillow tubing was easy, after that everything got tough.

We were taught, you see, that even though the pillow tubing was crooked as a dog's hind leg it could be evened up on the bottom by 'pulling threads'. This procedure wasn't always foolproof. Then one end had to be French seamed which meant that you first seamed it up on the right side, turned it inside and trimmed the seam down and stitched another seam. If you misjudged the width of the seam you had raveling sticking out and for this mistake, the woman in white made you rip out the whole business and start over.

We were threatened with 'F's on our report card until we finally made it down to the hems. "Put in a three-inch hem," she ordered.

Simple? There is no such thing as a simple hem. Some of us got so flustered we sewed the hems up on the outside. Some of us measured and marked and ended up with three-inch hems on one side and two inches on the other. No one could find a pillow to fit the finished pillow slips. So you can see how it was.

Yet, when summer came, we girls cheerfully got out our cigar boxes of doll clothes materials, buttons and lace, sat cross-legged on an old comfort in the front yard and sewed up some of the nicest garments for our 10 cent celluloid dolls you ever saw.

The birds sang in the trees and as we stitched we laughed aloud at childish jokes. We even got ambitious one summer between ball games, jacks, fishing, and rope jumping to make a four-patch quilt top.

Any girl can sew if she isn't in sewing class!

Next: The 8th grade cooking class (if you can stomach it).

March 1970

Perils of Learning to Cook By Trial And Error Method

The Grammar School cooking room was on the sunny south side of the old yellow brick building, on the top floor. You would naturally think, then, that the 8th grade cooking class

49

would be more cheerful than its 7th grade counterpart, the sewing class.

Wrong. It was another disaster area – only here we ATE the disasters!!

The previous story was about the perils of a sewing class back in the days of yore, and this one is about a cooking class (also back in the dark ages) where we learned the rudiments of cooking (under fire) and by the trial and error method, mostly error.

Those of us, who had fearfully made it through the sewing lessons the spring before, approached the end of summer vacation with sickening dread. We knew what to expect – complete annihilation by fire and brimstone. We were certain that before the first six-week period ended, all 8th grade girls would go up in smoke from charred Egg a la Goldenrod.

And even despite the apprehensions for our own welfare, we felt genuine concern for the poor little innocent 7th grade girls who would be going into sewing classes. How fragile and trusting they looked.

The same 'woman in white' presided over the cooking quarters at the east end of high work counters placed in U shape. For each pair of cooking partners there was a two-burner gas stove plate and a small amount of counter space. There was also a stool for each of us and an ill-fitting tied-at-the side apron made of the versatile flour sacks of that day.

If I gave you three guesses as to how close MY cooking spot was to the teacher's high official pedestal, you'd be right the first time. Exactly within swatting distance to the left.

Most of us, unfortunately, didn't know any more about cooking than we did about sewing. Making mud pies after a spring rain hadn't exactly prepared us for mixing up a batch of baking powder biscuits from scratch.

As I recall (and my memory is pretty good where unpleasant school happenings are concerned), our cooking partners were assigned, not chosen. Usually we were about as compatible as a cobra and a mongoose.

Nonetheless, I will always remember my partner, Mary, and hold her in high esteem no matter where or what she is doing today, because she had the guts to survive cooking class (no thanks to me) and I made it through, too (all credit to her).

Mary was a tall bony girl with very little breeding and a flagrant disregard for the niceties of life. She was older than most of us and cussed like a trooper. Most teachers, even the invincible woman in white, shied away from her. Before 8th grade graduation she dropped out of school. It wasn't the cooking class or the daily tirades that finally got her. It was a pregnancy.

My loss was devastating. I was afraid to go to school. The terrors of cooking alone without Mary are still numbered among the most horrifying of my life.

It was she who had measured a teaspoon of something and praise heaven, she could break an egg without plopping it all over the countertop. She wasn't even afraid to light the gas burner which hissed before they erupted in Old Faithful belches of blue flame. Indeed, she approached the monster gas range in whose oven all our collective baking was done with all the bravado of St. George facing the fiery dragon.

Anyway, back to the cooking class. One day we made plain custard, a relatively simple dish of eggs, sugar, flavoring and milk. All recipes first had to be broken down into amounts for two. The custard recipe was reduced laboriously to somewhere around two tablespoons of sugar, three drops of vanilla, four grains of salt, 5/8 cup of milk and half an egg. The other half egg was to be shared with the cooking team on the left.

How do you divide an egg?! (We didn't dare ask questions in cooking class either.) Mary and I decided to beat the thing up and innocently gave them the top half and kept the bottom part. They never quite forgave us because 'foam' doesn't make very good custard.

If you keep in mind that these were the Depression Years, you will better understand the seriousness of making mistakes. "Waste not, want not" was the motto of that era. If your allotted egg for custard flew the coop or something drastic happened to your flour, atonement was swift and final. You did not get another egg, but you did get a 'F' for the day, an audible smack on the posterior with a spatula and the assurance that hanging by the thumbs was too good for you. The tears shed in cooking class over the year would add another percent to the Rathbun Lake water level.

Did I keep my old cardboard recipe file? I found it last week in the bottom of my mother's old sideboard. We saved everything in those days because we were brought up that way. In childish penciled writing were recipes for creamed cabbage, white sauce (thin, medium and thick), prune whip and of course – hot cocoa.

You wouldn't believe the trials and tribulations we had making two cups of cocoa. Here was a complicated process, worthy of highly skilled technicians in a laboratory. Mix sugar, cocoa, salt and a little water together in one pan. Boil one minute. To what was left add the milk - which got scalded. Ah ha!! Scalding is not boiling and, heaven forbid, not simmering either. The milk doesn't do anything but get hot, suddenly rise up over the pan, and scorch on the bottom. It also forms a thick white scum on top.

Even though we tried to drink that awful hot stuff quickly before the 'great chef' suspected, scorched milk has its own revenge in odor and leaves its own evidence in an unwashable pan.

Well, the year of cooking was finally over. We were supposed to have been making everything at home that we had made at school. Grandma always got around this by explaining that to do so would be a sinful waste of hard-to-come-by groceries; a waste also of P & G soap to wash all the dishes I would dirty up and besides there was never any left over meat to grind for the croquettes. One family member even offered me some penny candy to 'forget' to make the biscuits for supper.

We 8th grade cooking class alumni are relatively certain that it just had to be a male member of one of our families who invented the idea of pre-packaging biscuits in tubes and devised the box of Nestlé's Quick cocoa mix.

Something good surely must have come out of Grammar
School cooking class.   *April 1970*
                              &&&

Several have called and commented how my writing of
Grammar School brought back memories of those 7th and 8th
grades. We had that building all to ourselves and needed it. We
were too big for the little kids and just 'runts' as far as the high
schoolers were concerned. It was a difficult age group, even
back then.

Strict was the word for discipline at "old yellow." Those
were the days (commendable or not) when teachers could and
did back up their mouths with action. Or the principal tended to
the job.

Some things always stick in your mind somewhere. I
remember one particular episode. One of the teachers saw a boy
spit on a girl in class. She grabbed him from his seat with both
hands by the collar and literally threw him against the
blackboard, shaking him until his teeth rattled. He was a trouble
maker and she'd had enough. As I recall, he dropped out of
school in the 8th grade and later ended up in the penitentiary for a
knifing job.

Another teacher told a boy to stand up while he recited. He
refused in a belligerent manner. Three times. Teacher broke a
yardstick over his shoulders. He stood up.

As I recall, these episodes were few and far between and most
of us toed the mark because we knew what would happen if we
didn't. We also studied our lessons.

54

I'm not advocating physical discipline, mind you; I'm just telling it like it was in Old Yellow.

Remember the big study hall on the second floor? It also served as our assembly room with a raised stage platform at the south end.

The 7th graders all sat on the west side and the 8th grade on the east. Students were seated by divisions, A B C and D, with the smart kids in rows A, of course. I usually sat somewhere in the middle.

Sometimes we would have Assembly and there would be programs and group singing. To this very day I can remember the words to two songs we always sang: "My Name is Solomon Levi" and "A Spanish Cavalier." They were the kind of songs that both grades could sing at the same time. They were supposed to come out even at the end though the tempos were different. They started like this:

"My name is Solomon Levi
And my store's on Second Street,
That's where to buy your coats and vests
And everything else that's neat."

"A Spanish Cavalier
Stood in his retreat
And on his guitar
Played a tune, dear"

I'd still like to sing that duet with someone. Or harmonize on

"Santa Lucia" or have fun with rounds like "Row, row, row your boat."

At least I remember something I liked about Grammar School. And remember Miss Tillmont and Miss Sidles? They were neat English teachers!

Stage Fright

Whenever I hear someone on stage giving a musical solo, or a speech before an audience, I marvel at the talent (and guts) it takes to be able to get up before a group and perform.

As one whose mouth seems to do its share of talking in group conversation, I have never yet given a successful performance alone on a stage nor even in front of a group of Alpha Study friends with a book review. I get petrified and don't even remember what the subject is. I even get tongue-tied when it's my turn to introduce myself to a group and have to stand alone.

But probably the worst fiasco I ever endured occurred back in my junior year at CHS.

It was the custom back in the '30s for the president of the Student Council to give the Welcome Address at the annual Homecoming chapel.

Well, that particular year the council had elected husky football hero, George Ellis, to head it. Now about the only place that George wasn't shy was on the football field. He refused to accept the 'honor' of giving the Welcome. He balked. He wouldn't tackle it. They couldn't threaten him with an 'F' if he didn't do it. But they threatened me, who was vice-president of the Student Council, and made me write a welcome and deliver it. (Everything I have ever been vice-president of has turned out this way!)

I wrote a short speech, adding what I thought were real knee slappers to liven it up, and proceeded to memorize it word for word.

Came the day. I donned the new blue twin sweater set my mother bought me, and a pair of blue glass earrings borrowed from my friend and seated myself early in the front row of the auditorium. I went over my speech 50 times.

Suddenly the place started filling up with rows and rows of restless teenagers, parents and alumni. They all had one huge eye in the middle of their foreheads, piano-key teeth and horns. Evil gremlins were at work.

They stopped up all the doors, windows, exits and air vents and caused steam to poor in so I couldn't breath. Frankenstein Superintendent loomed in the center of the stage and thundered, "Marjorie McGuire will now welcome our homecoming guests." I started to rise, but the gremlins had poured a layer of bubble gum on the seat. I finally pulled to my feet only to discover that the vile creatures had covered the four steps to the stage with egg shells. The crunch of my footsteps riddled my eardrums. Somehow the platform became two miles wide and the rostrum had disappeared. From the rim of the stage bright red lights were turned on me, burning my face. From the rear, the mile-high maroon velvet curtain whipped up such a cold wind that my teeth chattered and my knees knocked. I opened my mouth but I didn't have any words to say. I grasped at my left hand with my right hand and tugged at my notes. Someone had rewritten them in Hebrew.

I could see hundreds of Cyclops leering beyond the footlights. I could hear snickering, then laughing noises. I couldn't just stand there and die.

Then the air was clear as a ball, the red light was turned off and the steam was gone. Two girls in cheerleader costumes of red and black were up on stage with me. One said, "O.K. Marge, now lets welcome the good old alumni of Centerville High!"

My speech came back to me. I don't remember what I said now, but I couldn't (and wouldn't) do it again in a million years. I don't need to worry, I'll never be asked again. *October 1968*

Graduating Class of 1935

Marjorie L. McGuire, daughter of Mrs. Pearl McGuire, attended Lincoln and Central Ward schools and Grammar School. She studied the Normal Training courses. She was a member of the Teachers' Pedagogical Society, being treasurer, and vice president of student council. She would like to go to college and prefers teaching as an occupation. Marjorie always receives high grades and is mentioned whenever dramatics are concerned. She was in the senior play.

Student Iowegian, May1935

&&&

To get your teaching certificate after you graduated from the Normal Training course in high school, you were required to do some practice teaching in a rural school under a bonafide rural teacher.

My assignment turned out to be the Leslie school in the Exline area. I was really lucky because teacher Lavinia Scott was a top-notch young lady with brains who set high educational standards for her pupils.

I sure learned a lot in those two weeks teaching and how to mix the geography with a sense of humor. The text books I had been studying didn't point out how to handle 27 kids of all ages (some of them bigger than you) in a one-room school house.

I remember the spelling bees and how I always felt sorry for the youngster who couldn't spell orally.

The spirit of competition during recess at Leslie school was strong. We played Flying Dutchman, Ante Over, Dare Base and Dodge Ball.

To get your teacher's certificate, you had to be 18 yrs. old and I wasn't 18 until a while after I graduated. I got a job at Frankel's store and later the local newspaper office – the Iowegian. I haven't been sorry, yet I will always wonder if I could have built and kept up a fire in the school stove, refereed family fights, fixed skinned knees, tended to the outhouses, kept eight reading classes separate or taught anybody anything. Well, we'll never know.

45th Class Reunion

What can you say about a school class reunion that hasn't already been said by about every alumnus who ever attended one?

That it was an exciting experience? That you couldn't put some faces and names together? That everyone sure looked older than you remembered them? Or that you were hugged by fellows who couldn't see you for sour grapes when you were seniors?

Nope, you've heard it all before.

Our 1935 Centerville high school class found that all of these descriptive phrases (and more) fit the big event to a T when we met for our 45th reunion.

Forty-five years had gone by since we trod the hallowed halls of ivy and wore our caps and gowns.

Forty-five years!

That's a long time. A lot of "water over the dam." Forty-five years packed with joys, sorrows, disillusionments and achievements in each of our lives.

Oscar Gavronsky did us proud as master of ceremonies. His voice could be heard by all 116 alumni and friends present. If he skipped an item, wife Sarah cued him in. "Don't know what I'd do without that woman," commented Gavy as he set a light mood for the dinner and evening.

Introductions were made around the dining room as each of the 48 grads present stood and told about himself/herself and about their work and family. It is significant to mention here that not a single person mentioned the state of his health or any ailments that had befallen him ... arthritis, stroke, hearth disease, diabetes, or the loss of a limb ... during the past 45 years. No one compared operation scars.

Instead, the get-together was jovial and plenty optimistic as the group enthusiastically mentioned tentative plans for "the big one," the 50th in 1985.

We broke two rules expected in polite society! We pointed at people and whispered behind their backs, "Who was that?"

August 1980

Chapter 4

THE BEES, THE BIRDS
& CREEPY THINGS

The Bee Story

"How would you like to write a bee story?" a friend asked me this summer.

"Not particularly," I answered, thinking of the time I stepped on a bumblebee and grandma wrapped up my swollen foot in bacon fat and damp cabbage leaves.

I don't like bees and they don't like me.

But some writers will apparently face anything to get a story. So it was that Robert Wells of Moravia, Iowa, a beekeeper, was rounded up for an interview at the office where there are no bees.

Bee Inspector

Mr. Wells and his fearless 14-year-old son, Bobby know a lot about bees. They tend around 40 hives stationed in various parts of Appanoose County. Wells is a member of the state Apiary group and is presently serving as apiary inspector for the State Department of Agriculture. As bee inspector, Wells has 10 south central counties under observance and his job is to look for Foul

Brood, a disease that can infect and destroy a colony and all its young. Foul Brood is contagious to other bees and sometimes infected hives have to be burned.

Wells and his son this year attended a three-day Bee Farm school in Doylestown, PA. where they met with other beekeepers from across the nation and learned the latest in hive construction and beekeeper methods. They also took a glass hive to the fair and planned a program for a local KTVO television station this fall.

"I've been fascinated by bees all my life," Bob told us. "Every farmer should have a box of bees as they are the world's best pollinators and honey is the purest food there is."

Since I was never fascinated by bees, I knew very little about them except that they sting. But I do now. For instance each hive is actually a home. The Queen is the mother and the undeveloped females (the gals who didn't quite make it to the royal jelly dinner) are the worker bees.

The males are relatively useless members of the honeybee cooperative effort. Their only function is to fertilize the queen after which they ultimately get thrown out of the hive, or slaughtered or left to starve.

The workers perform multifarious tasks of the hive, involving building, storing, feeding, cleaning, ventilating (by fanning their wings) and defending its portals.

And defend it they do. It seems that a brave but foolhardy bumblebee decided to enter the honeybee's hive. He was pounced on and thrown out. Picking himself up, dusting off his bedraggled wings, he started to enter again. He got beat up.

According to Mr. Wells, bees are never quiet a minute. They literally work themselves to death in six weeks.

Lots of stuff about bees. So far, so good.

Then somehow it was suggested that no bee story would be complete without some photos to go with it. Like, say, good close up shots of Wells and son poking into a hive.

The bee story writer prevailed on the city newspaper editor Clyde Holbrook to go take the picture for her. He said, "Go to heck," or words to that effect. Theda Long and society editor Gladys DePuy were begged to go to the bee jungle with the cameras. "No way." Even the janitor wouldn't help although he was offered assistance in picking up waxed column scraps from the composition room carpet. He didn't know how to use the sophisticated camera.

It became evident that the office force was enjoying the situation certain people get themselves into for the sake of a story.

There was a brief reprieve when Wells said that we had to wait for the right kind of day before visiting the bee hives. The day should be clear, with no sticky humidity so that the bees would be busy gathering nectar and wouldn't notice us.

It was fortunate that a long, disagreeable period of wet weather came along.

Picture Day

However, then came the day of doom and the beekeeper and son showed up at the office with a pair of white coveralls, and a net "bee hat" and a long pair of extra thick gloves.

65

"Now don't worry, you won't get stung," they comforted. "We can guarantee it."

"They can guarantee it," parroted the office crew.

We reached the Herbert Norris farm where several of the bee boxes are kept. They suited this female reporter up in coveralls and paraphernalia, and started the smoker bellows going strong to tame the buzzing insects.

"You won't get stung," they repeated.

I happened to glance down at the lacy summer shoes I was wearing and saw bees crawling around.

"They won't notice your feet."

I panicked when I saw a dime-sized hole in the coveralls.

I asked to be allowed to take the pictures two or three hundred yards away, but there was no telescopic lens on the camera and no one heard me above the noise the angry bees were making.

It isn't easy to trip a shutter button with leather gloves on, but you learn fast rather than take the gloves off. A large bee zeroed down and stung the black camera strap, leaving a dangling stinger. That was close enough! A lot of ground got covered in a hurry.

Mr. Wells is not only a good beekeeper but he has a sense of humor too. He thought it would be a good joke on the office crew if he caught a drone (which has no stinger) and put it in a little match box for me to take back to the office. The idea was that I was to nonchalantly take Mr. Drone from the box and let him crawl up my arm, proving that in one hour's time a certain bee hater had lost her fear.

Too bad that everyone had gone home because by morning

the fuzzy critter had conked out in his box.

It's October now, and probably the Wells' bees have kicked out the drones to starve. All I have left of my adventure is a certificate with my name which reads that I have faced with extreme fortitude millions of untamed bees on 2B Honey Ranch.

Just in case anyone wants a story about the birds, it might work out. The worst is over. *October 1974*

&&&

I don't recall having heard so many bird tweets as I have this year. You wouldn't think that right here in town the feathered friend population would be so thick, but the morning air reverberates with the chirps of martins, sparrows, robins, blue jays, wrens, an occasional cardinal and of course, the raucous shrieking of the starlings.

Iowa is a beautiful place to be in the spring and early summer.

Family of Wrens at 4th of July Outing

Gary and Marguerite Crowell planned a carefree weekend at the lake and when securing their boat up on the boat trailer, they noticed that a family of wrens had taken up residence in the open tongue of the trailer.

What do you do? Pull the nest out and scatter the fledglings to the four winds? Stay home and forget about boating?

The Crowell's took the tiny birds with them, and when they returned home, the little feathered friends chirped and sang as though they had enjoyed the outing. The Crowell's said that the wrens can stay in the tongue of the boat as long as they want to.

July 1978

&&&

Out at sister-in law Miriam Horstman's house, there is a very vain robin. Or else he's a lonesome bird.

Everyday now, Sir Robin Redbreast hops up on her car hood and around to the rear view mirror on the side. Cocking his head back and forth, he prances and preens and is obviously pleased with himself. Or maybe he's found a new friend.

&&&

The moon was shining and in its glow, silhouetted atop one of the tallest trees back of our house over on the next street, was the biggest bird I ever saw, its wings flapping in the night wind. Was it a Yellow Bird or Super Nighthawk?

By the light of day I saw it was still there, perched high. Only this time it seemed to take on the appearance of a huge kite caught in the tree top. This all goes to show that what you see isn't always what it seems to be.

April 1979

&&&

Sometimes it's the apparently insignificant "little" things that happen at your house that put the sparkle of interest into life. The bigger events like weddings or births and deaths, of course, make up your life, but meaningful little happenings are the things that give your daily life that extra zing.

For example, like at the Judge Powers home last week. Judge and his wife Etta were having company: their daughter Mary, husband Jim, and their children Pammy and Timmy. It rained hard and son-in-law Jim noticed that the deluge had washed out a robin's nest from the crotch of a tree in the back yard. He brought three baby robins into the house. This started a flutter in the Powers household and Etta, who can't stand to see something that needs help not get it, took charge of the situation.

Despite the fact that the tiny, featherless birds had turned blue with cold, Etta put them in a box, warmed the oven and brought back the glimmer of life. It wasn't long until three beaks were opened wide and insistent, hungry cheeps came out.

The children were excited. What would grandmother do now? Well, she went out and dug fishworms, that's what! Then she called Zylpha Price who suggested hard boiled eggs, and since Zylpha knows about these things, eggs went on the menu with the worms. Soon the tiny creatures got real perky and feathers started sprouting.

They were moved to a basket topped with screen wire and it wasn't long until they climbed up the side and perched on top.

Mrs. Powers says that the mother robin still scouts the empty tree crotch and they are hoping that when the babies are put back out doors, that she will teach them to fly. They'll probably miss their boiled egg diet and the human companionship they are used to. Who knows? And as we said, it's the little things in life that keep us going. *June 1973*

There is a sequel to my story last week of the three baby robins rescued by Judge and Mrs. Powers. The thriving creatures are receiving Meals on Wheels, no less, delivered to the Powers home by Vern and Zylpha Price. Freshly dug worms, that's what. The Prices also have nurtured orphan birdies in their time.

&&&

This is the first spring in at least 17 years that we've been able to attract a family of wrens to our back yard and I'm on top of the world when I hear their lilting trills each day. I had almost given up. We have made, bought and hung many different types of wren houses, but all they seemed to house were nests of wasps.

We've tried Log Cabin syrup cans, cut-off plastic bottles, little wooden creations and a variety of boughten jobs to no avail. We've put them in the willow tree, under the eaves of the garage and on a post. The neighbors get the wrens. Even a coconut shell (which was practically guaranteed by an old-timer) was shunned by the wren scouting party in the spring.

You know what they're living in now? A miniature tin rural mail box complete with a tiny red flag and plainly lettered on the outside box: "Mr. and Mrs. Wren."

&&&

If your doorbell should ring at three o'clock in the morning, you wouldn't know what to expect when you stumbled shakily to the door. Is there trouble? Is somebody sick, or has there been a wreck nearby? Somebody out of gas and wanting help?
Or is it only a raccoon ringing your doorbell? Don and Lana Tracy knew you'd think that their story about a raccoon ringing

doorbells was ridiculous if they told it.

The Tracy's doorbell did ring at 3 a.m. the other morning and they did get shaky, especially when they opened the door and there wasn't anybody there except Deputy, the dog, straining on his leash on the back porch stoop and barking.

Puzzled, Tracy peered out the window and spied a half-grown raccoon clinging desperately to the side of the house near the back door, silhouetted in the shadows of the porch light. Each time the coon slid down almost near reach of the dog and scrambled up again he activated the doorbell.

Tracy chased the culprit off into the night leaving a puzzled dog still sitting on the doorstep, cheated of his nocturnal adventure.

So the next time your door bell rings in the night it just might be ..... *June 1978*

&&&

Mitzi

We have a dog named Mitzi. She's 15 years old this spring and sharp as a tack. She lives in a shed attached to the back of the garage and has a fenced in "run" behind it.

I don't know what breed she is and I don't care. We found out years ago that she could climb an 6 foot fence or dig out under the fence in jig time. She liked to catch balls and Frisbees with the kids when they were home.

We had to put her on a long chain which allows her to sleep in her washtub full of straw, or run, or nap under the weeping willow tree.

71

She hasn't accepted the idea that other dogs can gallop through the back yard and barks in resentment at the unfairness of the matter.

Mitzi has never been a "house dog" and has weathered the zeros and snows of 15 winters and the heat of 15 summers. She is by far healthier and has outlived countless other pampered canines.

Mitzi is a good dog. Yesterday I gave her a hambone as a fitting reward for valor above and beyond the call of dog duty. She killed a snake in a spot where I might have stepped the next minute. I know it was the size of a cobra, but when my husband saw it, it had shrunk to the size of a little garter snake.

&&&

Maybe you won't care for this tidbit, but then, maybe you will. Anyway, one of our faithful readers writes us that she has a friend in California who went on a tour of Africa recently. While there she became acquainted with a Texas lady who was also on the tour. Well, every other day, the Texas gal placed a call to the Lone Star state at a cost of $40 … to talk to her dog. Maybe the little critter perked up his ears at the sound of her $40 voice, but I'm sure hoping he didn't say much. A talking dog could run up quite a phone bill, especially if he caught on to direct dialing.

&&&

Fox hunters came to Unionville, Iowa again this Labor Day weekend to run their hounds in the annual hunt. More than 100 hounds were numbered with paint and turned loose in the Soap

72

Creek hills to hopefully score points by trailing a sly and fast fox.

Hound owners, who came from states around, were in the height of their glory as they followed the barking hounds in their cars and trucks, relating progress to other CB'ers.

Each hunter seemed to know his own hound's barking from any of the others. The running and chasing went on for three days, with trophies given for the dogs which scored the most points.

Unionville is a Mecca for fox hunters who camp during the weekend in Unionville's picturesque park.

"Fox hunters are born, not made," one veteran hound owner said. "Fox hunting becomes a passion for some and obsession for others and to many it has been described as a disease for which there is no cure!"

It has been said that there are just as many hound dog owner widows as there are golf widows. These are the gals whose husbands own one or more hounds and they like nothing better than to go hunting for fox, coon or coyote.

If they like training dogs to hunt, then their wives just have to let them.

Some hunters are even known to just let their hounds loose to run just so they can hear them howl. They (the hunters) will sit by the hour in the cold of the dawn or the dew of the evening to listen for the bays of their hounds running through the woods. It's music to their ears. Football widows, hound dog widows. Work can wait, supper can wait. It's a lost cause.

&&&

If it ever gets through misting, we might be able to see the "Hunters Moon" over the horizon. It's already raccoon hunting season, and pheasant shooting has begun. Next it will be deer season. We have seen a large number of deer at sunset as we were driving and kept hoping that none of the creatures would leap up and straddle our car hood. I have never gone hunting, shot a gun, nor killed an animal. I have been known to swat flies and step on spiders, though.

&&&

I see where the good folks of Cincinnati are having their share of "animals in gardens" problems again.

Last year the town council got a bit weary of such complaints and passed an ordinance to the effect that all dogs, chickens, ducks, etc. had to be tied or penned up.

It made quite a front page news story for the Iowegian.

Well, this year, among the first complaints to the city council have been about "hogs getting into gardens" and rooting up the plantings.

Nothing like adding the hogs to the 'tied up' amendment, Mayor. *April 1976*

Evict Unwelcome Creatures From Your Attic

Do you have bats? We know some people who do, and this is how it is at their house.

The bats in their belfry don't seem to worry them much – they're sorta used to them by now – it's the bats in their attic and walk-upstairs storeroom attic that bother them.

You see, when they first bought the house, they liked it so well that when they found a few dehydrated and very dead bats in the storeroom amidst the old corsets, assorted debris and an old red purse with three cents it, they were a bit shook up at the time, but promptly forgot the whole thing. This proved to be a mistake.

The winter went by and spring came with sweet songs of the robins and twittering of the friendly purple martins flying over the clean sheets on the line. They began to hear, also, some discordant sounds at twilight coming from upstairs.

Thinking they had mice, they got a cat. That good old cat almost single-handedly, rid the entire north section in town of mice, yet the squeaks continued.

The whole business came to a head when a few of the flying rodents decided to move downstairs with them. This, in itself, points up the fact that bats are pretty stupid.

How did they get downstairs? Well, this neighbor says, one evening after the last light was out, down from the space above the old cherry-wood sliding doors in the dining area swooped one of the fellows. You could notice how that the doors are now sealed with masking tape which does nothing to enhance the décor but certainly kept the bats out of their living area.

Some time later, down in the laundry room in the basement, as she was peacefully throwing socks into the washer and her family upstairs was engrossed in the televised *Run for Your Life* show, a bat dive-bomber narrowly swooped down and barely missed her head. He then shuttered to the floor.

She remembered having read somewhere that bats, once on

the floor, were helpless and could be smacked with a broom. This, no doubt, was written by the same guy who insists that bats hibernate all winter. Actually they hibernate louder between your walls than you would ever believe.

The upshot here was that this creature took off from the floor, and (contrary to yet another fallacy about bat super-radar) whammed into a shelf, knocking off a box of fuses. With a shriek that would have done credit to a banshee, Mrs. X sailed upstairs, shut the door behind her and leaned against the wall, exhausted and pale.

She insists that nary a soul raised his eyebrows from the harrowing escapades of Ben Gazarra to see what had happened to her. It was plain to see that it was up to her alone to get rid of the bat before the family ran out of clean clothes.

This feat required my friend to sit outside the house by the screened-in basement window armed with a can of bug spray. Each time that ugly monster crawled up the screen searching for a way out into the night air, she let him have it with the spray. After two hours, Mr. Bat was out like a light. How *Run for Your Life* finally came out she has no idea.

It may interest you to know, at this point, that they sought help for their dire situation. A fellow in the Extension Office put forth the suggestion that moth balls, strewn 'round about the attic, might repel the bats. This they tried with hopes held high for complete annihilation. The bats stayed and they were the ones who repelled.

Not yet undaunted, they wrote to Iowa State University whose first directive said clearly – find out how the bats are getting into your house. It made sense.

A tour of the roof revealed that the chimney, a new brick one, was in good condition, the slotted ventilator was in crackless state and the asphalt tile roof appeared to be in pretty good shape.

The family thinks you will be glad to know, as we are, that the problem has been solved.

The other eventide as the neighborhood children were jumping up and down in backyard water puddles, they saw a flock of bats fly from the corner of the house. At last!

The next night, at exactly the right time at dusk, they watched. All the neighbors watched them watch. One, two, three and more big ones flew out almost under their noses.

Some of their less understanding neighbors, who have learned to expect almost any strange shenanigans from them, are going to wonder what they are doing on their roof tomorrow night – lugging hammers, nails, a supply of wood and a large powerful beam-light. Their procedure will be to wait until all the nocturnal creatures fly out of the spot where the eaves join the wall, then quickly board it up.

None of us knows what the bats will do when they return to find that they have been evicted. The family hopes they won't go to YOUR attic. *(Compilers note: "Mrs. X" was Marjorie, writing of her own experience.)* *May 1967*

&&&

Fright Story

It's upsetting enough to see a snake in the grass, but when you walk into your bedroom and there is a four-footer all coiled up by the wastebasket, like he owned the place, then you can shake with fright!!

That's what happened at the Bobby Sowder farm a few miles southwest of Centerville last week.

And the bedroom setting for this fright story is on the second floor of the home, occupied by the youngest Sowder children, Thad and Leslie.

Thad had gone upstairs to change his clothes and suddenly he was shrieking at the top of his lungs. "SNAKE, SNAKE" he was yelling.

Mother Linda Sowder, home alone with Leslie and Thad, unbelieving, nevertheless dashed upstairs and there it was in the corner, head raised, ready to protect 'his' domain.

"Get the hoe," she yelled, even though she had never been confronted with killing a reptile before.

"I killed that thing fifty times, I guess," Linda told us. "But there was enough of it left to take a picture of to show the rest of the family."

After it was all over, then came the worst part. Thad, 8 years old, and Leslie, 11, could not sleep. Their bedroom had suddenly taken on a horrifying atmosphere.

So the entire room was taken apart – mattresses off the beds, furniture moved, drawers inspected and closet emptied.

"The old saying about where there is one snake – you'll always find two – haunted us," Mrs. Sowder said. "But we didn't find any."

Then came the questions. Did the snake slither up the steps to the second floor bedroom? Why not one of the lower rooms?

There are several theories. It might have come up from the basement when the door was open. The children had aired their sleeping bags on the clothes line the night before and they sort of dragged the ground. Looking for a nice place to sleep, the bull snake may have crawled into one.

Can a snake live upstairs in a bedroom for a month? This is the most terrifying theory of all.

Leslie had gone to camp a month ago and returned with her bedroll and gear and parked them in the bedroom. Mr. Snake could have been in the gear, and worst of all, could have been inhabiting the children's bedroom all this time.

But no matter what – there hasn't been much sleeping going on at the Sowder farm. And there are quite a few inspection tours going on.   *July 1975*

&&&

Sometimes I think that wintering in Texas might be nice, like some of Centerville's population do, but now that I've heard that you have to shake scorpions out of your shoes and bed, and scoot lizards out of your cupboards, I'm not so sure. And tarantulas. "Heaven forbid!"

&&&

It seems that people are talking about sewers these days, a welcome change from elections and Iranian oil.

First, there was the front page Iowegian article about the purported funds to come into the city which will renovate and update the city's disposal plants and sewer systems.

Then the other day the Iowegian's own Bill Weaver wrote in his column concerning his experiences working as a plumber's helper during his summers spent in California.

So it behooves me to tell about sewers ... the one we have at our house.

I wasn't going to mention our recent sewer problem. It's an indelicate subject to say the least, and when one writes about bathrooms and stools, one has to be super careful about the wording. It would be ideal, perhaps, to tell a sewer story with innuendos, letting the reader draw his own mental picture of the situation. I got a strong mental picture, for example, from Weaver's wording.

Anyway, since I've decided to tell it, here's what happened at our house:

I was sharply awakened one morning when my husband shouted, "There's a RAT in the stool!"

Now usually I'm not one to "snap to" in a moment's notice. This morning I "snapped to" in one second.

"It's trying to claw up out of the water," he told me, adding, "but it can't get a foothold on the slick porcelain."

"Do something," I commanded, taking charge and doing nothing myself.

He did, bless his heart. He grabbed the can of lye-based stool cleanser and dumped the entire mixture down on the head of the sewer rat.

"How big is it?" I queried, turning down his insistence to "come see for yourself."

I finally broke into action (always run deadlines) and boiled six teakettles of water for him to pour on the still scrambling rodent. Husband used yet another can of plumbers' helper and finally the critter sank to the bottom of the stool, the deadest sewer rat in town.

"Flush him down now," I ordered, reasoning that what crawls up a stool hole should go down again.

He wasn't sure. "I tried that awhile ago and the water swirled so high he almost got his claws onto the lid."

"He's dead now, surely."

He flushed. Soused rat disappeared down into the depths of the dark, smell pipes of the city sewage system where he came from. (We haven't even entertained a mouse in our home in many years.)

That was the end of the sewer rat, but it isn't exactly the end of our problem.

How long do you think it will be before we quit peering down into that porcelain cavity every time?   *September 1980*

Apology

I deeply regret having written about the sewer rat in last week's column.

From comments I've heard about it, I couldn't have "put the fear" into more people had I announced that I'd seen a little green man from Mars in my bathroom.

It was a case of not using good judgment as to what to write and what not to write. It happened over a month ago and should have been left there.

I apologize particularly to those widows and live-alones who were frightened after they read it and to anyone to whom it caused worry. My column is meant to be lighthearted reading, and the worry was unintentional.

I'm sorry.

Excerpt from Glady's DePuy column, Iowegian
I notice in Marge McConnell's column today that her recent treatise on sewer rats caused fear and consternation in some homes in the city.

I never once thought about one getting up into the bathroom, but I haven't had courage to go into the basement alone since reading about Marge and Lowell's experience with the little varmint as there is a flour drain down there that would make it easy for a rat to get into the basement.

I used to go down without even turning on a light, but now I leave one on 24 hours a day, hoping to convince any lurking creatures that someone is down there.

Marge apologizes in today's column for causing unnecessary fear. Personally, I'm glad she wrote about it, because I certainly would have hated to run into one of the creatures unawares.

Now that I know it's possible for one to get into house pipes, I'll be a little more careful. And it wouldn't be quite so bad seeing one, knowing that it could happen, but to run into one without any warning at all … shudder, shudder, shudder!

I'm sorry it had to happen in your house, Marge, but I'm glad you told us about it.   *September 1980*

&&&

82

Scientists are studying great things these days in the Geophysical Laboratory at the University of North Carolina, or so I read the other day. Instead of making headway isolating the germs that cause the common head cold, these super-minds are delving into theories about why catfish leave muddy waters and why horses refuse to go into their stalls.

But possibly the most earth-shaking discovery to come out of this southern lab is that cockroaches can foretell earthquakes.

Yes sir, reports from the National Earthquake Information Service indicate that cockroaches get restless just before a quake. Very restless.

So the next time you see cockroaches going up your kitchen wall after you turn on the light, be sure to notice whether they are just walking up your wallpaper or if they're skittering heck-bent in every direction. Keep your eye on the cockroach. Restless cockroaches may save your life some day or at least they could give you time to batten down the hatches before the quake hits.

Such scientific findings make me shudder – not, as you may think, because of a portending quake or the cockroach himself, but because these scientists may be on government study grants and using MY tax money.   *June 1977*

&&&

I never cared much for fish, but during my children's growing up days, I had fish anyway. Some store was always having a special goldfish sale offer, plus a bowl, plus a packet of fish food thrown into the bargain.

"We want fish. We want fish." They all wanted fish, and of course they'd take care of them. Fish are supposed to be educational too.

After a week, the great fascination wore off and the bowl got dirty. Their fish became my fish. We had millies, swordtails, goldfish, zebras, platy and little bitty guppies that ate each other. How was I to know that most of the things would be male and bully the rest of them?

Somehow, though, our fish lived longer than most fish do. They were overfed, changed with chlorinated water, dropped in the sink and weren't allowed snail service. I finally had to give them away to a little neighbor kid whose mother didn't have any fish.

Paddlefishing

I just got back from a four-day jaunt by camper with friends to the Big Bend Dam area at Chamberlain, South Dakota.

I thought you might like to hear about paddlefish snagging up there since two young local men caught several of these unusual fish out here at Lake Rathbun recently and had their pictures in the paper. I was unable to reach either fellow to find out how they caught theirs (said to be the first paddlefish to be caught at Rathbun). But I can tell you it is a whale of a sight to watch fishermen "snag" these huge, long nosed mammals along the sides of the dam outlet in S. Dakota.

Big Bend Dam is a power dam and every so often a whistle blows as water is let out the gates. This rushing water alerts fishermen that water from the Missouri River will be rushing through and the fishing will be good – especially for paddlefishing.

Here's how they do it. They put a half-pound lead weight, plus hooks on their lines (no bait), cast out, yank back fast, reel up, yank back hard again and again. Then they start all over. It is hard work fishing for these big ones. I thought that the paddlefish took the half-pound weight just like another fish would take a doughball, nightcrawler or minnow, but what do I know? Instead you accidentally snag into the paddlefish somewhere while you're yanking. They are big ones and have been known to pull the fisherman into the water with their fight. We saw a 96 pounder brought to land after a rousing struggle, and by his tail at that!

They are ugly critters and have only a cartilage-like backbone and a few rib-like cartilages. They say the fillets are delicious. Some people call them Spoonbill catfish but according to the fish expert, Mr. Marrone, this is not the correct name as they are not catfish but a relative to prehistoric sea mammals.

At Big Bend there is a 2,000 seasonal limit on paddlefish and when this is reached, the season is closed. A fellow is on hand to check on number of catches and weighs them. I believe the record paddlefish poundage is somewhere around 113 pounds.

Our host said that paddlefish are native only to the Missouri River and its tributaries as far as they know, and it is very difficult to hatch their eggs in fisheries since so little is known of their natural habitats and other pertinent factors.

How paddlefish got into Rathbun Dam is mere speculation. Local fishermen theorize that the high waters and overflows of

many rivers and streams might account for this type of fish in Rathbun Lake. Anyway, they are here too.   *July 1973*
&&&

The following fish story is true – only the name has been omitted in the story to protect the unfortunate (the unfortunate in this case being a local fisherman). It seems he was out seeking bass not too long ago when he hooked into a big one. A short time later he brought the lunker within about eight feet of the shore. It was at this junction that some very bad things began to happen. First of all, the bass spit out the plug and let it fly through the air. The plug whacked the angler right smack in the face, slid down his glasses and deposited the hook squarely in the man's nose. So the fisherman had hooked himself and was now in some kind of pickle. He cut the plug loose but still had the hook dangling in his nose. After a journey to one doctor who wasn't there and then to another doctor, the hook was removed. Only a sore nose and wounded pride were the net results. Moral: Keep your fish on the right end of the line this summer.

(Lloyd Finks is responsible for this story.)   *June 1972*
&&&

Horsey

A horse, a horse. Daughter Nancy Ewing finally has a horse. A nice chestnut brown riding horse at her home in Unionville, Iowa.

She is 22 years old (Nancy is) and for at least 20 of those years she has wanted a horse. She has begged, cried, cajoled and saved pennies for a horse.

While other kids were saying "kitty" or "doggie," Nancy was saying "horsey." The Centerville Drake Library finally ran out of horse story books for her to check out.

Instead of cutting out paper dolls, daughter whacked out horse pictures, and to make matters worse, papered her room with them.

Never ever allowed to ask anybody for money, Nancy somehow managed to have a little horse bank around in plain sight so that when visitors would remark "what a cute bank," Nancy would respond immediately (and she thought innocently) that this was her HORSE FUND. Once she built the fund up to $6.21 before giving up on having a horse and spent it for more attainable merchandise.

Her horse souvenir collection grew so large that she still doesn't have room in her mobile home for all of them, and I, who don't care a hoot for horses, have to dust the critters on the shelf in her former room at home.

Our excuses for not buying her a horse were many. We couldn't keep one on a 62 x 150 lot in town and couldn't afford to feed one.

We were invited out to see "Chief" the other day. Nancy's husband, Dave, is the one who finally couldn't withstand her wheedling and pleading to make her lifelong dream come true. He is the one who has the Soap Creek hill room and the oats to feed a horse.

Chief and Nancy ride into the Iowa sunset every chance they get. *July 1976*

Gertrude Goose

I wondered when they were going to get around to me for an in-depth Personality of the Week story. Other personality columnists had plenty of time to ask me for an interview, but instead kept choosing VIP people.

Actually, Marge McConnell wouldn't have asked me either but she kept getting phone calls and notes telling her what a character I am in the Terry street neighborhood and what a different personality story I'd make. She finally came. I don't intend to disappoint you readers with a run of the mill story of my life either.

I suppose I should start out my story like they all do. I was born out on Route 3 at the Melburne Baethke farm a year ago last May. Maybe I was hatched. Anyway, some ducklings were hatched at the same time too (ugly things), and the Baethke's son brought a bunch of us to school one day.

The kids all wanted us, but a kid by the name of Mike Wright chose me especially and from what I heard, paid a fancy price for me.

I moved right in at the Wright home and have been one of the family ever since. There's Mrs. Wright (Gladys Lou), tall Harold, Louis, Mike and Cheryl. Lou Ann married and moved to Missouri, darn it.

Had a great life

I've had a great life and mostly done as I pleased. I'm stubborn, born under the sign of Taurus the bull, you know. They first treated me like a silly gray goose, but now I've educated them to the place that they know who is boss around here. It wasn't easy.

At first they all fondled and handed me around so much that I about lost all my tail feathers. That was because I was so pretty and soft and cute. They called me Gertrude which was O.K. because they didn't know then that I was a gander and neither did I.

It wasn't long before I tangled with a couple of tough guys on the place who thought that just because they were there before I was that THEY ran the place. Pat and Pep the dogs were the ones. They would growl, show their teeth and knock me for a loop. I vowed that when I got bigger I'd teach them a lesson. I learned to flap my wings wildly, stretch out my long neck and let out a high-pitched hiss that hurt their ears. A nip or two on their necks convinced them that I was there to stay.

The Wrights even bought me a little rubber wading pool for the back yard but that was kid stuff. I'd rather swim at the town reservoir where they always let me swim way out. Several times I suspected they might go off and leave me, so when I heard the car door shut, I swam in and scrambled up the bank.

I soon knew everyone in the neighborhood. Some of them obviously didn't like me because I was different from them. Somebody called the dogcatcher to come and get me. All I was doing was chasing cars, blocking traffic, attacking the mailman and keeping people from going into the new Episcopal Church across the street. I don't think it was Father Irwin Foster who called the dogcatcher either.

One day I decided to follow Mike to school at Central. I had plenty of time before the last bell rang so sauntered down Drake Avenue. I didn't realize how important I was before, but there were cars lined up on both sides of the street two blocks back looking at me.

In the pen

It was about that time that the family decided to build me a pen. But when you've been a goose on the go, the wanderlust gets you and you find a way out of the pen. But I did learn a few things there. You have to be agreeable with people to get along in this world.

One of the Catholic Sisters who lives cater-cornered across the street from us was raised on a farm and she teases me by flapping her skirts and saying Shoo, Shoo. I don't let her get my goat - I just flap my wings back at her and she laughs.

How do I keep fit? Well, I owe it to exercise and the right diet of grass and rocks. I swear by fresh air and live under the carport winter and summer.

But I must tell you something rather sad about our future. We might move to Marshalltown where Mrs. Wright may accept a music position with Anson Junior High School there next fall. The kids are protesting the move loudly and I'm squawking, too. After all, a goose has to consider losing her familiar surrounds and friends, too.

I heard Mrs. Wright say to a neighbor that SOMEBODY certainly can't be taken to Marshalltown and SOMEBODY will sure hurt their chances of renting or buying a house. Apparently SOMEBODY isn't going and I was hoping they wouldn't leave

Harold, Louis, Mike or Cheryl behind. I know Mrs. Wright wouldn't leave ME. Well, I hope there is a nice Welcome Wagon lady in Marshalltown with a basket of goodies.

Writer's Note: Gertrude the goose is the SOMEBODY who will be left behind. Mrs. Wright wrote to the head of the Des Moines Children's zoo to see if they would take the big gray goose. But today, we learned that it will have a new home with the Ronnie Exline's of Centerville. Good luck!

July 1972

Update

Gertrude Goose received a letter from Iowa Congressman John Kyl the other day in care of Mrs. Wright. He liked her life story. And in case you're wondering how Gertrude is faring at the Exline home, she's doing fine. Took to Ronnie like a duck takes to water. Ron played it smart, though, and built her a pen to curb her shenanigans.

Chapter 5

OUT IN THE COUNTRY

Vegetables of Their Labor

I should be ashamed of myself. Here I am this summer, blissfully eating the fruits and vegetables of other people's hard labors, when I've barely scratched the earth in my own scroungy little garden plot. It only produced a crop of multiplying onions which were hot enough to burn a hole in the ground down to China.

Our good fortune lies in the fact that the man of the house is a rural letter carrier who brings home a lot of vegetables. When he opens a mailbox these days to insert the junk mail, he's liable to find a sack of fresh-picked sweet corn or a bag of green beans, baby beets, turnips, cucumbers and green peppers. They have practically kept us in zucchini squash. I'll continue to eat tomatoes until frost time and then I'll eat fried green tomatoes.

Even in zero winter, Route 3 people put bags of frozen gooseberries, corn and rhubarb into their box for the mailman. Once there was even a plump roasting hen. There are so many nice people on Route 3.

One time, a patron cut a square of comb honey for us and bees flew out of that mailbox into the mailman's car for a solid week afterwards.

We never had it so good at the table nor reaped the results of so many gardens. We even rated a delicious rhubarb pie from Mrs. Mary Lou Hamilton and she probably thinks we ate the pie pan too, because I've not returned it yet.   *August 1972*

&&&

It hasn't been too many years ago that every farm wife had a flock of chickens and the egg money was hers to buy pretties with.

The chickens didn't seem to cause much trouble and ate table scraps, vegetable peels and did their own scratching for pebbles and bugs. Sometimes they got corn.

Oh, those fresh breakfast eggs and crispy fried chicken.

Farm wives usually sent for their baby chicks in March and there was rivalry as to who could have the fattest hens or the first fryers on the table.

We used to have a few chickens right in town (as did most of the neighbors). I think ours were white leghorns because grandma was fussy about having white eggs instead of brown ones.

There is no question that chicken tasted better then, and there was no hint of 'medicine' in a chicken leg.

&&&

I have come to the conclusion that people with regular

paychecks just don't understand the people with speculative money coming in like the farmer, for instance.

"I lost $2,000 last year on soybeans," a farmer told me.

"How could that be," I asked. "Soybeans went up past unheard of prices last year?"

"Well," said the farmer. "I sold mine for about $15,000 dollars but lost $2,000 because I didn't wait a couple of weeks when they went up again."

No sir, we don't speak the same language. I think he meant that he didn't MAKE $2,000 rather than LOST $2,000. But what do we regular paycheckers know?

Two Weeks on a Farm

Some people take farm living for granted. I don't, and you wouldn't either if you had never lived on a farm in your life. The longest time I spent on a farm was a two-week summer vacation back when I was thirteen years old, and if that period was any indication of how I'd do now, then I'd better stay right here!

Down through the years at our house there has been talk about how nice it would be to move to the country. This stems from the fond memories the man of the house has about the summers he spent working on his Uncle Jessie's farm place near Udell, Iowa. I accuse him of forgetting the hard work like baling hay, planting corn, cultivating, threshing, hitching up horses, milking cows, and the slopping hogs and remembering only his Aunt Olga's hot biscuits and country sausage.

Anyway, I don't know sic 'em about running a farm and I'm scared of the animals (even chickens). I don't know a thing

95

about grain markets or how to stop erosion. I have heard, however, about corn borers and working from sun-up to sundown and watching clouds for wind and hailstorms that can ruin your soybean crop in one fell swoop. The worrying part I could adapt to.

I remember my two weeks on a farm just like they were yesterday. Each day was like a Friday the 13th, and *The Perils of Pauline* movie was almost nothing compared to what I went through. This particular farm was below Cincinnati, Iowa, set back from a narrow road in the hills and boilers. At night it was pitch dark and "things" howled, croaked, hooted and rustled in the trees and undergrowth. And when the sun came up the situation didn't get better, it got worse. "Things" crowed, flapped, buzzed, snorted and bellowed.

The first thing that happened was a ferocious encounter with a white Leghorn rooster which came at me, spurs flying, the minute I stepped onto the back porch to drink in the beauty of the pastoral scene. When I went to the barn lot, the pigs chased me; when I picked wild flowers in the pasture, a bull pawed the earth and sent me high-jumping over a barbed wire fence; when I looked for eggs in the hen house, I touched a big bull snake; when I went up to play in the hayloft, I was stung by a bee and couldn't see out of my right eye for days.

Besides all that, I saw a gunnysack of unwanted kittens tossed in the pond, a mare have a colt, a farm hand's toe run through with a pitch fork and a cow kick the milking stool out from under the farmer's wife.

If I'd stayed three weeks, I probably would have died of

fright. Come to think of it, maybe rural life with all its peace and quiet isn't for me. *August 1972*

Farmer's Wife Not Happy with Farm Story

When you write anything for a newspaper – a column, an editorial, a letter to the editor or even give advice to the lovelorn, you run a big chance that somebody isn't going to like what you wrote. They might not even think it was humorous when it was supposed to be.

Well, it happened to me the other day. A local lady not only didn't think my column "Two Weeks on a Farm" was very funny, she wrote me a six-page unfunny letter about it! I was thoroughly chastised, trounced, upbraided and squashed when she got through.

For instance, here are some excerpts from her letter:

"Yes, Marjorie, some people take farm living for granted. Others take city living for granted. The government builds a huge lake so you can get out of town. Why? Farm people come to your town to spend their hard-earned money to keep the townspeople alive and have food to eat.

The noise you speak of on a farm is a natural life. There is hay to bale, corn to pick, chickens to feed, cows to milk. You name it and the farmer can do it and he will. His wife will bake him biscuits and sausage and townspeople will go to supermarkets to buy the very food this poor farmer has made possible.

At night when it is dark, as you mentioned, things howled, croaked, hooted and rustled in the trees, etc. All of these sounds are sounds of nature – God-given animals we raise to feed the hungry. The things that crowed was from the chicken house where eggs come from. Cows bellowed for their morning feed so they would have milk to feed the hungry.

You saw a sack of unwanted kittens drowned in a pond. Perhaps the townspeople dropped them by after dark. Farmers do get hailstorms that ruin their crops. Centerville has more fires than farmers get hailstorms. Right? Count them.

Now let's take a look at city or town life. On farms we do not have paved streets, broken sidewalks for children to play on and where it is necessary to have signs saying 'Stop, Yield, Children Playing, Drive With Care' or city ordinances like 'All dogs tied up April 1 to October 1.' Ha! Who pays the dogcatcher and for what?

I now live in Centerville. Came to town to retire. I spend my money here, pay taxes, drive a car and have anything anyone could ask for. But when nighttime comes, you have to wait until all race cars are off the streets. No one can read the signs at night so we have car races, snort, have loud mufflers (or none at all) to rock you to sleep.

Oh yes, after the dog catchers day is done, all dogs are turned loose to come to your place to see that your yard, garden, flowers, etc. have been taken care of.

Oh yes, we (in town) had a goose that made headlines in the Iowegian because he stopped all traffic for two blocks. If he were out in the country, city folks would have run over him.

Then a Honda came into the same street for children to ride. Law says you cannot ride on sidewalks or streets, so around and around the hour, four children take turns riding. Quiet? Would you call this quiet city life?

When you were 13 years old you spent two weeks on a farm. You only got a child's view. There are fine people who live on farms and work for their living. Not many get handouts. There are no Christmas baskets for the poor delivered to farm people.

Their children are bused to school. Some leave home at 7 a.m. in the morning and do not get home until 5 p.m. Check with schools and find out if all farm people's children are uncared for or hungry.

In town, if it were not for our clocks (which we have to turn ahead so townsmen can play an extra hour), our radio or TV, all we do in our spare times is nothing except see only the same house across the street, the mailman and swat a few flies, bees and wasps.

It's a great life, but don't get old. I am sure farm life is not for you, Marjorie. You did not see the good. Thanks for putting us straight."

Well, she made her points crystal clear, and she was right on many of them. But hey, farm folks, you know I like you. You know that, and I did not say your kids were uncared for.

Has Farm Living Changed In 50 years? *(1917 – 1967)*

A good person to answer a reporter's questions on the changing farm scene was Mrs. Wilbur Hollenbeck who has lived on the same farm place near Udell, Iowa for over fifty years.

Tall pine trees stand near the house which is approached by a winding drive. The house, sparkling white, the well kept buildings and the remnants of a bountiful summer garden present a pleasing view.

Almost all homes in that vicinity are quite old, yet structurally sound. Most have been completely remodeled and modernized with electric and water as has the 110 year old Hollenbeck home.

Our children listened intently as we reminisced about the "old days" and it is plain that they considered these the biggest fiction stories of all time.

"I met my husband when he came to the house with the fellows for a 'wood-sawing'," Velma began.

"Each year at the drop of a leaf, farmers cleared out their timber of dead wood and stunted trees and hauled the logs on horse-drawn log racks. The entire winter's supply of wood was sawed by the farmer and his neighbors using the strong-arm method. The big pieces were for the heating stove and the little pieces fed the cookstove. A few hickory trees were felled to supply that smoky, full flavor to the hams and bacon hanging in the smokehouse."

Velma insists, and she'll probably get no argument from anyone over 35, that winters were colder, snow drifts were bigger and the winter lasted longer than it does now.

To help turn away the cold winter blasts, fresh straw was sometimes layered beneath the rugs or old newspapers were laid out. After the fires were banked for the night, the goldfish and flowers were moved next to the heating stove so they wouldn't freeze.

Youngsters hopped upstairs to bed-down under a pile of home-made quilts and comforts to sleep warmly until called at 5 a.m. to tend to the milking and other chores. Ticks were made of straw and pillows and mats of goose feathers.

A farmer always took good care of his horses. They were the machinery and no matter how much field work had to be done, these horses were rested in the shade for an hour at noon and fed clean oats and hay.

Without benefit of brochures from an extension office, commercial fertilizer or modern farming tools, the farm land yielded crops of corn, wheat and oats. Soybeans were considered hard on the land. All grain was kept on the farm and fed to the stock, which in turn provided about the only profit the farmer received.

A farmer farmed to make a living. He and his family ate, canned or stored all the vegetables they grew and all the fruit from their orchards. They consumed, canned or cured all the meat they butchered. Extra timothy or clover seed might be sold, or cream or eggs.

The cave was the ultimate for food preservation as well as providing a shelter in a storm. Potatoes were dug and put in gunny sacks, turnips and parsnips went into barrels and cabbages were pulled up by the roots. Apples and kraut, beets and pears lined the cave walls.

Staples were bought on a weekly trip to town and it was a long awaited treat which sometimes ended in the purchase of a new shirt or dress, or perhaps some material. Pin-money came from the sale of eggs, cream and chickens.

The most important building on the farm 50 years ago was the shop. This building was the most utilitarian of them all because it housed the smoke room at one end, the gasoline motor which powered the washing machine, the churn and the forge in the center and housed the workshop and tools. The old bathtub stood in one end and summer Saturday night baths were always taken in the shop until the tub was moved to the house come winter so you would not "catch your death!"

The stove reservoir was the hot water system.

Chores for the children were as certain as the rising sun in the east. The work was hard but their farm parents saw to it that they were educated. There was no end to the fascinating games that were invented and handmade. The farm pond provided swimming in the summer and skating in the winter. Hillsides were for dreaming and haymows were for playing on rainy days.

But to quote Mrs. Hollenbeck, "Deliver me from the 'good old days'." *October 1967*

&&&

Time was when old boards from a tumble-down house or barn weren't good for anything. They were full of splinters and rusty nails. But now weathered boards bring a price. They're using them for things like picture frames, decoupage and for paneling a kitchen.

Recently I saw a remodeled kitchen whose walls were of those wide boards of oak, weathered to a shade of silverfish gray. Planing the wood must have taken a lot of elbow grease, but the effect was unusual and gave the kitchen an old–timey look.

Unionville, Iowa. Population 150

Yesterday was the Fourth of July and we spent it at Unionville, Iowa, where they were having their first 4th of July celebration since the year 1899!

It was a beautiful summer day and this oldest of Appanoose County towns, really drew hundreds of people and campers from all surrounding towns and from neighboring Missouri communities. The annual Unionville Fox Hunt had nothing on this new holiday event.

The celebration yesterday was masterminded by Mrs. Ronald (Letha) Cormeny, a young Unionville homemaker who said she worked so hard on it because "the local folks wanted to celebrate the Fourth and kind of expected me to take hold of it."

Letha did just that, starting months ago when she, with the help of other community minded folks, earned money by sponsoring bean soup suppers and ice cream socials. She single handedly baked 16 cakes for the cakewalk, helped in the concession stand and swept up the cement floor of the shelter house for the big square dance at ten o'clock that night. She gives credit, though, to her hardworking committee. Prizes were donated by merchants in Appanoose and Davis Counties.

Like their counterparts in Cincinnati, the young women of Unionville decided to revive their small town and they really make their communities hum.

The Unionville celebration drew so many folks that more than 90 pounds of ground beef were served in hamburgers and several trips to Centerville were made for extra buns and cases and cases of ice cold pop.

As it was, those who came got to see a parade; saw a tricycle race; heard the Happy Valley Ramblers perform on stage three times (a fine country-western group from Missouri); saw a real live Frog Jumping contest in which Rodney Stajcar's long-legged creature finally decided to jump two feet and one inch to win; a greased pig contest in which young Billy Joe Smith landed on a squealing critter in a matter of minutes; and a pony race which became mighty exciting when pretty Susan Ewing rode her pony and copped prize money in several events away from some of the young fellas who were competing with all their might.

And the Ma Kettle contest! You should have seen that. The two judges had a time picking the winners from a group of "beauties" wearing gunny sacks and frowsy creations. These Unionville gals were really hamming it up on the stage to the delight of the audience and I think they finally decided on Belva Ellison, Ora Smith and Bev Babbitt. But I'm not sure, since those who were not chosen created such a commotion.

I'm looking forward to next Fourth of July, mainly because I can't imagine what the ladies at Unionville will cook up next!

July 1973

&&&

Cincinnati's Labor Day holiday celebration added interest to this area. There was a wedding in the ball park, a better-than-average carnival, and a little-but-mighty Nashville gal singer, Barbara Mandrell, who belted out country western music in true professional style. Her band, dressed in purple sequined suits was top-notch. Big name entertainers will too come and perform in a small town!!

&&&

Well, it's not too soon to be thinking about Pancake Day. Maybe Centerville is a small town, but if a much smaller rural town like Cincinnati can get a top-notch singing star like Barbara Mandrell to come to their town and put on a dynamite show, and Unionville, Missouri can entice Dotty West, why can't we draw big crowds with some super-entertainer instead of some third-rate comic who tells dirty jokes?

I'd suggest Elvis, of course, but would settle even for the Everly Brothers or the Osmonds. (These are hints to the Pancake Committee.) Can't afford someone like Barbara Mandrell? Cincinnati did. She put on a stupendous show on Cincinnati's little stage. Mrs. Glen Hawkins, a member of their busy Labor Day committee, said that the entire committee had dinner with Mandrell and her entourage and found her to be a real sweetheart. *August 1977*

Take the Family Nutting This Fall

It isn't time yet to go gathering nuts in the woods.

The frost isn't on the punkin and there is no crisp chill of autumn in the air. But in about another month, you can take your gunny sacks (if there are any these days) and tramp off to the wooded hills and shake down a few hickory and walnut trees.

Getting a supply of nut goodies these days isn't as easy as it used to be. Much of the most productive nut tree land went under water when Rathbun Lake was formed. Especially gone are the big, succulent river hickory nut trees that grew along the river banks.

We used to gather these big fellows on shares at the Bohm farm. We could easily get a winter's supply in one exhilarating nutting expedition and still dump Bohm's share in a mountainous pile in their backyard. The people who let you gather nuts on their properties not only shared their supply with you, they profited by selling bushels of nuts in town. It was a good arrangement.

If you have never been nutting in the fall, then you've missed something. As youngsters, we considered the nutting forays the highlight of the fall season, along with Halloween and the harvest moon.

You could only drive your car so far into the woods, and there you were on your own – on foot, plodding deeper, and more mysteriously into the woods. It was a new experience and one you never forgot.

As you went deeper into the forest, you could imagine you were in a land far, far away. The sunlight filtered through the trees and the leaves crackled under your feet as you searched for the right trees. There were also lindens, white birches and the beautiful oak trees. When you came to the clay-banked creeks, there were unusual rocks to stuff into your pockets.

There are two kinds of hickory nut trees. The big river ones were scarcer than the regular sized smaller ones. They tasted different, too. My favorite was, and still is, the smaller nut which was harder to crack and pick out, but had a more distinct flavor. The city park at one time had many of the smaller nut trees and they didn't mind if you picked up a sack full. The squirrels did, though, and usually managed to sort through them and left you the ones with holes in them.

The farmer had it made, usually. He had enough supply on his own land to yield several quarts of walnut and hickory nut goodies. There were usually hazelnuts too, and at one time some butternuts.

After the nutting came the hulling and drying of the nuts. This was a messy job and most kids showed up at school with walnut stained hands. Even Fels Naptha soap wouldn't take it off.

Old-timers always said that the walnut crop was generous only every other year, and surprisingly, that has proven true.

The black walnut was unbeatable for flavor in cookies, cakes and chocolate fudge. Many walnut trees are being logged for the great demand in lumber for furniture making, but Appanoose County is said to still have many trees left.

Did you know that there are proper ways to crack the nuts so that the kernels come out almost perfect? Brother-in-Law Walter Horstman, Mayor of Rathbun, tells us that you should always crack walnuts flat and hickory nuts on their sides. And don't smack them so hard that they squash the nut meats all to smithereens.

Picking out the nut meats was always a job relegated to anyone who would do it. Usually grandpa did it, but after he'd cracked and picked out the kernels, he passed the job of looking for bits of shells over to somebody who could see better. It was unpardonable to find a walnut shell in your fudge.

Take your family nutting this autumn and they'll think you invented a brand new type of recreation. It's a family affair. It's also educational because they learn to identify each tree in the woods by its leaves. Also take a basket of sandwiches along because you'll get mighty hungry trampling in the woods.

And just like hunting on somebody else's property, ask permission first.

There is one thing though that must come as a disappointment. Your kids my not have much to do with Euell Gibbons after they find out that Grapenuts Cereal really doesn't taste like wild hickory nuts!   *July 1975*

&&&

Went hazelnutting Sunday at the Donald Ewing farm near Unionville, Iowa. It sounded like fun and something I hadn't done since I was younger. So it didn't matter that I had forgotten what a hazelnut bush looked like; that the nuts grow in thick pods in clusters; or that they grow in tangled underbrush. Got a plastic bucket full and by the time I hulled them out, I'd had enough of the nutting business.

Chapter 6

CHILDREN OF THE 1970'S

First Hours in Isolette for Baby Girl

I am Baby Girl Crouch, and even though I was just born a few hours ago at St. Joseph Hospital, I am already something of a celebrity!

They tell me that I'm the first newborn baby to use the new Isolette here at the hospital, and let me tell you, it is a mighty fine contraption. Sister Mary Doreen says it is a generous gift from members of the Hospital Auxiliary and can have lifesaving advantages for me and other babies yet to be born.

Well, I was doing just fine here in my new space age home, cooing and trying to look around a bit, when this lady in a white gown and white mask came up. I was getting used to that of course, but this one, instead of giving me anything to eat or changing me, made a bright light flash. Well, I sure cried, because I'm not used to anything like that. She said she was taking my picture for the Iowegian. Ah, the price we celebrities have to pay!

If you like, I could tell you about this new incubator I'm in, but then, perhaps Sister Mary Doreen should tell you, because she uses some pretty fancy words about it.

Sister Mary Doreen explained it this way: "While it is not like the first home you ever knew, Baby Crouch, it is a unique piece of equipment designed especially to control your body temperature. Since moist air is easier for infants like you to breathe, the Isolette maintains a stable degree of humidity with warm air passing over the humidity reservoir."

Now for me, the first baby ever placed in it, this was not essentially a life-saving measure. But for any little preemie (a baby under five pounds), or one who is having respiratory difficulties, the doctor will use it.

I saw Sister Mary Doreen showing the other nurses on the O.B. floor, and the staff of doctors, too, how this Isolette increases the oxygen concentration. "Most babies do not need more than 20 percent oxygen which is found in atmospheric air," she said. "But should the doctor feel it is necessary, oxygen can be regulated using the oxygen flow meter and the oxygen analyzer. Even a 70 percent concentration can be done."

As all of you know, we newborn babies are especially susceptible to bacteria and germs, so the air flows through a filter in this Isolette, making the air I am breathing right now relatively bacteria free.

Now what more could I ask for? A comfortable bed, warm moist air, no bacteria and just the right amount of oxygen.

But you know, the Isolette manufacturers did think of something else! It's the Infant Servo Control. That's the temperature thing they have taped to my tummy. Doesn't hurt a bit and with this thermometer next to my skin, they can tell exactly how much heat should be turned on or off at just the right time. An alarm would ring immediately if it didn't and that would probably scare me and I'd cry.

Sister explained to my mother (she's here in the hospital too, you know) that there are a good many other things about this new incubator that the old one didn't have. There's even a thing to get the mucus out of my throat. They can even change me and give me excellent care and still not handle me too much.

Well, I'm leaving the hospital any day now with my loving parents, Mr. and Mrs. Floyd Crouch to live in Numa. By that time I'll have a name all my own.

They say I won't remember a thing about being in this Isolette or even the Hospital, so I am going to smile a little for the nurses to let them know I'm saying, "Thank You."

Right now I'd like to rest, please. These interviews we celebrities give out are very, very, tiring you know!"

November 1967

&&&

In picking up a magazine the other day and skimming through it as is my usual method. I ran across an article with the intriguing title "Don't Try to Do Your Child's Thinking." Right away I was interested, especially when the author suggested in the first paragraph that we mothers should avoid telling our children what to do.

This little gem of an article was written by a school counselor who also happens to be a mother of three daughters and a son.

111

I've always wondered anyway why youngsters seem always to tell school teachers and counselors things they wouldn't think of confiding to their parents. More puzzling they seem to be more satisfied with the results.

"Counseling is simply listening" explained the author. "It is listening while the counselee tells how he feels about things, listening while he puts his problem into words and decides what to do about it."

"The goal of counseling" she emphasizes, "is the same as that of child rearing – to help the person learn how to make choices." The clue here is probably the word 'listening.'

It was also pointed out in the article that children who have a great deal of practice in weighing small decisions will find larger issues less shaking during their growing-up years. In other words, unless an individual decides for himself on a given course of action, he probably won't respect anothers decision or profit from it.

Parents are told to cultivate empathy with their children and try to see the world as they see it. (Flat statement.) How DOES a youngster see this world?

The next suggestion was to establish rapport, or a warm relationship between parent and child. (This does not mean that the adult approves of the child's behavior.) Well, this makes some sense.

"Have faith in the child," the article next said. "Try to see him as a worthy individual with the ability to work out his problems with a minimum of adult guidance. And don't threaten." I suppose they mean that you are not to strike your

112

son Johnny while trying to get him to apologize to little Hiram for hitting him.

The best suggestion in the whole article, that I could see, was to learn to listen. It even went so far as to expect a mother to withhold advice until the child has examined his problem and reached his own conclusion. Usually she is way ahead of her child's story and has the conclusion all figured out.

Now a case in point, as told by the author. "Suppose your little Mary was not invited to a classmate's birthday party. Your daughter explains the problem with narrowed eyes, a crushed voice, tears, and a look of vengeance that would put to shame any villain on a horror show.

Mary's decision, which she arrives at herself, is that she will not (absolutely, positively NOT) invite this other traitor to her birthday party when it comes around next year."

Now since the counselor has repeatedly suggested that the mother must encourage Mary's ability to work out her problems as a worthy individual with a minimum of your guidance, you sit back and listen, not imposing your adult value system on your child.

You can only hope that Mary doesn't notice that you also are sitting with narrowed eyes, a crushed look and a vindictive smile.

We never did find out what the counselor told that girl to do or whether or not little Mary decided to invite the other girl after all. Guess we'll have to play these problems by ear – just like we always have.   *November 1968*

&&&

113

We must continually realize that the children of today have grown up in a different world from that in which we adults spent our childhood. We must be aware of these differences, we must understand the new conditions and the new needs in order to be able to aid and guide our children and grandchildren.

&&&

Practice is starting out on the Ray Dooley ball field on Park Avenue. Soon mothers and fathers will be on the bleachers to watch the young'uns get up to bat. I hope they mind their manners this year, the parents, I mean. Last year I was ashamed of some of the mothers who cussed out the umpires, berated the little boys who were doing the best they could, and sounded like shrieking banshees when their own Junior dropped the ball. Baseball must be a nightmare for the little tyke who is only playing because his dad wants him to be great in sports because he wasn't!

Happiness is baseball. Let them play the best they can, and if they strike out when the bases are loaded – well, it's only a game. *April 1977*

&&&

At about 11:15 the other night the phone rang. It doesn't usually (and better not) ring at that time unless necessary.

A child's voice asked, "Lady, what is your shoe size?" I asked, "Why do you want to know?" There were some giggles in the background and then he (or she) said, "Well, this is the shoe department." More giggles and muffled snickers. Those kids not only needed to be in bed asleep at that time, they needed new script writers.   *August 1975*

&&&

With summer barely underway, apparently some of the school kids don't have enough to do.

One young girl (or boy whose voice hasn't changed yet) thought up something to do with her time. She phoned people.

I got a call telling me that I had won $50 at Centerville's radio station KCOG. She continued gleefully that I should hurry on up to KCOG and collect my cash before 2 p.m. and be sure to use the "east" door.

I smelled a mouse.

In the first place, it isn't like me to win $50 anyplace, and in the second place it was already past 2 p.m.

"This is a prank call, isn't it?" I interrupted. I asked her name and she promptly gave me one but I'd never heard it before.

I dismissed the call as a time-wasting prank. But about four o'clock the old newspaper curiosity took hold. How many people, I wondered, had the prankster called? How many fell for the $50 prize and trotted up to the radio station to claim their money?

Naturally I called the radio station. The receptionist was clearly surprised. No one had called (except me); no one had used the "east" door because there isn't any.

I was "it" in this little game.

So I'm asking bored girl to come by the house and I'll give

115

her plenty of housework to do. Perchance she may win $50, but use the south door please. *June 1980*

&&&

A gangly boy, probably around nine or ten years old, rang my doorbell one snowy mid-morning.

I noted when I answered the door that he was warmly dressed against the cold, but I wondered why he wasn't in school.

"Lady," he began slowly, digging at the doormat with the toe of his boot. "Lady, I'm collecting money for the blind and crippled children."

"Who are you collecting the money for?" I asked him.

"I don't know."

"I mean, who sent you out in the cold on a school day?"

"Nobody. It's for me."

"You don't seem to be crippled and apparently you can see."

"Yeah, but if I can get some money I can buy pop and candy and stuff that I want."

"I'm sorry, fella, but I won't give you any money this way. Don't you know it's not right to go around to houses begging for money?"

"Why not? People and women and other kids go around to houses asking for money for hearts and to put in *(UNICEF)* cans on Halloween night." He looked me straight in the eye as he added, "They give them the money too."

I watched him trudge through the snow to the other houses in the block.

I guess I shouldn't have been surprised when later that

morning I saw him in the neighborhood grocery store, just four houses away, drinking pop and choosing a chocolate bar from a well-filled sack.

When he saw me, he didn't bat an eye, but the look he gave me plainly said, "Ya see, lady, why can't I?"   *December 1976*

&&&

I don't believe there are very many stores left where a kid can take a fistful of pennies and come out with a choice selection of penny candy. In fact, there aren't many grocers who want to fool around selling it to the kids.

Today, thank goodness nearly every piece of candy is wrapped. There are lemon drops, cinnamon balls, caramels, peppermints and all kinds of candy bars (which seem to have shrunk in their wrappers over the years).

As I watched the kids ponder over their selections, I noticed that the biggest sellers seemed to be the long tube-like spirals containing a grainy sugary stuff in different colors. They just bite off the end and squish the sugar into their mouths. I tried one – like eating powdered gelatin.

Then they like "Sweet Tarts" which are big, flat pill looking creations which have a strong sweet-sour taste in lime, orange, etc. I don't like them either.

Bubblegum! Oh boy, do they have a selection. They used to sell only one kind you remember – a big rubbery pink glob that stuck to your nose when you tried to outdo a friend in a bubble blowing contest. Well, now there is grape bubblegum, sour apple, watermelon and "Sputnik." I bought a "Sputnik," much to

117

the consternation of Joe the grocer. "That's bubblegum, you know," said Joe. "You'll need more than one to do it right." Well, Sputnik tasted more like spitnik to me and I have certainly lost the knack for blowing bubble gum. But then, I'm not a kid any more.

Another of the big current sellers is boxes of Pop Rocks (little pieces of confection that you put on your tongue and they snap, crackle and pop). Ingredients include carbon dioxide which makes the sugar rocks explode in your mouth.

Only kids would waste 20 cents a package on such foolish stuff. Right? But one adult column writer got curious and bought a package. The cherry flavored Pop Rocks are the best.

&&&

We have little Evel Knievels in our neighborhood. Take Paul Richmond and his friends. Paul is so entranced with the dare-devil spirit of Evel Knievel and his up-coming jump over the canyon in the west, that he is 'practicing' his own act by hurling his bicycle over a pile of gravel in a neighborhood driveway.

Paul starts out half a block down the street, pedals up to an impressive speed, and then makes his leap up and over the gravel. He has only landed on his face once. The neighborhood is getting quite a show (for free) and so far, not one soul in the block has even considered profiteering by selling television rights. *1974*

&&&

So it looks like its going to be an "Electronically Yours"

118

Christmas for the kiddies. There are Math Marvels that offer push button games that challenge a child's mind with more than 40,000 problems. They reward the child's successful answer with a musical salute.

There are electronic word machines, spelling games, and so on.

Star Wars stuff – where did you go?

&&&

I asked my neighbor boy, Paul Richmond, what he wants for Christmas this year.

"I'd tell you," Paul answered, "but you're sure going to be mad at me!"

"What did you ask for ... a Florida alligator or a siren for your bicycle?"

"I want a set of drums and I'm pretty sure I'm gonna get 'em."

Well, now, Paul. I hope you get the drums and I hope you will practice like Ringo Starr all winter and play Little League baseball all summer when the windows are open.

Just funnin', Paul. I wish I had learned to play drums myself!

(I may get up enough nerve this week to ask his younger brother, Stevie, what he wants for Christmas.)

&&&

The neighborhood kids, Paul and Stevie Richmond and their cousin, Chad Slavin, really made some great discoveries the other day. They each had found icicles hanging from the eaves

119

that measured six feet in length and we gave them one of ours which had dripped and frozen the length of 6 ½ feet. They could scarcely carry them around to their snow fort. Ah, winter!

February 1978

&&&

I overheard two pre-teen sisters engaging in a heated "discussion" the other day. Was it something earthshaking?

"It's YOUR turn to unload the dishwasher and put the things away."

"It is not. I put all the dirty dishes in it this morning for MY job."

Poor overworked little lasses.

&&&

Easter means many things to many people, but perhaps good will to our fellow man was one of Jesus' most significant teachings.

So with this in mind, and in the spirit of true friendship, the two first grade rooms at Lincoln School joined together for a friendly Easter party.

Miss Nora Bratschi's first grade students, numbering 27, were hosts at the party, and their guests were the 27 first grade pupils of Mrs. Jewell Traxler.

It is a tradition with the two rooms to have two friendship parties each year on such special days as Valentine's Day, Thanksgiving, St. Patrick's Day or Halloween.

Both Miss Bratschi and Mrs. Traxler feel that these occasions are invaluable in teaching the children the niceties of getting along with each other and the particular conventional requirements of being good neighbors as well.

"We could talk and lecture on how to do these things," said Mrs. Traxler, "but we could not possibly get it across as well as by actually letting the children do it themselves."

Since Miss Bratschi's youngsters were to be hosts this time, preparations were begun several weeks ago. This involved writing, counting, spelling and working.

Invitations were written and sent to the other first grade. Were they the regular who-what-when-where type of invitations? No, not these!

Each child cheerfully worded his own invitation, printed it carefully and delivered it personally to a first grader in Mrs. Traxler's room.

This preliminary item taken care of, Miss Bratschi called for suggestions on how they should go about making party plans. How about room decorations? What could they serve? (Every party must have refreshments.) How could they entertain the other children and make them happy while they were guests?

All these questions were to be resolved in a fun sense, yet with the true spirit of fellowship carefully tucked beneath.

Decorating the room took a lot of work, but when they were through, the results were outstanding.

A large bulletin board was devoted to the symbols of spring. Large flowers made from pastel ribbon, such as is delivered with a potted plant from the florist and handmade paper birds and trees bespoke the spring season.

An Easter Egg tree was a room project. Blown eggs were colored and placed on a real tree branch at the back of the room. A large, colorful Easter Rabbit poster and special window decorations completed the decorations.

Sit-down games were planned such as "Jelly Beans" (a counting exercise) and songs like "Bunny Rabbit" and "Blue Bird" were sung, complete with whistling and other sound effects. It was noted that almost all the children could whistle a tune.

Several of the pupils rose to read their original paragraphs on the "real" meaning of Easter. Tomorrow they would write their own ideas of what they thought was important about Easter. The imagination and talent of a six-year-old is always impressive.

Refreshments of Jello in individual paper cups and sugar cookies were proudly served by the children on placemats they had made from washable wallpaper. As they ate, they wore bunny rabbit hats.

It was a gay party and an unforgettable adventure in friendship.

But before the closing bell rang, there was yet another lesson to be learned. Each child brushed away cookie crumbs, gathered up the dishes, and tidied up the room.

As the thank-you-for-the-nice party goodbyes were said by Mrs. Traxler's room, you felt there was inner satisfaction in every little heart. You knew that two excellent teachers had furthered, at least for today, an undeniable feeling of good will and respect for others. *April 1968*

&&&

Rural Country School Easter

They must have a lot of fun while they're perfecting their reading, writing and multiplication tables in Mrs. Helen Marvin's 4th grade room at Mystic elementary school.

"We do plenty of fun things," they said as they greeted me at the door last Wednesday afternoon. Their faces showed it, and their cheery room showed it too. We had come for an Easter feature story after a mother had told us about the fabulous Easter egg tree the children had made.

In the center of the room, planted solidly in a large container covered with green paper and bunny rabbit decorations, was a real live tree ... not just a branch gilded with spray paint ... but a leafed-out wild choke cherry tree. The children had gone on a field trip as part of a nature project and selected the tree in the brush and brought it back to school. It became a part of their room and received careful watering. It appeared to reward the youngsters with tender green leaves and half-inch long formation clusters of choke berries.

The 4th graders began saving egg shells for their tree about a month ago. They "blew" the whites and yolks out through pin holes. Dying them a myriad of colors was the most fun.

"We would have had 256 eggs altogether but he (pointing at one of the boys) broke one!" said one of the girls.

A few tiny little banty eggs were scattered here and there on pipe cleaners. Before Easter, each child will take home some of the pretty eggs for a little Easter tree of his own.

How tall is their tree? Well, they didn't exactly know. So a yard stick was brought out and the class had an arithmetic lesson

123

in measuring. It was officially 9 feet, 2 inches tall and reached almost to the ceiling lights.

Evidence of spring was all around the room. Windowsills boasted blooming geraniums and here and there a sprig of pussywillow. One poster board featured a big red kite.

Mobiles

Mobiles with softly moving spring symbols hung from the ceiling. There were flowers, birds, eggs and fish, all of colored tissue paper. We learned about the fish because we forgot to remember that an adult never asks a child what he had made. I said (foolishly): "My, what a pretty mobile this one is. Such bright chirpy cardinals."

"Those aren't birds, they're fish." So they were fish.

They do a lot of reading in Mrs. Marvin's room, both at school and at home. For example, the children had read that there is nothing better than sassafras tea as a spring tonic. Why not try some. So Mrs. Marvin got some sassafras bark, brewed up a strong batch and sweetened it plenty. They all drank some on the first day of spring.

Sassafras for Snoopy

Then came a momentous decision. If a spring tonic is good for people, why wouldn't it also be fine for the class pet, a hamster named "Snoopy." So the little palomino colored rodent got several slurps of sassafras and became sassier than ever.

And about Snoopy, he is truly a class pet. Each member of the class has taken him home for at least one weekend. Even the boys and girls whose parents were less than enthused about having a hamster in the house permitted its presence for one weekend.

The class was enthusiastic about what they had done to make their room more cheerful. They were, however, a little surprised that a woman reporter showed up instead of a man. After all, aren't all big city reporters on television men like Huntley and Brinkley?

But Mrs. Marvin saved the day. "Remember, children," she said softly, "Jackie Kennedy was an inquiring reporter before she married John F. Kennedy."

The 4th graders smiled and accepted me gladly. I smiled too, because, other than the reporter bit, there is no other resemblance between Jackie and me. *March 1970*

Where Six Fish Were Painted and a Silvery Tree Shines

We are six little boys and girls and we go to school.

Our names are Myra, Debbie, Phillip, John, Sheryl and Larry and our teacher is Mrs. Delma Smith.

While there isn't anything unusual about children going to school, ours is a very special school. It is called Hope School (the Centerville Community Board of Education set it up just for us) and we all ride on the bus to get out here on Highway 60.

They say we are different children because something happened to us before or after we were born to keep our minds from learning as fast as the others and to make our bodies a bit clumsier than most kids.

But let us tell you about our school. We have some happy

times here at Hope from 9 in the morning until 2 o'clock.

Now take today for example!

Today Mrs. Smith wore the prettiest dress – just the color of cranberries. We like bright colors, you know.

Today was the day she said we could put up the shiny tree. Each of us put round balls on it, ever so carefully so they wouldn't break. Some of them did fall and break but we just tried again. The balls are as blue as the sky when you look up to watch a bird in a tree.

And it was today that we could paint with real paints on our plaques for mother's kitchen and on our "fish" for the bathroom at home. Mrs. Smith first put down plenty of newspapers on a table and then you should see us get started to paint. (A few paint puddles don't matter much.) One fish is blue, one is yellow and one is pink like the inside of a shell. There is even a spotted one.

Everybody has a plaque painted 'maple' that says "A Kitchen Prayer." Teacher made them out of plaster in a plastic mold just for us.

This is the day we will see slides on our new projector that some generous Centerville organizations and donators gave us. There is nothing better than seeing colored pictures.

Now you can meet us:

Here is Myra. She has only been to our school three weeks. She likes music and will show you how the piano sounds and where our record player is. She doesn't talk very much yet, but you can tell by those big brown eyes that she is going to try any day now.

Debbie, you'll notice, has a crippled up leg and hip but you should see her go across the room to the play telephones and the book shelf. She likes to hear stories and look at pictures.

Phillip carried his favorite toy. He particularly likes things that move because he moves a lot himself. His attention span is short but he is interested in finding out about what everybody is doing.

John is a curious fellow and inspects this puzzle and that chair with great care. He likes to do things with his hands and his painted fish is going to be very pretty.

Sheryl's main delights are the puzzles and she can make the large pieces fit into a zoo animal. She chatters quite a bit, we think, but she is only trying to be friendly.

And there's Larry. He is older and such a nice boy. You'll like him. He can read some words in Mrs. Smith's practice book and can even print some words and do some numbers. He helps Mrs. Smith, and he helps all of us.

Say, now, in a while a car will drive up and there will be a nice hot lunch from the Centerville High School cafeteria. We like to eat and it tastes good. You can stay if you want to.

Well, you see how it is with us here at Hope School. We are happy out here and when our mothers clean us up every morning, we can scarcely wait for Mrs. Brownie Johnson to come by in the school bus. She helps us and sometimes makes us laugh.

We know that when we get to school Mrs. Smith will have time to show us things and there will be music and singing, games and stories, and best of all – we are learning to take care

127

of ourselves in the bathroom and how to put on our own mittens and boots.

We are learning that if we want to be happy we mustn't kick, scream, pound, break, or grab things from each other.

It's time for the bus to come and Sheryl will probably get her red boots on the wrong feet (she won't get her feet wet anyhow) and Phillip will need help from Larry in zipping up his warm coat. But these things don't matter much.

We are glad to go home but we will want to come back. That is the way it is with the six of us at Hope School.

December 1967

&&&

We watched our last two youngsters; Craig and Nancy, march down in cap and gown Monday night and receive their diplomas from high school. We were proud. We predict that the members of this large class, as a whole, will do O.K. because it held some personal talent in almost any field you could name. Great potential there.

Congratulations to all the high school graduates. They are now part of the "reminiscing" group. "When I was in high-school," they'll be telling, "we didn't have a swimming pool."

And wait until their 10th class reunion! They'll be talking over "the old days" just like the rest of us. *May 1973*

Chapter 7

THE DARING SEVENTIES

According to my latest copy of Writers Digest, there is money to be made writing commercials for television. They're even crying for material to spring on an unsuspecting audience for 30 or 50 seconds, says the magazine. But if hitting a lucrative market means writing stuff like that toilet bowl commercial I saw the other night, then it's as clear as the handwriting on the bathroom wall that I won't make a dime at it.

You know the commercial – the one where the well-dressed lady goes into her hostess's bathroom to snoop. Anyway, either before or after the cause, she snoops. She lifts off the top of the toilet tank and peers down in. And what does she see? Well, there's the cutest little man floating merrily along upstream (or downstream, whichever) in the darlingness little boat on the prettiest blue "bowl cleaner" water. The snooper is ecstatic and she wants you to snoop too. "People do snoop in your bathroom, you know," she smirks.

Ah yes, well, I've got news for any snooper who lifts off the lid of my toilet tank. We already flushed down our little man in his little boat. I checked today.   *July 1977*

&&&

I really can't help listening to commercials when the television is on. One rerun of some of them is one too many.

Take the asinine one currently running.

A baby product advertisement on TV features a baby care class for mothers-to-be. One gal pipes up, "What does it mean when baby's diaper gives off an ammonia odor?"

The instructor beams and jumps at the chance to answer that one. She holds up the baby care product, smears it over the appropriate part of the anatomy of a doll they're using to practice changing diapers.

After some inane folderol, the mother-to-be picks up the doll and says, "Now doesn't that feel better?"

Now I probably would have answered the ammonia smell question by saying that the baby wet its pants. Things like that seem so simple to me. But what do I know? I didn't have Dr. Spock nor television commercials to answer my "what does it mean" questions. Thank goodness!   *August 1978*

&&&

My grandma Leigh would have liked television had she lived to enjoy this invention. Especially if Bing Crosby were performing.

She skimped and saved on the household and food bills to go to the picture show at the Majestic. She liked child star Margaret

O'Brien and loved to hear Bing sing. She eked out enough to buy records for our wind-up Victrola and they were usually Bing's songs.

She would have liked the musicales on TV and variety and comedy shows. "Going My Way" was a favorite.

But I wondered the other night how grandma would have reacted to some of the commercials ... especially the one where the girl is wearing the panty that doesn't show seams under her tight jeans and says, "Makes me feel like I'm not wearin' nothin'." Or the English Leather commercial where the girl says, "All my men wear English Leather, or they don't wear anything at all." Or the personal items advertising the beer commercials or the sleazy bedroom scenes.

She would have been aghast at the subject matter of *Mary Hartman, Mary Hartman* and would have croaked over the dialogue on *Maude*.

Come to think of it, grandma might have thrown the television set out the back door. *1977*

&&&

How times change. I went to a movie at the Majestic and by the time it was over I had scooted down so far in my seat that I could have picked the chewing gum off its underside. And some of the stuff you see on the tube makes you self conscious in your own living room.

Words

POT – Time was when pot meant the kettle you cooked your

131

Monday morning beans in, or pot meant the vessel that was kept under the bed. Nobody ever thought of having a "pot party."

TRIP – Taking a trip back years ago meant going on the train to Kansas City to visit relatives. It was usually a good trip, hardly ever a bad trip unless the train jumped the track. You could also trip and fall down. Now they trip out on LSD.

GRASS – Something that you use the lawnmower for. Now they smoke it.

MAKE OUT – When we used to refer to a couple as "making out" we probably meant that they were doing all right financially. Couples make out now, but it hasn't got much to do with the financial situation.

SLAMMER – Due to the preponderance of cop and robber TV shows, we now use the word "slammer" when someone's in jail. A slammer used to mean someone who slammed the screen door.

FAIRY – There was the tooth fairy, fairy godmothers and fairy tales. They were pretty ladies in flowing white gowns carrying a magic wand. Now they are men.

PLAY HOUSE – We neighborhood girls used to get out our favorite dolls and play house on a comfort under a shade tree. Now, couples play house when they live together.

BOOBY – Time was when club hostesses gave booby prizes to the ones who had the worst bingo or bridge scores. There were also booby traps set out during WW II. But today Racquel Welch would probably win the booby prize in a contest.

April 1976

&&&

I crossed the paths of three young men who I didn't know on the local square the other day. They were saying to each other, "We need some money, man." "Gotta get ahold of some bread, man."

Then one of them glanced my way and said to the others, "We could take that lady's purse, man."

'That lady' quickly went into the nearest store, man.

&&&

Every now and then a siding company person calls from Des Moines.

"This is Linda calling to tell you about So and So's exciting siding offer."

Then before you can open your mouth to say you don't want any, she reads off a sales pitch that is designed to keep her from coming up for air or for you to interrupt.

I always listen because I'm not accustomed to hanging up on anyone. However, at the end I always give my stock answer, "We have a brick house." That usually stops them cold.

Not so, Tuesday. Linda informed me that brick houses pose absolutely no problem anymore. "We cover right over those unsightly bricks," she said, not concealing her pleasure and unaware that our brick home is not "unsightly." "When can our representative stop by to consult with you?"

Now I'll have to think up another answer or learn to hang up.

&&&

I recently received the book "When I Say No I Feel Guilty" that my daughter Rosemary thought I should read. This was a bestseller on Assertiveness Training by Manuel J. Smith, Ph.D. and I must say it was interesting reading!

For example, it asked: "Do you let people walk all over you?" "Are you asking for a raise and not getting it?"

So far, it has taught me to say NO to the telephone solicitor from Des Moines who insists that I buy siding for my brick house; NO to selling greeting cards door to door for a worthy cause; NO to the Junior High kids selling magazines because my supply reaches the ceiling now.

The book taught me how to say no, but is hasn't made me conquer a twinge of guilt.

"You don't have to give a reason for saying no," says the author. If an encyclopedia salesperson gets a foot in your door, just say "no" over and over until he leaves. Even if he says that you don't care if your grandchildren do grow up to be dummies without his encyclopedia, you keep on saying that you're not interested. That's called the "Broken Record" resistance, and it's supposed to work every time.

And if people try to manipulate you, you have the right to offer no excuses or reasons to justify your answers or behavior.

And about the question "Are you asking for a raise and not getting it?" Well, I haven't asked the boss for a raise for my column writing yet. By the time I finish reading the book and get practiced up on being assertive, I may ask him. I hope he won't feel guilty if he says "NO!"   *January 1978*

Convoy

So now some radio stations won't play the truck song "Convoy" anymore? And C.W. McCall could be making fun of the state highway troopers and calling them Smokey the Bear, eh? And it's scary to some that a convoy of semi trucks might be taking over the highways at 98 miles an hour - is it?

Well, now, many listeners say that it's silly not to let them air the recording, judging from some of the other objectionable garbage that's being played by disc jockeys for music these days.

The truckers are only funning. It's all a big joke. But maybe the guys who nixed the record have driven a couple thousand miles or so on the highways since the 55 mile speed limit law went into effect. Maybe they were passed by every semi from Alabama to Iowa so fast that they couldn't even see the name of the company on the rear end of the truck.

We were. You don't see those semis again, even though they are loaded to the rafters with steel fence posts or something like that and the Tennessee hills are pretty rolling. But there's always more coming from behind.

Trucking is big business and we need it. Wheeling the interstates probably would get pretty dull for a truck who stuck to 55 miles an hour. After the 3rd trip, seeing the scenery around Dogpatch, Arkansas, might get boring. Turning his little CB on could add spark to the travel, or playing "Pass the Other Truck" game might relieve the boredom a bit.

These anti-"Convoy" record banners might have gulped diesel fumes through open car windows last summer and have forgotten that the fumes sort of prime up your lungs in case you go to

California.

Naturally, the 55 per hour drivers figure that Smokey is sure to stop them if they dare go 65. One careless, foolhardy, lead-footed car driver went around us doing about that speed when sure enough, Smokey curbed him and wrote him a ticket. The tailwinds from a passing semi blew the ticket right out of his hands.

There was one place, though, in Indiana where everybody was piddling along at 55 mph. It was a weird sensation – there you are between five semis ahead and about a dozen steaming along behind. Perfect synchronization in motion. Weird. For 25 minutes CB 'ears' were out on sticks on that heavily patrolled Indiana road. Then zoom, the first line is out of sight and the ones behind you rock your car as they pass around you.

So you can see why that "Convoy" song doesn't bother me. No sir. I know it's all in fun. Who's going to believe that a big bunch of trucks are going to go through Iowa at 98 miles an hour? Most drivers know for a fact that it's doggone hard to keep those big babies at 75. And who's gonna believe that truckers are bullying interstate drivers or finagling the State Troopers? Tut. Tut.

And besides, Sonny Pruitt of TV's *Rolling On* is one of my favorite actors (Claude Akins), and the show is one of my favorite shows. Sonny Pruitt can roll his rig down the highway any time he wants to.   *January 1976*

*Compilers Note: "**Convoy**" was a 1975 novelty song performed by C.W. McCall (pseudonym of Bill Fries) that became a number-one hit* *in the USA (no. 2 in the UK) and helped start a worldwide craze for citizens band (CB) radio. A few lyrics:*

Yeah them smokies 'as thick as bugs on a bumper
They even had a bear-in-the-air
I sez callin' all trucks, this here's the Duck
We about to go a huntin' bear
Cause we gotta great big convoy, rockin' through the night

Well we laid a strip fer the Jersey Shore
An' prepared to cross the line
I could see the bridge 'as lined with bears
But I didn't have a doggone dime
I sez Pig-Pen, this here's the Rubber Duck
We just ain't a gonna pay no toll
So we crashed the gate doin' ninety-eight
I sez, let them truckers roll, 10-4
Cause we gotta mighty convoy, rockin' through the night ...
Convoy ... Convoy
   Song by Bill Fries and Chip Davis
     &&&

There won't be any cheese when astronauts Armstrong and Aldrin become the first men to land on the moon – and eat on the moon.

Although the spacemen will be able to munch cheddar cheese sandwiches going to and from the moon, NASA officials say there won't be cheese of any sort during the approximately 30-hour stay on the lunar surface.

While on the moon, Armstrong and Aldrin will each eat two meals. One will consist of bacon squares, peaches, sugar cookie cubes, freeze-dried coffee and instant breakfast drink. The other will be made up of cream of chicken soup, beef stew, date fruit cake, grape punch and orange Tang.

The freeze-dried items eaten by American spacemen consist of two basic types of items. There is rehydratable food – food that must be reconstituted with water – such as coffee. There are also solid, bit-sized cubed foods which are eaten directly from the package such as cinnamon toasted bread cubes.

All rehydratable foods have an injection valve at one end and a sealed eating tube at the other. For "cold" foods, the astronaut inserts the cold-valve nozzle of a metered water dispenser into the package and injects the water (55 degree F). For "hot" foods, the hot-valve nozzle is used (155 degree F). The astronaut knows exactly how much water to add from the instructions printed on the package.

As he removes the nozzle, the valves in the water dispenser and the package seal themselves, preventing spillage. The astronaut then squeezes the food from the package into his mouth through an eating tube.

In addition to the two meals, the lunar module will contain extra drinks, dried fruit, candy, bread, ham salad spread and turkey and gravy.

Freeze-dried foods are becoming more popular on earth and constitute most of the items served to our astronauts.

Regardless of what minerals, plant life or food if any is on the moon, at least there will be food in the module. Some persons still insist that there is life on the moon. We don't know. But there will be – when the astronauts touch down!   *July 1969*

Compilers note: The lunar mobile "Eagle" landed on the moon July 20, 1969. Six manned moon landings were carried out between 1969 and 1972.

A Break From Viet Nam

Like great silver birds, planes leave the mainland and fly over the Pacific Ocean to the beautiful Hawaiian Islands, their jet streaks fading away as they skim down at Honolulu's bustling Hickham field.

And 24 hours a day, these huge aircraft carry hundreds of young wives to Hawaii, where they will meet their husbands from who they have been separated many anxious months.

The soldier will be on a well-deserved Rest and Relaxation break from the hostile fighting and mortar fire in South Vietnam. Hawaii is considered about half-way between the mainland and Vietnam and an ideal meeting place …

Sgt. Hawkins

A soldier sits under his 'hootch' on a firebase in the Ruong Ruong Valley (Vietnam). It is raining and it has been for the last few days. He is cold and wet and caked with mud – it has been a miserable day.

And although the monsoon season is always dreaded, Sgt. Donald W. Hawkins of the 101st Airborne Division is finding a measure of comfort in brief reflection on six wonderful days of Rest and Recuperation leave he spent in Hawaii with his wife, Elizabeth, and baby.

He writes: "With a sigh of relief, I settled back in my seat as the giant Pan America 707 began to roar down the runway away from the Ton Son Nhut Airport in Saigon. This was the moment I had waited for - my R and R in Hawaii and a reunion with my wife and baby daughter I had heard so much about, but had never seen."

Hawkins related that he tried to read a book and take a nap during the 13 hours of flight time, but his excitement wouldn't let him do neither. He tried to visualize what his baby would be like, but couldn't even visualize his new role as a father! He thought of his wife and how beautiful she was when they said farewell more than seven months ago in Des Moines.

Then Vietnam kept floating in and he wrote: "I thought of the intense heat, the intolerable insects, the heavy rucksack and I could hear again in my mind the sharp crack of an AK-47 bullet. Places like Hue Phu Bai rolled in and ambushes at Phu Loc; the 'Hook,' the 'Bowling Alley' (the place along the coast referred to as the 'street without joy'). There was the nightmare of Ashau Valley and I winced at the memory of the buddies I'd lost there.

Then there was the Elephant Valley, Back Ma, Hill 592, and the Ruong Ruong Valley."

"Then," Hawkins wrote, "The big plane set down in Honolulu and taxied to a halt. Customs was quick and efficient."

And then he saw a mob of women at the reception building. It was like running a gauntlet, with every few feet a woman

140

giving out a shriek and jumping into the arms of some GI walking past. Then he saw his wife, Liz, and his baby Michelle was crying. It was a very happy moment.

"I couldn't believe the motel room – wall-to-wall carpet instead of wall-to-wall mud – and the bathroom. I thought back on all the cat holes I'd dug the last several months so I flushed the stool again and again and again just to hear that sound!"

There were other things this American soldier and the many others like him serving our country will never forget about their six-day Rest and Recuperation leaves in Hawaii. The country is breath-takingly beautiful, the food is deliciously different and the rides around the island were impressive.

For a short time, Vietnam faded from his mind. But in the night, sometimes a soldier will waken sharply because guard duty is still in his sub-conscious.

On the plane again for Vietnam and two more months in that swampy field of hostile action.

And thoughts lean toward Christmas …   *September 1969*

Compilers note: Fortunately Sergeant Hawkins did make it back home. More than Fifty thousand Americans lost their lives. The last remaining U.S. troops were withdrawn in 1973 and the war ended in 1975. Three to four million Vietnamese from both sides also lost their lives.   *(Wikipedia.org)*

Chapter 8

THROUGHOUT THE YEAR

It's January. And as one who appreciates living in a state where there are four seasons and who believes that there is a deep need for all of them, I don't really mind cold, snowy, icy January too much.

I made a few New Year's resolutions this year. I try not to make the same resolutions each year so that I don't break them more than once.

Books: Read some.

Quit watching the *Gong Show* and my soap opera: It upsets me when they change faces on me. I want the old Monica, Heather and Karen back. And when they killed Lana off a few weeks ago without any prior notice to me, I didn't like it. And as for the *Gong Show*, I'm mad at Chuck Barris because he doesn't pull his hat down farther over his face and I don't like the things lewd J.P. Morgan says.

Keep house better: Pick up the litter in the living room so that I don't have to leave people standing in the doorway more than 10 minutes. Breathe the air; Get out doors and walk out to the dog house every day.

Establish a writing schedule: Keep a firm writing schedule every day and stick to it no matter if the fire truck goes by or the neighbors all gather for coffee to discuss things without me.

Be nice: Especially to the women who get new towels, living room suites, carpeting and dishwashers this year.

I'll make other resolutions as I go along the rest of the 364 days.

&&&

It was Ground Hog day Sunday and according to the experts, the little critter didn't see his shadow for the first time in 15 years.

And that means that we will have six weeks of beautiful winter instead of bad winter.

And I figure we might as well depend on the ground hog as anything else because everybody knows that the things like a ring around the moon means a change in the weather. Or a red sky in the morning – sailor's warning.

The weather men haven't done too well lately forecasting the weather. I think they work in little rooms that don't have any windows. Thus, they give us this 20 percent chance of rain prediction while it's raining cats and dogs outside.

It might as well be that the ground hog tells us what's what as anybody.

&&&

St. Patrick's Day is almost here again. Being about one quarter Irish has always made me enjoy the wearin' o' the green.

144

Did you know that March 17 is the anniversary of St. Patrick's death, not his birth? That his burial place is unknown, but it doesn't matter, for Patrick, Ireland's patron saint, is wherever you set foot in Ireland?

Ask an Irishman, "Do you believe in leprechauns?" He'll say, "No, but they're there."

&&&

"You should have seen me on St. Patrick's Day," City Clerk Tom King told us the other day.

Yes, we should have!

It seems that King really went in for the wearin' o' the Green that day, not stopping until he had tinted his white, wavy hair as Kelly green as he could get it with food coloring.

Imagine the stir he caused when people came into city hall on municipal business to see a leprechaun sitting behind the city clerk's desk.

&&&

If you depended, as I did, on the calendar to proclaim spring, we sure got fooled. Or the first robin who hopped, red breast deep in the snow. But when neighbor Grace Adams brought over pussywillows Monday, I knew it was spring. I put them in a green potter vase (without water) where they will last in all their pristine pinkish-gray glory until next spring.

The martin scouts have arrived in the backyard of neighbor Adams, looked into every nook and cranny of the high rise bird house apartments with their white "coolie" hat shaped roofs,

145

staked out a free rent apartment and left to return for their families. Spring has surely arrived!

The next episode in the moving process will be the big feud! Not between the Martins and the Coys, but between the Martins and the sparrows – those reckless backyard boys.

We've watched the mix-up for many springs and can predict that the outcome will be that the Martins will take over three-fourths of the high rise and the sparrows will fight for the rest.

So goes the summer.

&&&

Over in the open spaces near the county fair grounds during the recent windy weather, the youngsters launched their kites on a hill. On one particularly colorful afternoon we could see The Jolly Green Giant, Chinese Dragon, Yellow Bird and The Red Baron cavorting together in the big kiteways of the sky.

And seeing the kids with their high-flying kites reminded me of the last time I held a kite string in my hand. We lived in Charles City, Iowa at the time and our first child, son David, was in elementary school. He decided to get his brand new box kite into the air during school lunch hour. Assisted by his friends, he tied on a nylon stocking tail and an extra ball of kite string.

They did such a grand job getting it up into the air that the yellow box soared into the wild blue yonder. We could barely see it. Then the school bell rang and son handed me the string and they all ran off to the school grounds, leaving me with a string that tugged so hard I thought I was hanging on to a tornado tail.

The neighbors never did let me forget the day I stood out on 6th Avenue flying a kite. It took nearly two hours to land the thing and how was I to know that it would eventually get caught on the telephone wires and flap into sheds?

&&&

To me April is like a beautiful, trusting child ... it comes with no pretense ... with the whole world bursting into bloom, trees misty green with tiny leaves, skies blue with patches of furry white clouds. It's easy to believe in such a world.

I'm glad spring is here with its green grass, crocuses and tulips popping up. In fact, I am getting quite enthused about hunting again for those Dutchmen's Britches and wild violets in the wooded place of my childhood.

Centerville also has its gorgeous Tulip trees making splashes of April pink in yards all over town. The one in Lucille Kauzlarich's yard is particularly lovely.

&&&

Easter was celebrated in the spring in recognition of the rebirth of nature.

The Council of Christian Churches in the year 325 decided that Easter should be on the first Sunday following the Paschal full moon. Believers making their way to the yearly Easter festival needed the light of the full moon to aid their travels and this was the principal reason for so establishing the time of Easter.

The longing for the colorful flowers of spring following a

147

long cold winter motivates the use of flowers at Easter time. The tulip, crocus, daffodil and the early blooming forsythia bush make us know that from lowly dirt, trampled and cold, will come renewed life.

Our churches in our many communities and cities across the nation will receive us for holy week and communion. We are given Monday, Thursday, Good Friday and Easter Sunday that we might know the meaning of Easter – the risen Christ.

Its deep religious significance transcends flowers, fashions, customs, eggs of rabbits, even as the Son of God transcends the little incidentals of our man-made ways.

&&&

A dear friend of mine is one of those people who somehow find the time (and the inclination) to do nice little things for others. This Easter, for example, she sent Easter cards and tucked down in each was a crocheted pink bunny lapel pin.

Little thoughts do make a difference.

&&&

I've always liked the month of May and when we were kids we always saw to it that this great time of year was ushered in with fanfare and homemade maybaskets to our friends.

I had almost forgotten this beloved tradition until the other night. The doorbell rang and I was presented with a beautiful genuine, homemade May basket filled with wrapped candy treats. The giver was pretty teenager, Debbie Mitchell, daughter of a school day friend, Mrs. Mary Mitchell. Debbie said: "My mother and I read and enjoy your column every week and we thought you'd like a maybasket as a token of our appreciation."

Did I!! This one was made with construction paper all prettied up with butterflies and a fancy handle. It was folded with four stand-up points just like in the old days. Debbie's basket brought back memories.

We used to make ours out of scraps of leftover wallpaper. When Frances Peterson's folks papered their parlor in green leaves and gold plume spray, we knew that paper would sure make glorious maybaskets and we saved the scraps. When my grandma papered her bedroom walls with "tiny pink roses on ivory background," we thought we had it made. A big bonanza came one year when one of the more aggressive kids wheedled a big sample wallpaper book out of a paperhanger friend.

There were lots of ways to fold a maybasket and hold it tight with flour and water paste. The rolled cone shape was easiest, and it held more flowers. And those flowers! We walked to the end of the street to our favorite spot by a tiny creek and there, on the hillsides, we gathered Sweet Williams, purple and white violets, blue bells, Dutchmen's Britches, anemones and buttercups.

We would put the baskets beside the front of the door or hand on the doorknob, knock and then run!   *May 1973*

Mother's Day *(1938)*

As Father Time winds his way with the world in his arms into another month, we find ourselves looking out into a season which we sometimes think is the most beautiful of all. Wild flowers are flourishing in Mother Nature's fields and woods and tame and equally beautiful buds and plants are blooming or raising their sprouts above earth which has lost its cold and frost.

Someone knew that this was the ideal time of the year to honor God's greatest gift to mankind, "Mother," and so, although each one holds a personal honor for his mother deep in his heart, tribute is paid publicly each year to "Motherhood," as clubs, societies, churches and organizations take part and add to the loveliness of that day.

May you and yours have a happy, precious Mother's Day next Sunday.   *May 1938*

Memorial Day

I remember back when May 30th was called Decoration Day. That's exactly what we did – decorate the graves of loved ones. Now it is known as Memorial Day and has been sneaked up to May 29th by a congressional bill designed to give us three-day holiday weekends. Surprising what can be done when they put their minds to it. You see, if a traditional holiday doesn't fall on Saturday, Sunday or Monday, they fix it so it will. It's the new order of things and we'd best move along with the changing times or find ourselves waving the flag on the wrong Fourth of July some day.

Anyway, we youngsters always considered Decoration Day a very special enjoyable holiday despite the solemn reason for its origin. It always marked the end of school, a respite from work and the arrival of lively visiting cousins who could share fishing spots and a picnic at the city park.

We felt good about placing our flower offerings in fruit jars on graves of our ancestors early that morning. Few of us had the money to buy fresh floral sprays and big fancy wreaths. We couldn't afford showy copper urns or professionally planted shrubs. Instead, we picked our own early roses, iris, and lilies of the valley and whatever peonies happened to be in bloom at the time.

I know that we middle-aged folks eventually get used to three day weekends. Aren't we the plucky, versatile bunch who adjusted so well to Daylight Savings time and took the moon walks in our stride? Didn't we get over our frustration when they changed Armistice Day to Veterans Day and moved it from November 11 to an obscure date in October last fall? Well, at least Christmas is still red lettered on the calendar as December 25th.

May 1972

&&&

We keep reading a lot about tornadoes and are reminded that storm weather is near.

Now we are told that the southwest corner is not the right place to be if a twister strikes.

We are also informed that there will never be a tornado if the ground isn't dry. The day will be warm and humid and eerie yellow and black clouds will darken the sky.

The warnings are so many and so complicated that they include: Don't be in a school building; watch the TV screen – if it turns a brilliant white like Liberace's teeth, watch out; listen to the radio – tornado sighters may have seen the clouds funnel up;

151

get under a sturdy workbench or table in the basement; get into a closet.

Preparedness pays off. The best place to go is to an old fashioned cave. (We don't have any.) We probably won't remember to watch the TV screen. And if time runs out, we won't remember whether it's the southwest corner or the northwest.

The closets are definitely out because they are so full we could never get in, likewise the workbench in the basement. By the time we'd get the stuff removed from underneath, we'd be feeling the wind down our necks.

If worst comes to worst, we may find space in the first floor hallway.

&&&

The Fourth of July weekend is coming up. I remember when it was almost the greatest thing in the world to go to the 4th of July celebration in the city park. We always had wienies and watermelon that day. Somehow the magic of fireworks has dimmed and the planning for holiday festivities isn't what it used to be at our house.

&&&

It's my birthday tomorrow and I'm not bragging, I'm complaining. My birthdays have long ceased to be earthshaking events worthy of five-gun salutes and making wishes over the flames of pretty pink candles. Things have gotten so tame, in fact, that if anybody shot off guns now, I'd think it was the

152

premature opening of the pheasant season and if the family lit 55 candles we'd have a major conflagration on our hands.

Actually, though, I plan to arise Thursday morning as usual, just as though nothing terrible had happened overnight. I'll pretend all day that I don't give a hoot that I am getting so old I can't accept an invitation to a Japanese tea because I'd never get back up off the floor, gracefully or otherwise.

I intend to make a great sacrifice on my day – make a chocolate birthday cake (which my family prefers) rather than the angel food cake I'd like. We mothers who are getting old just have to face these things, you know.   *Age 55 August 1972*

&&&

I noted in Clyde Holbrook's Tuesday column that I had a birthday last week on Ridiculous Day. Sure, I knew which quartet called me at 7:30 in the morning and sang the Happy Birthday song. Where else but at the Iowegian news office are voices trained to be heard over the Associated Press teletype machines, two electric tape punchers, four clanging typewriters, a battery of ringing telephones and the arguing in the composition room about the results of a softball game played the night before? Only Theda, Gladys, Clyde and Alex can sing like that.

Actually, the birthday was really great. I was also sung to by Imogene Tissue of Moravia and Mrs. J.L. Shankster and kidded by experts like Leona Long and Mary Knowles. The phone rang all day.

&&&

153

Age 60

Well, it's the Chinese Year of the Serpent and according to Chinese astrology, this is my year, the year that fortune will shine down on me. I was born in the year of the serpent.

(The year of the rat doesn't sound any better – or the dragon or the boar!) I can use a favored year.

In the last few years, since I've somehow joined the legion of Iowa's greatest majority – the senior citizens, I've tried to pretend that I don't have a birthday anymore.

This year, for instance, I left the calendar on the July page with its pretty covered bridge scene until someone noticed that July only has 31 days and that they were gone.

These ploys would probably work very well, I suppose, were it not that I like birthday presents. Everybody knows that you have to "hint" at least a week in advance or you don't get any. I really hate to have the family run to the store at the last minute and get a jar of rejuvenating face crème when what I'd really like is a pre-paid cruise to Jamaica or someplace.

When you've lived more years already than you've got left, that's a pretty good sign that you are not as young as you used to be!

Sure, I knew the day was coming, but I really wasn't prepared to be catapulted into another decade when I had definitely planned to "stay on hold".

And apparently I'm not aging gracefully. I stubbed my toe on the bedpost just because I was trying to avoid looking in the dresser mirror this morning.

Once I used to bounce out of bed, now I clamber over the

side, testing both feet to the carpet to see if the old knees are still hinged to the rest of my legs.

A friend reminded me that "today is the first day of the rest of your life." A right nice philosophy to hand someone who is already "over the hill."

Another said cheerfully, "Well, you are only as old as you feel." I hope not.

Actually, life is like building with blocks. You try to start with a solid foundation, and then add each year to the next. Some of the blocks tend to sway and some almost crack under the strain, but you just keep going.

Perhaps we all should be aware that we are privileged to live through the Seven Ages of Man as Shakespeare defined. Enjoy each age to the fullest and let each one become a building block for others to follow. *August 1977*

September

"The goldenrod is yellow,
The corn is turning brown;
The trees in apple orchards
With fruit are bending down."

These are lines from Helen Hunt Jackson's poem "September" which I have always liked.

September is a rather nice month … a stepping stone from hot summer into placid autumn. Its flowers are very distinctive and royal in shades of purple and gold. In a drive last Sunday afternoon, we spotted purple thistle, and a lighter purple jimpson weed with patches of horsemint, splashy with a paler lavender.

And the most golden of all gold's is the goldenrod with its waving fronds of very tiny flowerettes. We saw huge sunflowers, little sunflowers, black-eyed Susan's and Spanish needles, and here and there, as an accent color to match the heavens, were vines of blue morning glories climbing the wood fence posts.

And of course there are grasshoppers which delight the cats, and a few yellow butterflies still flit around the purple butterfly spike in the garden.

September ... a special time of the year.   *September 1975*

&&&

By the 20th of this month the full Harvest moon will beam over the Iowa countryside and three days later autumn begins.

Cobwebs will drape across the Queen Anne's lace and ripening grapes smell so good they make you think of the purple grape pies grandma used to make.

The sunflower grown tall in the backyard is heavy with seeds but the neighborhood birds are pecking them away. Undaunted by cooler nights, the cerise and white petunias are blooming and won't stop until a frost or two. Maybe summer flowers are losing their splendor, but we'll have chrysanthemums and purple poke and vivid red sumac along the roadsides to enhance the scene.

Remember when we used to treasure a shiny, polished buckeye to tote around "for good luck"?

Bittersweet is still one of the brightest harbingers of the fall season and what's nicer than seeing a row of jellies and jams on the shelf ... the honey colored wild crabapple, red strawberry, purple grape and the newest color of beet jelly.

Maybe September is a month to sort of schedule our time because many of us spend time living in the past and worrying about how much security we'll have in the future when we ought to be living today to the utmost and in the best way we can.

&&&

October strutted in like a color guard leading the autumn parade. Red maple leaves are silhouetted against blue skies studded with white clouds.

&&&

All Hallows Eve

There'll be a knock on the door or the doorbell will ring, followed and repeated by 50 or more come next Halloween night as little monsters, spooks and witches will appear with sacks opened wide to receive a treat. The children love it and the oldsters tolerate it.

A harmless custom in the modern age, it was not always so, much to the relief of those who remember way back when horses mysteriously left their stables, hens crackled furiously after being given whisky-soaked grain, gates were unhinged, and carts would end up on farm roofs. Be glad it isn't that way now.

Now a carefree, fun-filled festivity for children, Hallowe'en started out in a very different fashion. In one of its earliest

157

forms, its purpose was to confuse and mislead the evil spirits summoned by Sambain, Lord of the Dead, as they roamed the earth on Celtic New Years Day.

Broom-born witches and devilish black cats struck terror into the hearts of innocent people whose homes shook and moaned amid whistling autumn winds. Some neighbors, with meanness in their hearts, availed themselves of this awesome atmosphere to don outlandish disguises and commit pranks and mischief which would be blamed on unholy spooks.

To add to the dread that Hallowe'en inspired, criminals were burned alive and animals sacrificed. Such barbarous rites were outlawed by the conquering Romans in the British Isles; however, their suppression was not entirely successful as women presumed to be witches underwent a similar fate as recently as in our own Puritan days.

Hallowe'en did not become popular in this country until the 1840's, following the great Irish immigration. In earlier days, its pre-Reformation religious aspect as All Hallows' Eve had affronted the predominantly Protestant colonist.

Anoka Minn.

One morning in 1919, the residents of Anoka, Minn., were awakened by what resembled fog horns or the mooing of cows.

The latter explanation turned out to be the right one; scores of placid bovines were crowding the streets. The invaders were seeking something to eat in homes where a door was unlatched.

As Hallowe'en pranks came, even in those days, this one had passed the limit of what Anokans were willing to endure. They decided, then and there, to resort to a whole program of contests, parades and other forms of youthful entertainment in order to channel young energies along more constructive paths on Hallowe'en.

Window soaping, for the most part, has been replaced by a sponsored window painting contest such as Centerville merchants promote. Children's parties and costume competitions are expected to minimize tire deflating and other senseless pranks.

Dummy Trick

Even mild-mannered, law abiding people like us, took part in some pretty stupid tricks back in "the old days." One idea, in particular, comes to mind and we are not proud of ourselves today for being in on it.

Most of the neighborhood children thought it was harmless fun, including Bob Stephenson, Dorothy Campbell, Frances Peterson and myself. Bob stuffed and tied a gunny sack to resemble a person (no small task) and rigged it up to a pulley in a tree overhanging the front sidewalk. The rope could be held while sitting on the porch by perfectly innocent children, apparently, to passersby, minding their own business. When someone came walking down the street the idea was to let the dummy down right in front of them on the sidewalk.

Shrieks usually greeted the whole business and loud remonstrations from the 'victim' who walked, unhurt, on down the street. Bob also provided Halloween fun by tying a cord to an empty purse and yanking it away when the unsuspecting

passerby stooped to pick it up
"Tricks or Treats" night isn't really so bad!   *October 1967*
&&&

When you ride through the Iowa countryside and instead of seeing red maple leaves and yellowed weeping willow fronds you only see abandoned bird nests perched precariously in the barren tree tops, then you know it's November – gray November.

According to the Farmers' Almanac, there are several foolproof signs of a hard winter:

1. *Woodpeckers sharing a tree*
2. *How high the hornets nest 'twill tell how high the snow will rest.*
3. *Muskrats burrowing a hole high on the river bank.*
4. *Unusual abundance of acorns.*
5. *Pigs gathering sticks.*

Thanksgiving

A time to reap the good of all our labors and a time to sow new seeds of compassion and love in our hearts.

We could never get our "Thank-You's" all said in just one day, so doesn't it make pretty good sense to remember to space a few of the things we're thankful for throughout the other 364 days of the year?

Thanksgiving Day was the one day of the year, I recall, that we could have all we wanted to eat of meat, vegetables, salads and desserts – all at one meal!

160

Mother and grandma always went all out for birthdays and holidays even though we may have eaten lots of beans and fried potatoes the rest of the time.

Thanksgiving seemed to be extra special. Mother had a set of pure white, paper thin Bavarian china and crystal goblets and William Rogers silverware. Grandma was the proud owner of a white linen tablecloth with a Thanksgiving motif woven in and when the round oak table was set with matching napkins and cut glass jelly and relish dishes, it was the most beautiful and festive table I had ever seen.

We didn't have roast turkey much in those days. It wasn't fashionable even for those who could afford it. Mostly we had roast chicken or duckling and once we had an oversized roasted goose. Just once we had a goose because after grandma finished cleaning the grease spatters from the coal stove, she vowed that that fat fowl would be the last.

We had the usual sweet potatoes, cranberries and trimmings, but our dessert was always English Plum pudding, made with suet, tied in a cheese cloth bag and steamed for hours. Being from England, it was grandma's traditional food from home.

We never knew there was any other kind of stuffing than homemade bread seasoned with homegrown sage, handpicked leaf by leaf and hand rubbed.

Food memories of Thanksgivings gone by somehow seem more poignant than they do now. Perhaps it's because food was harder to come by and we never seemed to have quite as much as we thought we could have eaten. Eating out and rib-eye steak dinners were something that they did in Hollywood. A treat for us was a nickel hamburger at Lute's.

So, along with you readers, I'm thankful for so many things this day … the best of neighbors, the many thoughtful, kind friends and a family who cares what happens to me.

My mother always said to live one day at a time the very best you can. I'm thankful I had such a wonderful mother, every day of my life.

&&&

There were some scrumptious food dishes at Erma (husband's sister) and Dale Scritchfield's annual family Thanksgiving dinner. The traditional turkey, dressing, candied yams, relishes, twice-baked potatoes, pumpkin pie. But where was the cranberry sauce?

No doubt everyone thought the other was going to bring it after what happened last year. Then we had cranberry relishes, cranberry salad, cranberry sauce, cran-apple juice, cranberry nut bread and cranberry sherbet. No wonder!

Now that Thanksgiving Day is in the past, it's clear sledding to Christmas. Smile when you think of Christmas, for if it weren't for this beautiful holiday season, December would be a mighty dreary month with its short days and bleak, cold nights.

&&&

Christmas

Christmas means a lot of things to us: Angels, anthems, crèche, decorations, presents, oranges, stars, stable, tinsel, old folks, Mary, wreaths, children, Jesus, friends, candlelight, evergreens, visitors, love. The very name of Christmas has sparkle in its sound.

It also has the shine of golden baubles; the fragrance of a northern pine; the smells of ruby jelly and ham; the rustle of secret gift wrapping; the tinkle of silver bells; the warmth of a hearth fire; the brilliance of the heavens and a reverence anew for the wondrous Christ child's birth.

&&&

Some people don't appreciate receiving Christmas "form letters" which relate all the good things that happened to Dick and Jane during the year.

Well, let me say this about that. I'd much rather get a form letter than a card which just has a gold printed John and Jane Doe on it when you haven't heard from them for a year.

My choice of Christmas cards so far is one from niece, Dr. Shirley Scritchfield and husband Tom Kodera, which depicted in stark white, black and red, a hand reaching for another which held a single poinsettia flower. It read: "If only every hand that reaches could touch ... LOVE."   *December 1978*

&&&

No, I haven't got all my Christmas shopping done. I intend to crochet an afghan apiece for my two daughters this Christmas. Maybe I should go out and buy the yarn.

&&&

Some things you don't need to buy me for Christmas:
A bean bag chair: Even though you can buy one for $14.96,

I don't want one. I managed to sink down low to the floor in such a creation at my daughter Rosemary's home and found that with my legs spraddled on the carpet, it was not only uncomfortable but disconcerting. Getting up out of it was worse. Rolling out over one side is the only way.

A Shrunken Head Apple Sculpture Kit: You can save $7.77 by not buying this kit for me, although the picture of Vincent Price on the box lid dangling shrunken apple heads in each hand is probably worth something. I have a distinct distaste for shrunken heads.

A Habit Rail Hamster and Gerbil Starter Set: Even though the little plastic cage thing includes an instruction book, all for $7.99, I can do without this gift. We had a hamster once. He became very smart. Besides spinning the little revolving wheel in his cage and climbing up and down the little wooden steps we made for him, he learned how to reach his little paw through and unclip the clasp on his little cage, thereby letting his little self out to roam the house. Where, oh where, did that little hamster go?

&&&

How have you arranged your Christmases? Have you placed each one in its own box – tied with red ribbon and set it in consecutive order down memory lane? Have you strung them like Christmas lights with only the brightest, happiest ones remaining lit?

No matter. All of our Christmases have been very different and they belong to us. Some of us have been lonely for family at Christmas, some of us were married at Christmas and others of us have known sorrow at Christmas. But most of us have known the feeling of being close to the Christ Child especially at this time when the eastern star shines brighter.

&&&

I've never thought there was much wrong with perpetuating the Santa Claus myth as long as it was fun for little children. I didn't believe in using Santa as a threat for good behavior. I did, however, point out the window to our willow tree where Santa's little elves just might be watching some particularly unruly children the week before Christmas.

Maybe you've realized lately that there have been a lot of comments about Santa Claus. The static seems to be whether or not we should keep the Santa Claus myth going with our young children.

One eminent psychiatrist of our day, Dr. Jonathan Salk (son of Dr. Jonas Salk of polio vaccine fame) wrote recently that he feels it is wrong to perpetrate the Santa fantasy on the basis that if we lie to our children about this, then they could rightfully think we lie to them about other things if we take a notion. He apparently frowns on the Santa Claus legend and intimates that we use it just to keep the little kids in line for a few weeks.

Well, the good doctor has a point there. Somehow I never felt guilty about it before. Nor do I recall feeling bitter against adults for my first voyage into fantasy land.

I later read volumes of Grimm's Fairy Tales, Aesop's Fables and nursery rhymes. My imagination was always pretty good. I read the fairy tales knowing full well that there was no

165

Rumpelstiltskin to take away the queen's firstborn if she quit spinning gold for him. Neither was there a chance that an honest-to-goodness Rapunzel existed who would let down her hair for a good prince to use as a ladder up to her prison tower.

Of course I even knew that there was no ugly troll under Billy Goat Gruff's bridge and that three little pigs can't build houses out of straw or anything else. I've never seen a fairy godmother appear with magic wand in hand nor a white knight rescue a fair damsel. But wasn't it fun being Cinderella? And climbing up the beanstalk with Jack to the land of the Ogre?

You can view the Santa Claus thing in your own way. Dr. Salk was right, I think, in saying that Santa's place in Christmas is only a make-believe game and that the true meaning of Christmas is in the Nativity, the conception and birth of a savior.

I think Dr. Salk would probably frown on another fantasy I built up one time when my son David was three years old. We were changing buses at dusk in Des Moines. He was very tired and started to cry. Passengers were becoming disturbed and I was embarrassed. Suddenly, as lights came twinkling on across the countryside that winter night, I told the boy, "Look at the little bunny rabbit houses, the lights are going on for supper." We watched for Peter Rabbit's house all the way home. I hope he never suffered any great traumatic experience because I made believe.

You have to come up with something sometimes, but it was a few years after that bus episode until he found out that bunnies don't live in electrically lighted houses across the fields.

As long as little boys and girls miraculously behave better

than usual in December because Santa's elves and brownies might be checking the list from a nearby treetop, then worn out parents will probably prolong the old Santa routine.

December 1972

&&&

I heard an older woman say the other day, "What's happened to Christmas?" Then she added, "Once it was such a happy season, but now it's turned into a hectic race to get cards addressed and buy expensive gifts which we're not too sure they're going to like or that we're going to get much of a thrill out of giving!"

Wouldn't it be great to see the Christmas tree once more through the wondering eyes of a child?

Mood Ring

If I might say so myself, I was quite flattered this Christmastime to receive a Mood Ring as a gift from my son David.

Mood Rings are a current "IN" fad with the younger generation and almost every chick has one. (That's why I was flattered that said son thought his over-the-hill mother had enough warmth to turn a Mood Ring on.)

A mood ring, as you probably know, is a raised glass creation which changes colors on your finger supposedly according to your moods. It starts out a lifeless charcoal shade, then, before your eyes, it turns opalescent (you're cool) to green (nervous and unsettled) to turquoise (in love) to blue (calm and serene) to blue violet (the ultimate happy state).

Some wearers never get it past the green, but I was extremely proud to watch mine run the gamut of emotions.

Proud that is, until the day I took Mood Ring off and laid it on the television set. Right off, that fickle old mood ring warmed up to the TV, turned turquoise (in love with TV), and went on to blue violet (ultimate happiness with TV). Rats. *January 1976*
&&&

I want to wish you a wonderful New Year, all of you. Your letters, phone calls and greetings on the street have meant so much to me. You readers have kept my hopes up and encouraged me to keep writing. My best wishes to all of you.

Chapter 9

CLUBS AND SOCIAL AFFAIRS

Ruth Circle

Sometimes you are particularly reached by someone else's words, and at Monday night's meeting of the Methodist Ruth Circle, Jeanette Coates gave devotionals that made all of us think about the rest of the year after the fanfare of Christmas is over.

Jeanette used these impressive word pictures:

"I tore the first leaf from my calendar today and dropped it into the wastebasket. The first chapter of my New Year is closed. Just 31 days ago the New Year started. It was alive and vibrant with possibilities. Oh, what all I was going to do with this New Year.

I had the New Year to help others, to improve myself, but I have already thrown one page away. Thirty-one days are gone and what have I done? What have I done?

There were days when we might have cheered the sorrowful; days when we might have spoken an encouraging word; days when we could have visited the sick or lifted the burdens of those oppressed.

I reflect. Must my whole year be a record of unused opportunities? And at the end will my record flutter into nothingness, to be forgotten, crumpled like the piece of paper?

For sometimes it isn't the thing we do, it's the thing we leave undone that gives us a bit of heartache. Perhaps there were kind words left unspoken, a letter we did not take time to write, a forgotten prayer at night. Perhaps the gift of a single rose would have gladdened the heart of a friend, or if we'd shared another's troubles maybe our own load would have been lightened.

All of our good intentions, all of our better impulses, all of our plans for sharing, let us do them now."

Thank you Jeanette for a meaningful evening that made us all realize that sometimes we can help lift another's head even when we think we can scarcely lift our own.   *February 1978*

&&&

You know how Ladies Aid church circle meetings are supposed to go ... there is old and new business, devotions, a lesson and refreshments ... all fitting and proper, all dedicated to the work of the church.

But once in a while Ruth Circle unintentionally deviates from the usual and the meeting turns out anything but proper and routine.

There was the time, for instance, that the hostess gave a slide presentation on her trip to Hawaii. Her muu muu had a split in its seams and later all of the slides slid off onto the floor, making the commentary impossible to match with the scrambled slides.

At last weeks club meeting the opening poem read by the

circle chairman is the ONLY thing that went right. Then the discussion began about the Women's Society annual May Breakfast. Ruth Circle and Mary Circle are to serve the food this year. Without any hassle, Mary Circle decided to serve Ham Soufflé. Our group will prepare the fruit. Shall we prepare a fruit cup with bananas, sliced sugared oranges, skewers of chunk pineapple, mandarin orange slices and maraschino cherry or fresh strawberries dipped in powdered sugar?

The fruit cup idea was batted around for 20 minutes after which it was decided that it had been served at too many other May Breakfasts and besides, some members didn't like the bananas because they turned dark.

The sugared orange slices suggestion might have made it past the discussion of the 17 members present if only it could have been decided whether or not to leave the skins on the slices. And if only oranges were cheaper.

The shish kebob deal sounded clever and tasty, but after another 20 minutes of animated discussion, one member pointed out that the women probably wouldn't eat the maraschino cherry because of the red food coloring in it. (That's the latest scare since saccharin, you know.)

Another member interjected the foolhardy thought that a simple cold glass of orange juice would go well with the Ham Soufflé. She was voted down immediately, the only quick decision made all evening.

Another hour went by before it was finally decided to serve large strawberries dipped in powdered sugar. How many to buy and how many to put on each plate? Would two apiece be enough? At this point one member declared that unless there were at least three she wouldn't be caught dead serving and would stay in the kitchen.

A guest and prospective member attending the meeting tried to conceal her surprise and amusement at such church circle procedures. She may or may not become a member.

The co-hostesses brought in refreshments which luckily had already been decided on and prepared in advance. The napkins started the hysterics when they turned out to be covered with pretty red strawberries.

And there was a finishing touch to the evening, quite apropos, you'll agree. The chairman's contact lens popped out onto the carpet. A flashlight was secured and a number of church women went down on their knees. Others nearby anxiously awaited the finding of the lens so they could "see what one looked like." It was found, untrampled, under the chair.

But that isn't all. There is more. Two members came late to the meeting after attending the Junior High music concert. They innocently asked us to "run through" items of business we discussed.

We couldn't possibly do it all over again. You can't talk when you're laughing so hard.

Although the group reached the strawberry decision by ten o'clock there still remains a huge workload for the circle chairman. Her job will be to go to the grocery store and count how many frozen strawberries are in each bag and multiply 3 x 125, allowing for some green ones. It won't be a snap decision for her to decide how many boxes of powdered sugar to buy, either.

We were lucky we didn't have to plan a five-course meal. Chances are that Ruth Circle will never be asked to plan anything again.

Now you 125 women who will attend the annual May breakfast at 9 a.m. on May 8th, enjoy your food. What you see on your plate is what you get. *April 1979*

Sugar Belles

I like a bit of socializing with people I care about tossed in with the humdrum winter fare. At Sugar Belles we made attractive pillow tops from double-knit material and ate our fill of pumpkin roll. A member of the Alpha Study club sang "One Day at a Time" hauntingly, without accompaniment and at the Ruth Circle meeting a member gave a superb lesson on "Giving Yourself". We drank spicy percolator punch with a luscious pink frothy concoction of a dessert made by another member.

You've probably read about the Sugar Belles Club on the Society page of the Iowegian for a number of years and may have wondered why they gave themselves this "sweet" name.

It all started when a group of friends with a common interest in cake decorating decided to meet together. From there they began making molded sugar doves, roses, swirls, colonel mints and of course – sugar bells. That is what gave them the name idea. *March 1969*

&&&

Pauline Donovan is famous for her amusing practical jokes and at her Sugar Belles party she pulled this one on her friends: When the unsuspecting gals used the bathroom, a deep, male voice said loudly, "Hey, I'm trying to work down here!"

(A recording gadget attached to the underside of the lid) produced the startling voice.)

You never know what that hostess will think of next.

January 1977

&&&

I was invited to a Mother's Tea last week at Russell, Iowa by sister-in-law, Reverend Wauneita McConnell, and haven't enjoyed myself so well in a long time.

The Russell Methodist ladies put on the cleverest program. Instead of giving flowers to the oldest mother, youngest mother, mother with the most children, etc. they gave to the "gaddingest" mother, the most "creative" mother and the "grooviest" mother, just to give you an idea. The narrator had compiled amusing anecdotes in prose and each choice was greeted with loud applause.

There was never a dull moment the whole evening. *May 1980*

&&&

Yes, Virginia, there is a TOPS club in Centerville!

TOPS stands for Take off Pounds Sensibly. A year and a half after chartering in 1969 it now has its limit of 20 members – all women. Some aren't as fat as they once were, some are still fat and some are fatter.

174

Almost everyone knows that TOPS clubs were formed across the nation to help people lose weight. Group therapy is the first and basic principal. What you haven't been able to accomplish by yourself, you may do in a group ... with encouragement from ladies just as fat as you are. The blind leading the blind, you might say.

If the group therapy format sounds alarmingly familiar, it should, because it is based on the one used by Alcoholics Anonymous to help drunks. About the only difference is that alcoholics have tipped the bottle too often and the fatties have lifted the fork too many times.

Both groups operate with the same theories.

For example, one idea is that A.A.'s are asked to call another member, day or night, if the urge to take a drink comes on. TOPS members are also asked to do this if an eating binge is coming on, but it doesn't always work so well.

A case in point: One member started thinking about pumpkin pie with whipped cream when she arose, kept thinking about it all morning until she knew she must have a piece of pumpkin pie for lunch. So she called another member and told her the consuming desire. The member was firm and pointed out several reasons why the tortured woman should NOT eat the pie. And she didn't. She felt smug about it until she found out that she had, in turn, implanted the compulsive desire for pumpkin pie to her friend who promptly made three pies and gobbled one up herself. What a shame.

The local club has officers, a motto, a piggy song for weight gainers, fines, contests and boos for anyone who might have added an ounce or two. Singing the piggy song (solo) before the group to the tune of "My Bonnie Lies over the Ocean" is supposed to be degrading enough so that you'll only sing it once. The words, however, seem to come easier the more you have to sing it until some of the girls fancy they missed their calling on the stage.

Dieting isn't easy and there are times you just can't start dieting – like Thanksgiving, Christmas, New Years, Fourth of July, Easter, Memorial Day, and Washington's birthday when you must have cherry pie. Weekends are not conducive to diet starts either.

The seasons in Iowa are rough on beginning dieters.

Winter is bad because after you shovel snow you go in and put a meal in the oven and have hot chocolate and doughnuts and all that sort of thing.

No one diets in the spring. There's gardening and planting to get done and everybody knows that the harder you work, the more you have to eat to keep up your strength. You'd hate to have your husband come home to find you face down in the rutabagas because of starvation.

Can a fatty be expected to shed weight in the summer when there are picnics and barbecued spareribs? Steak on a grill is not fattening, but steak with French fries, baked beans and raspberry turnovers is.

It would be fool-hardy, to say the least, to begin a rigid diet in autumn when there is all that beauty and tranquility of Indian summer – and chili and candy corn. Foolhardy!

To counteract all the negative things, TOPS comes out with a monthly magazine brim full of marvelous tips and pictures of 250 pound women who have trimmed down to 135 in less than a year.

TOPS, for example, tells you to eat off smaller plates and eat slower; buy a dress a size too small; don't be a human garbage can, eating all the leftovers; and this doozie – prepare supper, then go sit in the living room while the family eats, clears the table of all crumbs and washes the dishes. Then, and only then, should you go back in the kitchen. We women liked this suggestion fine, but our families didn't.

Hazards

We talk things over at our TOPS meeting each Wednesday night. We found out that we all like to eat and it is no joking matter. We discuss the hazards and pitfalls of dieters. One woman said that every time she goes on a diet a neighbor (who hadn't baked a cookie in years) suddenly trots over with hot doughnuts which she must try right now.

Another member swears that her mother-in-law is psychic because she never fails to ask the family for dinner and is hurt if she doesn't eat, as usual. It is strange how all manner of hazards appear such as husbands bringing home boxes of candy and new magazines arriving with pages full of food.

The fat woman's head is working on all wheels all the time. She reasons that since candy bars are so small these days, there surely can't be many calories in them. She consoles herself with the fact that fat people are jolly and skinny people are grouchy and that her family still likes her no matter how she looks.

And if these excuses for being overweight don't quite sell, she will even go so far as to say, "The devil made me do it."

As to will power, or the lack of it, one heavy member who has faced obstacles in her life that would floor a hardier soul, who has braved illness in the family and shown great fortitude in the face of duress, says at a TOPS meeting, "I have no willpower when it comes to eating." The strong become weak in the throes of dieting.

Having an incentive – a very, very strong unshakable incentive – could be the breakthrough.

It is a well known fact that to accomplish anything and do it well requires great effort. We are taught to think in terms of incentive. One of the girls wanted to lose 20 pounds because her son was getting married and she didn't want the girl's folks to think she was fat. She lost pounds, but after the wedding was over, losing wasn't easy because the incentive had flown the coop.

You'd think that some of the remarks and insinuations fatties overhear and some of the looks they get would be enough to turn the tables right there. Few fat women wince.

Most women would diet or die if someone said to them, "Why did you let yourself get so fat in the first place?" or "My husband would leave me in a minute if I got fat and didn't take care of my looks!" or "You have such an interesting face if only you weren't so ..."

The right thing to do, though, is to get mad – real mad – and stay that way long enough to show the hussies a thing or two.

Four of our group did get mad and developed enough

incentive from it to reach their weight goals. We are proud of them because they worked for it.

The rest of us, thrilled with their success, may start dieting – tomorrow!   *October 1970*

Compiler's note: Pleasingly plump, Marjorie did eventually succeed in losing weight and reaching her goal.

Country Club

Catching some of the few sunny, warm hours this spring, the first Ladies Golf Day was pronounced a success Wednesday, as foursomes teed off, and carts rolled over the lush green of the fairways. Thus the girls began a busy six months at the Appanoose Golf and Country club.

Men's Golf Day is Thursday. Both men and women conclude their 'days' by being served one of Rose White's fabulous dinners.

During May, you might get in several rounds of golf, bring guests out on Sunday for buffet, enjoy dinner-bridge, or perhaps dance to the Cliff Love Band on Memorial weekend.

The president and members of his committees have planned a calendar of activities that should appeal to all – even the non-golfers.

In June, you can get your teenager ready for the spring formal dance and the first of six family night dinners begin in June.

Free golf lessons start also in June, given by Centerville's better golfers. Here is your chance to learn a few pointers – or just learn.

Another June bonus is a rousing square dance with Dell Trout calling and scrumptious food later. Remember the fun last year?

July is the month packed with events, starting off with carnival time, where, as one of the attractions this year, a trained cow will do tricks. The big fireworks display will begin as soon as it is dark.

July is also the Ladies Golf Invitational, and there will be a swimming party at the municipal pool, with a Dutch lunch at the club later.

August finds the greens still green since Ray Dooley works to keep them that way. It will be hot, but the bridge games, golf, dancing and eating are still going on. Also in August is the annual style show and luncheon for guests. This is an excellent back-to-school style feature for feminine enjoyment. September arrives, and with it comes the annual golf tournaments. If you haven't watched the local fellows in a sudden death play-off, or watched Jim Craver sink a hole-in-one on No. 3 during a match, don't expect to see anything like it on TV.

There is still October – beautiful October. Some golfers prefer it, while other members just want to enjoy the last fleeting remnants of a busy season. Count it in for Sunday buffets and smorgasbords. The house committee has anticipated cool weather needs for a comfortable, well managed club house. Charlotte Beck, as house chairman, arranged attractive accommodations in this colonial-type setting for your enjoyment.

Should you care to do nothing else but sit on the large cool porch and look out over the pastoral hills, enjoying a bit of leisure, you'll find that here is the place for it.

If you've heard that you have to be "up-amongst-'em" to play golf or enjoy the facilities of the Appanoose Golf and Country Club, or that chasing a little white ball around for miles is pretty silly, just don't ever try it yourself. There is something about it that gets to you, and you find that it is a marvelous way to relax and get some exercise at the same time.

Why else would Buck Olsasky still be out golfing in November with his ear muffs on?

Republican Women

Almost every Iowan has been to Des Moines and taken in the sights of the big city. Thousands of persons have climbed the steps of the State Capitol, trampled the State Fair grounds, taken in a stage show at KRNT Theatre, or rooted for a girls basketball team. So what else is new?

Until you've taken an all-day trip to Des Moines with a bus load of Appanoose and Monroe County Republican women though, you might have missed something.

I was invited to go along, ostensibly to take a few pictures and write a story, and partly because the boss thought a change of pace might be in order.

The story I got – the pictures I didn't get. When the film was developed there was nothing except a faint outline of a chandelier in the Governor's mansion. Reason: unfamiliar camera and not enough know-how. Everybody felt badly about that, and they may feel even worse about this story.

Thursday dawned gray and dismal with a light rain falling which continued at the same drizzly pace all day. The bus arrived a half-hour late to pick up a cold, damp bunch of women, clutching cold, damp, paper sack lunches. A sense of humor prevailed, however, which was to stand them in good stead as the day progressed.

To Moravia to pick up several ladies and on to Albia. Several county GOP officers boarded the bus.

Arriving in Des Moines, the first stop was the magnificent new Art Center. This is a beautiful structure built after the most modern design with large expanses of glass looking out over wooded areas. The floors in the rooms where paintings are hung are not only carpeted, but the walls are covered with snow white short-pile carpeting to facilitate picture hanging.

The very proper receptionist who had booked the tour in advance said she "preferred" we all stand in a close group until volunteer guides could be secured; she also "preferred" we remain in close formation; she "preferred" to ignore several discreet (and finally urgent) feelers as to the whereabouts of the ladies rest room. She "preferred" too, that we admire only from a distance the huge carved pumpkin head on her desk. But in all fairness to her, we were probably only one of the disasters of the week.

We were divided into two groups and our guide was a very charming girl who told us she was a volunteer worker who was just sort of learning her way around the place herself.

In the main foyer of the Center, four or five eye-catching paintings were hung. One to a wall. We were told the Center acquired these huge paintings at great expense. One was a masterpiece of two enormous rectangles on canvas. Our guide pointed out that while the artist was exceptionally good at

182

painting other things, he "chose" to paint the two rectangles in orange and red. Another masterpiece was a Campbell soup can with the label almost torn to shreds. This painting too, she said, was what its artist "chose" to show.

There were some recognizable Van Dyke's and Renets and Picassos and Matisses.

The frames were, without exception, very beautiful.

The mammoth sculpture room boasted a ceiling mobile and several carefully selected figures including Rodin's male nude and a block of carved darkish stone which was labeled "Woman." Here was spaciousness and architectural beauty yet with perhaps only one object per fifty feet.

The finale was the Hobby and Curio shop where you could purchase an item or two. We were warned that if you accidentally knocked an article off the shelves or tables; you bought it! We were told the sad tale of a lady school teacher who brought her group to the shop and accidentally swung off an expensive item with her big purse. (Forty-three women were seen clutching their purses tightly under their chins.) Some of the mod "far-out" items you wouldn't want whole for $15, to say nothing of the pieces.

Outside it was still raining.

Sack lunches were eaten in the bus. Strangely enough, the dried beef or baloney and cheese creations we had slapped together at 6:30 a.m. looked mighty appetizing at noon.

The Governor's wife was expecting us at one o'clock at the mansion on Grand Avenue. She greeted us individually at the door and invited us to tour the home with an official hostess.

The home is lovely and spacious and Mrs. Ray has chosen colors of turquoise, soft beiges, browns, and gold. Tea and cookies were being served in the dining room when another busload of women arrived and after that a group of school children accompanied by teacher. As the many pairs of wet feet trooped in, Mrs. Ray somehow managed to keep her composure. She told us that besides all this, she serves more luncheons and dinners than teas! She bid each of us goodbye at the door.

Down the windy and wet driveway to the bus. But it wasn't there. The thin soles of our best shoes were soaking up puddles and the misty drizzle persisted. We thought of trooping back into the Governor's mansion but agreed that Mrs. Ray might faint at the sight of us.

We paced the driveway until the bus arrived much later. The driver ruefully explained that he had taken the bus out on Tonawanda Drive and had slipped off, gotten stuck on a short curve, had to call a wrecker and it cost him $15.

The last stop was at Salisbury House, a full-scale duplication of Renaissance luxury and grandeur. You have to see it to believe it. There are coats of armor, valuable books, monks furniture, priceless paintings, 100 Persian rugs, tapestries and many, many historical items in a setting of British and American culture of centuries ago. It was well worth the 50 cent fee.

Braving the rain, we walked back to the bus (it was there) and greedily ate the last remnants of our lunches. Darkness had fallen. One group member suggested a sing-along and the bus fairly rocked through a musical repertoire of old time religion, Stephen Foster tunes, and down through Christmas and Easter and the good old summertime.

At this point, the bus driver assured us that he, too, was a Republican. Before we stepped down from the bus we had forgotten that the bus had ever been late at all.

Chances are the driver will ask for a busload of nice quiet teenagers as his next assignment. He had plenty of time to think about it as he trundled the big empty bus back to Des Moines with the rain falling softly on the windshields. *November 1969*

Iowa Press Women's Convention

The Iowa Press Women's convention at Webster City, Iowa last weekend went well. In fact, this Hamilton County seat town went all out to make its guests welcome and the entire back page of their Friday's Daily Freeman-Journal was a tribute to the woman writers of Iowa.

Accommodations at the New Castle Inn were the finest and the food excellent.

Registration was at the Jane Young House which is of historic vintage and is home to various groups such as the Women's Club and DAR. It is furnished with such items as old sideboards and secretaries made of beautiful woods. It was here that the Webster City Women's club hosted us to coffee and homemade pastries.

DAR (Daughters of American Revolution) members presented a skit which was not only excellently written and acted out, but boasted some of the cutest bonnets and dresses (all authentic) out of wartime eras past. Watches on chains and old pins and lockets were proudly displayed and of great interest in a

185

time when nostalgia reigns.

And if you want to see a beautiful public library, the Kendall Young library in Webster City is it. Maintained by a trust fund from the Young family, this marble pillared building should last forever.

A spectacular display of the Foster doll collection is in the basement section. It was said that no doll in the collection was less than 100 years old. A fascinating display in a library of beauty and character.

A tour of the Fred Hahne Printing Company sounded so-so, but proved to be outstanding due to the charm of our guide. Here was a girl who made even the big Heidelberg job printing presses come to life. They were in the process of finalizing the printing of the Angus Journal at the time, and Nancy Kayser, our tour guide and assistant editor of the Aberdeen Angus Journal, could have sold any number of the publications to women who didn't know an Angus from a Hereford.

Talk about Public Relations people! We were sorry the tour ended. One of Nancy's bits of advice to the press women was: "Get where you want to go in writing; be aggressive but be a lady, so you will be treated like a lady."

Mrs. Kayser went on to say that she was a farm girl who showed hogs, cattle and sheep in stock shows all around Illinois and loved it. "I wore jeans, bred cattle, and walked in mud and manure, but I learned early that I could be as feminine and as much of a lady as though I was Queen Elizabeth."

There was no doubt in anyone's mind about that. Nancy Kayser was beautiful, intelligent, well-dressed, dedicated to writing – and a lady.

A Saturday afternoon panel of four on "It's a Women's World, Too" featured Dr. Faye Lewis, M.D. of Webster City who is also an author of a number of medical and fictional publications. Also Nancy Kayser again, plus Sue Leaf - a young Freeman-Journal staff writer, and Eve Rubenstein, KVFD-TV, Fort Dodge.

Now Eve Rubenstein was a very attractive woman who gave promise of contributing much to the panel since she was hostess for *Eve's Kitchen* show on the Fort Dodge station.

Eve not only used up her allotted 10 minutes of speaking time, but got carried away with her own conversation for five times that, consuming almost an hour in name dropping and incidentals which were only interesting to herself. Not a word about cooking.

The press women fidgeted, and some left the room to go to the bathroom, but still Ms. Rubenstein rolled on just as though the TV director was motioning with his arms to s-t-r-e-t-c-h the dialogue.

Finally, the gal in charge of the panel got up and stood by Rubenstein, looking daggers, but was Rubenstein intimidated? Nope, she just went on another five minutes, including her uninvited observer in the conversation.

Commented a nearby press woman: "How in the world do they ever get her program on TV over with?" That's easy. Quit working the camera.

The awards banquet Saturday evening was a high point. One hundred sixty 1st, 2nd and 3rd place awards in writing categories

187

were given out with the Iowegian's Theda Long and Gladys DePuy winning a goodly share.

And to the few people who asked me why I didn't win any – I didn't send any entries in to the Iowa contest this year due to the death of son Craig at entry time. Had I sent some in, I don't know what my excuse for not winning would have been.

As usual, something amusing has to happen when you go to a convention.

In our case, it was one of us who got locked in a restroom on the interstate. The lock was faulty, but not the vocal chords of the writer. She yelped for help after considering climbing up over the partition or squeezing under the door. Conventions are eventful.   *April 1975*

&&&

Loree Roach, retired Ottumwa Courier columnist, has started writing for them again and her column "Worth Mentioning" is fun to read. My Ottumwa daughter Rosemary sends them to me.

We Iowegian press women met Loree when we all attended the bi-annual meeting of the Iowa Press Women. She is a delight to know.

One of Loree's recent columns dealt with the unlikely subject of funerals. She wrote about one deceased person who left instructions that her last rites were to be anything but sad. The minister, who had known her for many years, was told to recite only the humorous and light-hearted high points of her life or she'd "reach down and whack him on the head."

Loree insisted that the mourners left the service happier than when they came.

Wish I'd written that.

Glad you're doing what you do best again, Loree.

National Federation of Press Women

I would guess that few people are as unimpressed with prestige and VIP's as I, so when I received an appointment to head a Protocol Committee, I was amused at the irony of it. Me – the one who doesn't give a hoot who sits at the right or left of a President at a state dinner, or whether or not there is a 'head table' at all. Me – the one who might seat Elizabeth Taylor between two ex-husbands and expect them to enjoy their food and make polite conversation.

This protocol appointment came from the state chairwoman for the Federation of Press Women which Iowa Press Women will host in Des Moines. Every Iowa member is expected to accept some kind of pre-convention job and for some faint reason the Iowa Chairwoman thought this job would be in capable hands with me.

She wrote: "You will work with the NFPW protocol director during the actual convention to ascertain arrangements are made for VIP's, greet conventioneers at points of arrival or at the hotel, and be certain that all manner of hospitality are completed. You will serve, basically, as assistant and liaison from Iowa to the National Protocol Director."

Well, Virginia, I reluctantly accept since I don't want any of the other jobs either. At least I have a year to read up on protocol and who's who to decide where they should sit. If all 50 state presidents attend, I certainly will have to know if you seat them alphabetically or the North on one side and the South on the other.

It's obvious that I'll need all the help I can get from the National Protocol Director. *May 1979*

Chapter 10

COME INTO MY GARDEN

In this morning's mail, nestled deep amongst the income tax forms and the blatant notifications that I may have won free trips to Las Vegas and Hawaii, was the prettiest little seed catalogue you ever saw, bearing the title, "What's New for Your Garden This Spring?"

So enthusiastic about the plants and seeds they were offering did I become, that I could almost see those plate sized petunias and jumbo marigolds growing in the dead of winter.

And it happens every January – this mirage – because I am not noted for my gardening prowess.

But I thought about my flower garden anyway – all 5 x 12 feet of it, lying peacefully now under the snow with nary a weed in sight, and I pondered that surely this summer I could embark upon a carefree dirt-digging project. Surely this summer the neighbors would be proud of me instead of skirting their back yard guests carefully from the McConnell side.

To no avail the neighbors have tried to make something of me by proffering handfuls of this plant and that, but are always stymied when I carefully ask if such and such is a perennial which will never, never again, need replanting.

Now this catalogue pointed out the necessity of planting things so that something is blooming from April through October. I do fairly well along this line, since my backyard is usually the first to display dandelions of prize winning size and hue, and they stay there longer too. Next to follow are the irises which have somehow multiplied over into my yard from next door.

The people from whom we purchased our home, and to them I will ever be grateful, left a Paul's Scarlet rose bush and four peony plants that never fail to bloom their heads off come June with no special care except from the ants.

By this rose bush I once planted a red regal lily which turned out to be bright orange and they bloom at the same time, turning the sensitive stomachs of the artistic.

With complete abandon, I dug in the good earth and planted giant zinnias and cannas on the "outside" and border plants such as verbena and ageratum on the "inside."

According to the catalogue, a good garden should have a bit of everything, and here's where I qualify. With a yearly hankering for fresh lettuce and white icicle radishes, I always make room for them somewhere. It would be hard to find showier little white daisy weeds or bigger, bluer wild morning glories (of the choking variety) than I have.

As Mr. Vandike (my neighbor on the south) is prone to say, the ring of the hoe has never sounded good to my ears. It is my contention, however, that weeds and flowers can flourish well, side by side.

And as to vegetable gardens, no one likes to hear the snap of a green bean or catch the magnificent view of a stand of green peppers better than I, but then I am a picker rather than a planter.

Come spring, though, our good neighbors on the west, the Walter Adams's, whose flower gardens are always something to see, will again attempt to get me down on my knees with a trowel. Mother Nature will likely smile up at me again by making two-inch "Golden Glow" seedlings shoot up as tall as the garage and I will enjoy another short period of satisfying gardening.

And Lucy Kauzlarich, another fine neighborhood gardener who knows my weakness for blossoms, corn, and roses grown by other people who have slaved all summer, will possibly indulge me again this year.

Long live the gardeners! I hope they all received the same inspiring seed catalogue I did.

&&&

The most unusual flower offered in the seed catalogue this year was the Mexican Shellflower, a sturdy two-foot high creation that has red-orange blossoms six inches across. It blooms from July through September.   *May 1972*

&&&

I like flowers! Any kind, any color, any shape. Some people have a favorite flower. I don't. I'm fickle where flowers are concerned.

In the spring I always proclaim that the lavender lilac is the loveliest. That is, until my double-pink peonies bloom.

In May when I pick violets in the woods, or bluebells and buttercups, I think I have never seen blossoms so dainty.

When summer's roses, gladioli and dahlias are budded out I declare that no other flowers are more beautiful. Then when autumn comes along with asters and mums, and December brings the vivid poinsettia then I'm fickle again.

I like to see the old fashioned flowers growing wild along farm fences, especially the tiger lilies and the brilliant hollyhocks. Even the red and purple clover. Anyone who likes roadside volunteers like tiger lilies and Queen Anne's lace or thinks dandelions are intricate and pretty, just likes flowers.

&&&

I went out in the back yard this morning to see if any flower plants had come up in the 5 by 12 foot space I casually call my garden plot. I wouldn't blame them a bit if they didn't. A flea on a dog gets more attention than I give to the bluebells and lily of the valley year after year. If my garden didn't come up by itself, it wouldn't come up at all.

It's disconcerting and probably unforgivable that I garden about like I keep house – in a willy-nilly fashion. My friends think I luck out pretty well on both counts. The neighbors on all sides of me worried about the dust on my furniture all winter. Now they are fretting because I am sitting in the porch swing instead of getting my hands in the good old dirt outside. They have been spading, raking and planting now for several weeks and I see them glancing my way. The happy looks of their faces do give me a slight twinge of conscience, but quite frankly, the ringing sound of so many hoes in action interferes with my reading concentration.

It isn't that they haven't tried to reform me. Goodness knows they've tried to make a gardener out of me down through the years by bringing little handfuls of this plant and that and ordering: "Plant it." I always ask, "Is it a perennial?" It had better be and they know it. I almost cured one neighbor of trying to make me into something I'm not. She handed me a start of Blue Flax and before she could give me professional advice, I promptly dug a hole, dumped it in, smoothed the ground and wiped my hands on my apron. "Heavens to aphids" she snorted, "you didn't plant those darling dainty blue flowers under the Paul's Scarlet rose bush did you? They'll never grow." They did though and I must say I thought the color effect was rather striking, especially when the orange lilies bloomed right next to the red roses.

The point is I just don't have any intention of getting so carried away with gardening that I would head for the nearest Agriculture office if I lost a chrysanthemum bush to the blight. Years ago I once saw a friend very unhappy just because the American flag flower sections she blue-printed didn't turn out right. The red and white petunia flag stripes did fine, but the larkspur blue field and white alyssum stars fizzled out. She took it as a horrible affront to her gardening ability. I'd rather hope for the best with my flowers.

So far, I've been luckier than I deserve. I noticed today that the purple irises are budded and there are ants on the peonies. Those things with the little white and yellow daisies have come up too. Somebody told me those are weeds, but time will tell. And anyway, I've got to plant tomorrow because someone gave me some multiplying onions. I wonder how they'll thrive in the yellow daylily patch.

&&&

I got a new "Green Thumb" houseplant book and it suggests that I should get a Bromeliad plant if I have trouble growing things correctly. The Bromeliads are called the "living vases" because their centers are little water tanks. I have one already. The book says that the blooms will last up to six months. That will be nice - if mine ever blooms.

&&&

The bluebells are blooming in the back yard, and the beautiful violets are coming out in the front yard and those luscious bright yellow dandelions are popping out all over the place.

"I hope the new people will be good neighbors and not let dandelions grow in their yard," said a biased neighbor of ours when we lived in Chariton. (She actually judged people by whether or not they had dandelions in their yards.)

&&&

I was sitting in our back yard the other afternoon and happened to look down and saw a four-leaf clover. My mother was the one who could find them. My old family Bible has a number of them tucked away, yellowed and dried, in its pages.

I could look for hours without finding one and usually made one by sticking another leaf on a three-leafer, but I never gave up looking in almost every patch of clover I saw. I thought of her when I found it.

&&&

The minute the flowers start blooming in the spring, you can start sorting out the two kinds of flower lovers ... those who pick and those who don't!

Those who pick a rose for a crystal vase or pluck a bouquet of nasturtiums for the kitchen table are the flower lovers who believe in two-way enjoyment of beauty and fragrance ... both close-up and in the garden.

Those who never pick flowers for indoors truly believe in enjoying the blooms in their natural settings where they will last longer and be enjoyed by the neighbors as well.

One of my neighbors, Betty Vandike, and I are members of the first group ... the pickers!

When my daffodils and narcissus bloomed in April, she got a handsome bouquet too. Today her lilies of the valley are perfuming both our living rooms.

"What good are lilies of the valley out of sight on the north side of the garage?" she reasoned. That's our theory in favor of picking.

Next we'll have iris, roses and peonies, and sweet pansies to sniff and observe close up.

Did you ever peer down into the perfect little faces of a

pansy?

Come on now, group two, pick a flower and enjoy!

&&&

I saw British actress Deborah Kerr advertising Old English Lavender soap and perfume on TV the other day and it made me recall that my grandma Leigh would never use anything else. Her roots were in England and she liked to tell us about their gardens in which grew the pungent lavender flower.

&&&

It's peony picking time just around the corner again, and I never see one of the beautiful blossoms but that I think of the year we didn't have a single one on four bushes.

The buds had been on the bushes all right, but when I saw them they were all over the grass.

It seems that my youngsters, Nancy and Craig had nipped every single bud off because "they had ants crawling around all over them."

The peony is one of my favorite flowers and because of its heavenly perfume, I have always hoped that Avon or Coty would bottle its fragrance, but they have never come close. I'd be first in line to buy some.

&&&

Henry and Frances Ellis picked a perfect rose for me one evening before the storms came. It was deep pink with an old fashioned rose fragrance.

I placed it in a pale blue glass bud vase and put it where I could watch it unfold day by day. Had it been County Fair time, this rose surely would have been judged perfect and without blemish.

The Occult Cereus

There are doubtless a number of Night Blooming Cereus plants growing in homes and nurseries in these United States, opening their spectacular blooms during one season of the year. However, it is doubtful that any other is like the occult, uncanny plant growing in this southern Iowa town. When a Night Blooming Cereus suddenly blooms in broad daylight, after forty-two years of habitual night blooming, there is a reason. Is it botanical? Scientific? Or is it, perhaps, metaphysical? Consider, then, the utter strangeness of the following true story:

It was in the year 1923, forty-two years ago in this county-seat town of seven thousand Iowans, which a woman known by the intriguing name of Birdie, rooted and placed in soil a small plantling of night blooming cereus. Webster's New World Dictionary notes: 'This plant is a member of the cactus family with large white flowers that open at night.' Birdie had seen such a plant and had fallen in love with the beauty of the magnificent ivory-white blooms. She wanted one for herself even though she knew they were unwieldy to grow because they often attained the height of five feet or more.

So the little seedling did grow, and its green foliage flourished. It was re-potted several times to accommodate its maturing stature. Each year, during late summer, usually late

199

August, buds came on and opened their petals at night. They put on their extravaganza after ten o'clock, later to close themselves slowly after several hours' performance.

Birdie was always delighted to have a guest in on the infrequent evenings. It was indeed a rare treat for the invited, since, if one gazed deep into the throat of the bloom, he could see a replica of the birthplace of Jesus. A soft silky fuzz symbolizes the manger hay holding baby Jesus, and just above, coming out on a pure white tiny pedicle, is a star flower. Surrounding the entire plant is a distinct heavenly perfume. An aroma, perhaps similar to frankincense.

Twenty-two years went by, and Birdie went about her duties with great cheerfulness. Children knew her as "The Popcorn Woman," since she had sold popcorn and sweets at the movie theatre for a good many years. Everybody knew Birdie, in fact. It could not be said that Birdie was an especially saintly woman, indeed she was too much the average small town homemaker for that. Democrats held her in awe, as she was a tireless worker for the Republican side. No election board was complete until Birdie was there.

So it was that one day in 1945, a neighbor, who had been especially kind to Birdie, admired the cereus and Birdie promptly gave it to her. "Take loving care of it," she told the neighbor. The neighbor did, and for twenty years now it has grown and bloomed at the Henry Ellis home, standing majestically in its octagon shaped wooden bucket. The Ellis's have also stayed up later than usual many nights each summer awaiting the beautiful display. Birdie herself could see it from her apartment window across the alley after Mr. Ellis moved it outdoors for the summer, sheltering it with a protective canopy erected next to his garage.

Birdie became ill during the summer of '65, and toward fall gradually weakened into the critical stage. The Night Blooming Cereus, which had been thought to have stopped blooming for the season, surprisingly began forming buds again. Ten in all. It was unusual, yet a pleasing thing, so the Ellis family left the plant outdoors in its usual place although October had coolly flipped the calendar over. Noticing that the buds were almost bursting on Saturday evening, October 2, Mrs. Ellis invited friends in to watch them open, but they did not open. Not that night.

The following day, Sunday, Mr. and Mrs. Ellis and children returned home from church to find that one cereus bud had opened wide and was giving off an even more pungent aroma than usual. "It just cannot be," they said. They were understandably taken aback by this plant that had never before, in forty-two years, bloomed in broad daylight. The telephone rang then, and the voice on the other end said that Birdie had died that very morning.

As her body lay in state, two more lovely blooms opened on Monday, with three more showing on Tuesday. Burial rites were to be held at ten o'clock Wednesday morning and four buds remained yet unopened. The sun tried to come out, but the sky drizzled a fine mist instead. Immediately preceding the service, three of these last four buds opened. On returning at high noon, Mr. Ellis found the tenth, and last, showing its rare beauty.

Those of us who saw this phenomenon have pondered it many

times since. What, we wonder, gives us this uncanny feeling that this particular plant somehow is of occult nature. Why did it suddenly decide to bloom in the daytime ONLY after the woman who had given it care and life as a seedling, had died? How was it that the plant apparently apportioned its ten blooms to appear consecutively the four days from death to interment?

Some say that, of course, there is a scientific reason for it, yet no one seems to know what it is. No one had ever heard of a Night Blooming Cereus blooming other than when it was supposed to. Several local gentry are of the opinion that perhaps the weather had something to do with it. Maybe so, yet each of the four days was different; one sunny, another very windy, the third quite cool and the fourth day misty. Not one of them though, in any way, simulated nighttime conditions. Perhaps its goodly number of years affected the odd blooming cycle, a local horticulturist suggested. But he was only guessing, as there were no facts to prove it. No one knows for sure. Those of us who saw it feel that surely something mysterious and touching was being perpetrated between the plant and the woman who first knew it.

Will the cereus bloom next summer? If it does, will it bloom in daylight or its natural nighttime? It has now been taken to its usual winter spot in the Ellis basement. The blooms have since withered and dropped off, but the foliage is still bright and green. Some say the stalk and leaves will surely die before another summer. It performed its "Swan Song", so they say. Others of us prefer to await the next blooming season with hope. Birdie would have wanted it that way.   *1965*

13 years later ...

Over at the Henry Ellis residence on North Park, the occult Night Blooming Cereus cactus plant outdid itself this year. It bore more huge blooms this year than for many summers.

I think the night blooming cereus is one of the most beautiful blossoms I have ever seen. It begins opening its waxy white petals around 10:30 at night. The cereus opens fully by midnight and emits a heavenly fragrance in little puffs into the night air. By morning, alas, the blossom has withered, never to open again. If you know someone who owns such a plant, ask them to call you when the flowering extravaganza begins. It is worth seeing.

September 1978

Chapter 11

MAN OF THE HOUSE

Honeymoon Blues

They say the first year of marriage is the hardest, but the first month gets my vote.

That 1940 December day dawned warm enough that we took pictures out-of-doors without jackets. We were married so early in the day because we had a long trip ahead of us to Lawrence, Kansas, where Mac was employed at the Gambles store. There were only family members present and grandma prepared an early roast pork dinner for us.

The old car we drove managed to chug and lurch the 250 miles or so to Lawrence. We got lost going through Kansas City, which didn't help dispositions any. We had very little money, which made matters worse, and by the time we arrived at our apartment (which I had never seen), the first day of marriage was nothing to brag about.

As we recalled the other evening over our T-bones, Mac's pay was around $70 for the month's work. That work included both day and night hours six days a week and sometimes Sunday. Out of that money came $22 a month apartment rent.

I cringe when I recall that apartment! It was a two-room nightmare in an old house. Actually, it was a former upstairs back porch with windows put in on three sides. And don't let anyone tell you that it doesn't get below zero or that the icy winds don't blow in Kansas.

There was one heating vent and somehow the other renters channeled the heat into their rooms before it got up to us. The stove was a three-burner oil job with an oven that wouldn't brown a piece of toast. I couldn't cook anyway, so I had an excuse for not baking bread like grandma did or roasting meat like his mother did.

One room was a bedroom and the other was a combination living room with an ancient horsehair sofa and a kitchen. There was one bathroom which was shared by three groups of renters. Everything in the bedroom was sloshed with bright blue paint. It appeared that they used left-over paint for the furniture. There was a blue bed, a blue dresser, blue walls, a blue chair, blue ceiling and the lone mirror was painted blue. To top it all off, the Iowegian had given us a beautiful blue chenille bedspread.

I became very blue, and since I had never been away from home for any length of time, I was not only blue, I was homesick. I finally blew some of our eating money on a phone call home, but I felt better anyway.

Yes, that first month was anything but great. Why did we stay there? Well, it was all we could afford. I finally went out and got a job at a dime store selling candy, and quit that because the manager gave me orders to weigh out an ounce less in each

206

package of candy than the package said. It wasn't long before we moved back to Iowa.

&&&

Thirty-some years married to the same person. An incredible feat inasmuch as the two of us are as different as night and day.

About the only background things we have in common are being raised in the same town (Centerville) and the Depression. In most everything else, we have discovered we are NOT as one.

For example, he will spend three hours searching for a misplaced shoe lace, while I will look only 10 minutes then either put on another pair of shoes, make a shoelace out of string, or go barefoot. (He is more persistent than I.)

He is a saver of everything. He saves string, aspirin bottles, oleo tubs and toothpaste tubes against the day when we might need such items. Why just the other day our daughter Nancy threw away a pair of old Eskimo snow boots, but they didn't stay in the trash long. Just think of the possibilities for utilizing the old sheepskin linings. He wished he had had such nice sheepskin to use for knuckle-downs when he played marbles as a boy. (He is more frugal than I.)

If there is any project that calls for detailed figures or planning, then that's right down his alley! Working out how many pennies each household electrical appliance costs to run per day is just his cup of tea. I personally would like to throw details out the back door. (He is more patient than I.)

One of our first big difficulties reared its ugly head the first Christmas we were together. He was reared in a home where

Christmas Day was the only day (come snow or high water) that gifts were opened. I was reared in a home where Christmas Eve was the magic time with frost patterns on the windows and the Star of the East shining in the yuletide sky. When mother came home from her clerking job on that magic night, we ate popcorn, apples, and drank hot chocolate as we opened our gifts. We went to bed happy, knowing that Santa would fill our socks and that we could play with our dolls and admire our presents again Christmas day.

We solved that problem by allowing the kids to open only one present on Christmas Eve and the rest of the celebrating to be done on Christmas day. We still do. (He is more adamant than I.)

And in the food department, he refuses to eat cooked onions, watermelon, sweet potatoes, cucumbers, green peppers, broccoli, squash, or boiled cabbage.

And I refuse to cook or eat the brains he relishes so much. And I won't make meatloaf gravy either.

We have found that we don't like the same colors, don't have the same decorating tastes, nor like the same music. We differ on television shows and get into it when he wants to chop down my weeping willow tree because it sheds branches all over the back yard.

It's a fact that we have some weeks when we don't agree on much of anything, but when you consider that we are still married, that's doing pretty well.

It seems that there is always some situation arising that puts us to the test. During the year just passed, he solved a crucial problem in his usual dramatic style.

He wanted to move the toilet tissue holder from the right side to the left side because it was always there when he lived at home. I'm bullheaded too, so I said, "No way!" But I should have known that there was a way because the next day he proceeded to install another tissue holder on the left side.

If any of our friends who have used our facility noticed that there were TWO holders, one on each side, they haven't said anything. Actually, they wouldn't be surprised.

Well, we plan to eat our anniversary dinner out Thursday night ... if we can agree where to go.

&&&

One of my friends glowingly reported to me the other weekend that they were really going to have a treat for dinner.

"What?" I asked, impressed. "Pheasant under glass or Baked Alaska?"

"Neither," smiled my friend. "We're having a whole platter of chicken gizzards, enough for everybody this time!"

I place chicken gizzards in about the same food category as brains and would about as soon eat fried lizard as fried gizzard.

Speaking of gizzards reminds me of the time my father-in-law, Ira McConnell, in his droll way, almost caused a riot at the McConnell clan dinner table one Sunday when I was dating his son. That's when I found out that I was marrying into a family of gizzard eaters.

Dad McConnell (who had already eaten the two chicken gizzards prior to dinner), told everyone at the table that

Marjorie ate the gizzards. He didn't crack a smile, and neither did I when I found six pairs of eyes turn to look at me. Had I stuffed all the silverware into my pocketbook, I could not have been looked at with more distrust. It was a great beginning for our romance.

&&&

I decided recently, after paying for our third fill of fuel oil, that we would turn the house thermostat down two degrees. My husband reluctantly agreed although he pointed out that the house wasn't too warm the way it was.

It wasn't long before I noticed that he was wearing his old blue quilted jacket, even to the dinner table.

He, in turn commented that my long robe and velour bedroom slippers didn't look too great with my pantsuits from sunup to sundown.

So, as with most of my brilliant ideas, we chucked and agreed to turn the thermo back up 2 degrees. "We're not going to be cold in our own house," we said.

He suggested that we cut expenses in some other areas to make up for the high cost of fuel oil. (His brainy ideas aren't any better than mine.)

We went over the grocery area thoroughly and after finding that our favorite vegetables jumped 10 cents a can last week, threw the food idea out. We don't want to forgo the wonders of electricity either, or read our Iowegian by the light of a coal-oil lamp, so cutting down on electricity won't work. The water bill? Nope. We still want to flush the toilet, take baths and drink water. That area is out.

So we'll pay the fuel bill as long as we can without mortgaging the house! Or join all the folks who winter in Florida, Texas or Arizona.

&&&

Well, the roses are red, violets are blue, the day just went by and I received a box of Pangburn chocolates and a fancy heart-bedecked card. It will probably always be Pangburn chocolates on Valentine's Day since that's the kind the first little heart shaped box was some 30 or more years ago.

"I didn't know what else to get you," he said, as he gobbled down the first five pieces and took the only chocolate covered cherries in the box.

&&&

Every woman knows you can't possibly do 12 months house cleaning in one week. Nobody but me would ever try. And I never learn – I do it every year. It all starts when I strip the kitchen bulletin board of its annual accumulation of trivia such as ancient dental cards, outdated cat food coupons and recipes for beef Stroganoff which I have never made in my life.

While doing this chore, I happen to notice with astonishment that I am to be hostess for two groups next week. I sprang into action, but after a year of lethargy and pretending I didn't care whether or not I could see out the dirty windows, it wasn't easy to get a move on.

I am known as the most unorganized housekeeper in the

family, in the neighborhood, and possibly in the north end of town. In fact, if they ran a Betty Crocker contest for lousy homemakers, I'd probably win it, broom down! I'll never lose this bad reputation and have yet to disappoint anybody who comes calling.

So all this week, every member of the family suffered and worked. Any teenage friends who made the grave mistake of dropping by for sugar cookies and cokes were immediately drafted into the McConnell Work Corps. One tall lad wiped the dust from the top of the refrigerator-freezer and remarked under his breath, "What does she do all day – sleep?"

I finally entertained 17 nice ladies of the Alpha Study Club and by the next morning everything was back to normal. Clothes were on chair backs, dishes were soaking in the sink and school books found their way back to the stairs. The only thing left to show for the party was the pink, lavender and purple centerpiece I spent my week's allowance on and the fancy decorated sugar cubes. The Sugar Belles club will meet here in two days and I'll have to clean up all over again. Anyway, the young people won't be dropping by, and the man of the house is thinking of taking our tent out to Lake Rathbun until Friday.   *April 1972*

&&&

I'd like to forget that the summer months are almost gone and once again I haven't accomplished one major cleaning job around the house. I did get so far as to walk through the house and up and down the stairs making mental notes of the one hundred things that needed to be done. I worked hard planning a

212

summer work schedule.

Top priority went to carpeting the upstairs bathroom which is a spacious nine by eleven feet. It wouldn't have gotten top priority except that we had bought the gold and black flecked carpet at a bargain over a year ago and it is still rolled up. We probably would have put it down except that we had to wait until we got a new toilet. After we got the toilet, the rug didn't match the peach colored walls which we couldn't paint until we fixed the little leak in the roof over the tub. Now we can paint the walls and install the bathroom fixture, and if the plumbing doesn't fall to pieces, we may lay the carpet. It takes time to ponder these major undertakings.

Then when our daughter Nancy heard that we might carpet the bathroom she complained that she feels silly when her friends come in her room and see the juvenile floor covering on her floor. We thought her vinyl flooring was rather unique and charming with the toy figures on it when we bought it 16 years ago. Actually, we hadn't noticed it the past few years because we tried to keep the door closed most of the time. However, at her insistence, we did agree to inspect it, and came away very pleased that we won't have to replace the floor covering or repaint her walls this season. Her floor space is so well covered with records, magazines, and socks and the four walls so well camouflaged with banners, horse collections, little felt feet, and Bobby Sherman photos that nobody will ever see either one. What a relief.

I knew the four big closets needed cleaning out by now, but I couldn't get in them to really do a good job survey. I am smart enough to know, too, that if I ever got all the stuff out of them, it would never all go back in and since there isn't any other place to put the old tennis shoes and World War 2 Army Air Corps uniforms, I decided the closet jobs shouldn't be tackled right yet. You have to be prudent when you make out a summer work sheet, you know.

We have a huge pantry off the kitchen which is a veritable storehouse for many interesting things. It could definitely use a re-haul job, changing the pots and pans, putting them where they should be and sorting the canned goods shelves. Then there is a stack of old recipe books. I know from experience that it would take me five days to go through all of them. I figure this is one job that can wait. I always say it is better not to start a project than to mess it up.   *September 1972*

&&&

Our house is full of old things. So is the basement, the garage and the walk-in-attic.

It has become increasingly impossible down through thirty some years to separate the collection of mementos and memorabilia from the junk.

When there is a man in the house who saves coffee cans because we can use them for something, sometime, and old rolled up toothpaste tubes because they can be melted down and used for solder or something, then you have a problem.

For example, the pantry was being tackled for a cleaning.

"What did you put in that sack?" he asked.

"Nothing," I answered. "Just some old bottle caps, some

214

cleaning rags and about 35 plastic covers from ice cream cartons."

"I'll keep the plastic covers" he decided. "Never know what you can make out of them someday."

One of us (not me) also relishes the great bargains in furniture and other people's discards (junk) that he proudly "bids away" from right under the other fellow's nose at a sale. Any sale.

"You never know when these things will come in handy and they'll look super after I refinish and work on them."

Thank heaven that most of them never get from the garage to the house.

We are still using a dinette set purchased 33 years ago in Chariton from some friends we played Pinochle with who wanted a new set so we bought it for $10. The reason it is still in use, is that it was made of such good sturdy wood that it never fell down nor did the six chairs fall apart.

We have two pictures in the living room that were acquired from a neighbor woman who asked him to get rid of them for her because the garbage man didn't pick them up.

Of course he would. The garbage never saw the likes of those pictures. But I did. Every day.

In the basement, in one dingy corner, stands an old bellows type pedal organ. This was a "gift" from a family who didn't want to move it to another state, so spouse paid somebody to trundle it down to our basement. The fancy carved wood has string lines of cobwebs crossed over again and again many times. The bellows pump has never been fixed. This organ was a great acquisition and will surely make beautiful music someday.

But there is hope that something will come out of this hodgepodge of old items (junk).

Spouse has plans to convert his "den" into a room out of the past. He thinks the old railroad lantern would look pretty good hanging from the gun rack which holds his grandfather's Kentucky squirrel rifle.

Somewhere he read that old rusty ice tongs make a nice wall hanging as does a washboard decorated up as a bulletin board.

He found an old wicker lamp shade somewhere and naturally they happen to be right in style now.

That rusty coal bucket in the basement will be painted to hold magazines. Won't this all look chic together? And add to this décor his antique coat rack with mirror and seat. No one else will have a room like this.

And while he was up in the attic, he brought down all my old Ladies Home Journals that I was going to cut recipes out of someday. He destined them for the trash, but when nobody was looking, they disappeared to the basement.

People shouldn't throw away valuable things like old magazines.

&&&

We're getting a little premature taste of how retirement might go at our house. (Husband has been house-bound for a few weeks due to a health problem.) And in just this short time we've discovered that all the advice we've been reading about preparing for retirement years hits the nail on the head.

Sudden togetherness, for 24 hours a day, can create a few

216

problems. For instance, I've been making gravy for years without a pair of eyes peering over my shoulder. I'm not used to stirring up strawberry shortcake with a running commentary from a kitchen superintendent, either.

"Have you fed the dog yet?"

"Of course," I replied. "She has never yet died of starvation."

And I didn't know there was a movie on another TV channel at the same time as my only daytime program.

Yes sir, I can see we've got to study up on this retirement thing before he leaves his rural mail route.

But in the meantime, I've been called to 2nd term jury duty, so I'll be listening to the lawyers argue instead. (Now he can watch his old movie and maybe even make his own gravy!) *May 1977*

New Budget Book

This has all the earmarks of being the year that we at our house are going to know where every penny that comes into it goes when it leaves.

Just because we've never been able to keep a flawless, detailed income and outgo book before doesn't mean that we'll fail miserably again this year.

Goodness knows we've tried to keep household books. In fact, every New Year always starts out the same way. He says "Where did all our money go last year?" I reply with a vacant stare, "I don't know."

This leads to his statement that "we certainly should keep track of our hard earned, sweat of our backs, cotton pickin' money" and I agree that "we should, indeed we should."

The next scene in the Happy New Year drama is the presentation of a handsome, hard-bound budget book from him to me. I'll have to admit that this year it is a beauty, the prettiest one we've ever had, all bound in scarlet and black, our old CHS school colors.

But you have to open a brand new budget book to really know what the sight of those crisp, neat pages can do for you. Here, before your very eyes are the pages of the New Year. You marvel at what brilliant mind put this intricate book together.

The first three pages grab you right where you live. "There is exhilaration" it says, "in keeping a daily expense record." And woe and dire disaster await anyone foolhardy enough to play willy-nilly with facts and figures.

Then you see January with all her 31 lines and spaces down the side and several categories across the top. What a breathtaking assortment of categories including Household, Utilities, Automobiles, Food, Insurance and Miscellaneous just to name a few. (I'm always pleased that my favorite category, Miscellaneous, has a bigger space than the rest.)

There are a lot of little squares for daily totals, monthly totals, combined category totals, totals to carry over into February. You can even make sub-totals clear down to December if you feel like it and add and subtract almost anywhere. It's absolutely mind-boggling.

Now January 1 gave us an easy start. The space was blank: Nobody left the televised Pasadena Rose Parade or the football game to go out and spend any money.

January 2 presented the first problem. We bought groceries

and naturally I put the amount down under Food. That proved to be an inky mistake which was promptly noted by him who snorted, "Didn't you see that the Food category is subdivided into 1) edibles 2) non-food 3) lunches 4) restaurants 5) parties, entertaining?"

So I scratched out the offending total under Food and painstakingly put the bread under edibles, the toilet tissue under non-food and the baloney under lunches. I didn't, however, know what to do with Fido's Gravy Mix so left it out. The Woman's Day magazine went down under non-food and the magazine, newspapers, books. I'm no dummy.

By January 15 I felt I was really getting into the swing of the Battle of the Budget. I was particularly elated to be the No. 1 in charge of the Book and in knowing that not one red cent was getting spent without my knowing for what.

My enthusiasm knew no bounds, while his seemed to lose luster. Every night I'd get out old scarlet and black, usually during *Charlie's Angels* or *Baa, Baa Black Sheep* or whatever favorite show he happened to be watching, and begin my rundown query of the day's expenditures.

One evening the NFL football game was on. All I did was ask him to run sort of a CPA audit of the first two week's entries.

This morning I can't find my budget book. It seems to have disappeared into thin air. Now I won't be able to write down that $22 I spent on clothes today. Too bad. There goes another year.

&&&

Since last weeks column came out about the Happy New Year

budget book ordeal at our house, I've been accused (by him) of telling everything I know.

Well, that's not quite true. There is a least one other little matter that crops up every once in awhile that you may as well know about.

It is the Battle of the Food Bill. This isn't one of those annual deals, but rather a sporadic tribulation that is brought on after he has seen a newspaper or magazine article on how to feed a family of eight on less than $25 a week.

"Aha, now see here," he bellows, pointing to the accompanying picture of an Amazon-sized ma and pa and their six strapping, healthy-looking children. "They don't look hungry to me. If she can manage that well, why can't you feed the two of us on $10?"

His comparison between this family of eight and just the two of us struck me as very ridiculous and very funny. Amusing, that is, until I realized that I haven't been able to buy groceries for two on $25 lately.

Something is wrong somewhere and I'm willing to read yet another article telling how to buy meat, potatoes and gravy for eight people on $25 dollars a week.

I hadn't read the first two paragraphs until I found out that the "Miracle" family considers all that twenty-five dollars as food and didn't count the other twenty-five they spend on soap and Raid as something else besides groceries. Our groceries are groceries!

I also note, farther down, that the Miracle workers raise a big garden and the missus cans and freezes everything from gooseberries to collard greens plus 45 quarts of chopped kohlrabi. That's another big minus for us – we don't grow that kind of garden.

And there, in black and white, looms another big reason why we don't seem to be holding the budget line like the magazine family. It seems that mother Miracle's parents just butchered a calf and two hogs and stuffed their freezer with steaks and chops. And they throw in dozens of fresh country eggs to go along with the ham. Naturally, these are just "gifts" and are not counted in on the $25 per week.

Another of Mrs. Miracle's clever little budget ideas is that the family does not have snacks – except for the popcorn which a generous neighbor grows and shares with them. Desserts are rare too and are something like "Prune Snow" for which she generously gives the recipe. (At our house we'd be sure to miss the fruit turnovers.)

Then the author of the article asked, "What do you feed company? Everybody has company for an occasional meal."

"Well," answered the mother, sheepishly, "we sometimes out-sit them or go to the door with toothpicks in our mouths like we've just eaten." Then she acknowledged that once in a while she did grind up stuff like eggs, pickles and leftover liver for sandwiches. (They probably never have to worry much about company coming at mealtime anyway.)

The clincher of the article comes when the author suggests that each reader plan a week of low cost meals just to show that the whole thing is possible, that you don't have to have Half 'n Half on your oatmeal after all.

He thought that this plan indeed, was the smartest idea HE'D ever thought of. "Plan a week of low-cost menus and give it a try. What have we got to lose?" he insisted, handing me a $10 bill. (We no doubt would lose weight.)

Luckily they were having a sale of canned spinach at Easter's that week, and tube biscuits for 10 cents at Hy-Vee, and ground beef at J & K Market. I made some beet soup and followed the Miracle household recipe for Medley of Okra and Rutabaga Casserole. Hamburgers stuffed with mashed squash are very filling and certainly do stretch the meat.

I think we might have made a go of it for seven days on that $10 if it hadn't been for the stewed tomatoes with the leftover biscuit pieces in them or the pressures from eating bean soup three days in a row. (Dry powdered milk mixed with water turns us green.)

Actually it cost him about as much to buy the plop-plop-fizz-fizz stuff later as it did the groceries. I expect that I'm probably safe from the Battle of the Food Bills until he spots another of those "How We Manage" articles written by a mother with 10 children – who lives on $22 dollars a week.

&&&

I've been thinking strongly of instigating a raise in my allowance. Actually, it's not a $12,900 increase I'm after, just a modest cost-of living raise. Say $12.90

Now ordinarily, I would have gone to the head of the house and cast my vote for my raise. I'm no coward. But since those Washington fellows had such phenomenal success getting their

222

salaries boosted without doing anything, it has occurred to me that maybe if I pretend I'm not looking, a generous bounty will just drop into my apron pocket.

It would seem apropos, also, that there should be some 'freebees' around for me someplace. Perhaps some free hair-do's, jewelry, letters mailed free and even a junket ... er business trip ... to the Caribbean where I could study the spiny shells for somebody while basking in the sun.

&&&

We probably aren't going to be one of the families who get a rebate from the government for buying a small, compact car.

President Carter is urging John Q. Public to purchase smaller autos which don't gobble up the gasoline.

We would like to comply, of course (if we were going to buy a car), but Mr. Carter should know that my tall husband just can't sit up straight in one of those 45 miles per gallon creations. They say that short men are touchy about their heights, but extra tall men don't always have it so good either.   *April 1977*

&&&

Being tall must have numerous advantages like being able to see the entire Pancake Day parade.

But I've found that when I ask my 6 foot 3½ inch husband to put staples and food in the pantry, I end up having to get the kitchen step-stool to reach the sugar on the top shelf. He also mixed up the vegetables with the fruits and it is nothing to find the tomato soup behind a row of grape jelly. Sometimes I can't

223

find the canned tuna because it's on the top shelf behind the sugar.

He's helping, of course.

&&&

Instead of a decorated cake for Father's Day, husband decided he'd like a fresh gooseberry pie better.

Daughter Nancy picked and stemmed enough of the tart berries from their property in Unionville, Iowa and he got his pie. It would have been a beautiful creation if the baker hadn't forgotten to turn the oven from pre-heat to bake the first 15 minutes causing the sugar on top to bubble on the dark brown crust.

However, he had a good Father's Day anyway since Nancy also brought in fresh country eggs, radishes, and frozen black raspberries.

&&&

I'm in the height of my glory when the temperatures are in the 90's, to sit under my big weeping willow tree and let its cool fronds fan the breezes back and forth. A dirty tree that should be banned to the back 40? Nay, I say.

I'd like to swing across the rivulet in the woods again from the branch of a willow tree, but I wouldn't dare.

&&&

Nobody told me not to plant a weeping willow tree on our property. They didn't have to. There was already one in good standing when we moved here. I took it to my heart and championed that underdog tree. Many times in the past 20 years I've wailed, "Woodman spare that tree!" I've protected it from the ax man, saw man and the evil eye. I've had fierce arguments over it and picked up after it like it was a baby. Several times I thought it was a goner and once the entire center was twisted out during a windstorm.

When I wasn't looking this week my husband launched into his annual "trimming" of the tree. The fronds get caught in his lawnmower, he says, and whap him in the face when he feeds the dog.

His "trimming" turned into a whack-fest to about ten feet off the ground. Needless to say, I could be heard in the next block.

I betcha Tree will send up twigs again next spring. He's been through everything else.

&&&

It was bound to happen at our house sometime.

One of my hanging macramé plant holders crashed to the floor in the middle of the night, dropping my Boston fern upside down on the carpet, spewing soil all over and crushing the fern that I have babied for five years.

And that's not all, on its way down, it managed to knock over a prized ceramic bowl, an old fashion Polka Dot plant and a glass bowl of philodendron. The hook just pulled out of the tall ceiling above the bay window. It was bound to happen someday. My husband said so.

&&&

225

Sometimes you don't rightly know what people mean when they say something. For example, the other day my husband and I saw a couple uptown. I didn't know her and she didn't know me, but the husbands knew each other. Anyway, she asked Mac, "Is that your wife with you?" He said that it was. She said: "Oh, Well, she doesn't look like I thought she would."

Yes, there are times when you don't know what people mean when they say something. And I was afraid to ask.

&&&

We didn't have much trouble putting up our Christmas tree this year (unlike certain other newspaper people), but when it came to stringing on the lights, things went from good to trouble.

None of the three strands of twinkling lights worked.

Naturally, the one who takes down all the decorations, boxes them and cleans up the debris afterward (me) was to blame.

"What have you done to the lights?" he blared, intimating that they had been stuffed into the boxes just like I stuff things into dresser drawers.

Two hours later, after finding the pliers, fiddling with the wires, checking each bulb, and repeatedly plugging into the outlet, he became a person that only Scrooge himself could love. The lights still wouldn't go on.

Only after I carefully suggested that something might be wrong with the floor outlet that we hadn't used in years did any light get shed on the problem.

So we moved the tree back into the same spot it always had.

The tree lights really glow now, and tomorrow he'll replace the other outlet and I'll put the rest of the baubles on the tree.

&&&

Had a stint in the hospital right at Christmas time. This is one way to get out of the work and bustle of Christmas preparations, but I don't recommend it.

Daughters Rosemary and Nancy are taking over Christmas dinner preparations this year and husband has run all over town finishing up last minute shopping and details. I needed a box of Christmas cards so he brings home one that has only "To Our Good Friends" inscribed. Are relatives good friends?

&&&

One Centerville gal (me) bought herself a beautiful Kewpie doll for Christmas because it brought back memories of the one she had many years ago. Her husband thought the whole thing highly amusing so she put it away in the closet.

Then he bought himself one of those battery-powered mechanical toy trains and she found this highly amusing and went around guffawing impolitely.

But he didn't relegate his pride and joy to a dark existence in the closet. No sir, he says he bought it for his grandchildren to watch!

&&&

There are probably some male column readers out in Iowegianland, and if there are, they are no doubt wondering why

I "pick on" my husband sometimes and write about his faults. (He never reads the column, but I guess people tell him about it.)

Well, I have mentioned a time or two that he "pack rats" everything and saves old toothpaste tubes in case there is a shortage of metal someday. And once I did mention that he insists on a strict budget book every New Years. Things like that.

Some fellows even defend his right to like scrambled brains and meatloaf gravy. They're the ones who would like to hear about some of my idiosyncrasies, and most certainly I would oblige if I could think of any right off.

Now actually, I don't think it a bit odd that I put the dinner dishes in the sink for a five-minute soak and leave them five hours while I peruse the new National Geographic and read all the articles in Reader's Digest.

Nor do I see anything wrong with squeezing toothpaste from the top and leave the cap off if I'm in a bit of a hurry.

And for the life of me I don't know why he gets upset because I yawn and squirm in my chair when he tells his World War II tales for the millionth time.

And as for being the world's worst bureau drawer stuffer, I believe that if his underwear and socks don't fit into the drawer, make them fit. The world won't come to an end if he has to get a spatula to pry the drawer open. And if things don't fall on his head when closet doors are opened, he can consider himself lucky. It's not such a big deal if boxes of old Christmas cards fall off the shelves now and then.

I'll have to admit, though, that serving hamburger four times in one week didn't prove to be such a great idea even if it did prove that I did know four different ways to prepare it.

If you consider that butting in on his lectures (when he's winning) is a fault, or that talking when I should be listening is so bad, then I suppose I do have a few idiosyncrasies.

But somehow, fellows, the peculiar things I do don't seem nearly as strange as installing two toilet tissue rolls on opposite sides.

Chapter 12

GRUMBLES AND GRIPES

It's a way of life that everybody, at some time or another, gripes about something that doesn't suit them.

Tom Tuttle grumbles and rumbles about situations he deems unfair in the community for all the readers to see in his column "Ramblings and Rumblings"; Russ Swanson hollers about Christmas candles still on the courthouse come springtime and gals with rollers in their hair in his "Russ lings" column; Theda Long, in her "Thimble Thoughts," tangles with governmental shenanigans and even Edwyna Fenton speaks her mind in "Chits and Chatters".

And of course Donald Kaul growls about a lot of things in his Des Moines Register column.

So I decided that once in a while I'd write on my grumbles and gripes.

&&&

Hal Boyle writes a syndicated column which appears in many newspapers. Hal speaks his mind on any subject under the sun and lets the chips fall where they may! But then, Hal doesn't always hear the chips fall – he lives hundreds of miles away from most of his readers. So it is with a bit of reluctance that I air any of my personal prejudices because when a hometown columnist lets fly with gripes, some of the chips might hit the fan and he (or she) might wish for residence in Timbuktu.

For instance, I've harbored a few personal ideas about funerals down through the years and they are not the opinions of this newspaper or anybody else's for that matter. Some of my best friends are funeral directors, so the prejudices have absolutely nothing to do with them or their excellent work.

Gripe No. 1: When someone in the line passing the casket whispers loudly, "My, doesn't she look so natural that she could talk to you?" I about jump out of the line. Either the morticians performed a face miracle or the poor lady didn't look so great when she was living. (I've always thought that a hidden speaker might just cure this type.)

Gripe No. 2: Mourners who can later describe in minute detail how everything looked. What color the silk lining was; whether or not the pillow had lace edging; if the corpse's hands were folded right over left or vice-versa; how many rings were on the fingers. (These people usually can't remember what they did that day, but develop eyes like a hawk and memories like an elephant on such occasions.)

Gripe No. 3: Glasses. Yes, glasses, because grandpa just

232

didn't look natural without them, living or dead. So how many people (neighbors and friends and relatives) had ever seen grandpa flat on his back in bed with glasses perched on his nose and with his best suit on?

This brings me to prejudice No. 4, which is clothing. New dresses and new suits and ties are bought for the service so people won't think the dear departed looks shabby at his own funeral.

I once knew a fellow who wore overalls because he worked hard and loved to be out-of-doors. His best outfit was a pair of blue serge pants which he bought to get married in. (You had to peer twice to be sure they were burying the right man in a fancy suit and red tie. He wouldn't have liked it.)

Other personal prejudices: People who comment: "My, they sure didn't put him down very nice considering all the money they've got." Or, "My, they must have gone in debt up to their ears for THAT funeral when they don't have a dime." And others who use old superstitions like: "Well, they buried him in the rain and that's bad luck." For whom?

Shop in your own hometown

You can call me a basic Centerville shopper.

I'm one of the "trade-at-home" devotees. In the first place, I don't go to Des Moines all that much and if I do, I only buy a few trinkets or something I honestly can't find in Centerville.

I've always said that if I had all the money I could use, I could find almost anything I want or need right here, from clothes and furniture, down to a skillet.

It helps our town to shop at home yet wives of local business men, whose bread and butter comes from right here, trek regularly to Des Moines to do their heavy buying ... Christmastime and otherwise.

I don't own a business here, understand, but I agree with Mr. Frank that many times they've paid more for an identical article.

Irate Response

Well, last Thursday I made mention that I am a Centerville shopper and if I had plenty of money I could buy almost anything I wanted or needed right here in local stores.

I heard about that remark, yessiree!

This is typical: One woman said to me, "I don't agree with you. We make our (doggone) money and we'll spend it where we (doggone) please for what we (doggone) please!" Or strong words to that effect.

Another told me, "Groceries are very high in Centerville so we buy our staples and canned goods in Ottumwa at a wholesale place which has good stuff." She added that "when you have a large family and can buy five loaves of bread for $1 and canned goods by the case a lot cheaper, then why not pool a car and go?"

A man commented, "We notice that Centerville merchants don't turn down business from other southern Iowa towns who could shop at home too."

So, to each his own way of thinking.   *November 1980*

Teachers Salaries

When I read the list of salaries (and proposed future salaries) for local school administrators and teachers in Bill Weaver's Iowegian article recently, I about fell off my chair. Centerville School District, you're certainly not a poverty area any more. Pay to keep good teachers and administrators? Of course, but pay to keep them all, mediocre (or poor teachers) alike under their bargaining organization? I draw the line.

A teacher's response

You may have noticed over the years that I generally stay away from using controversial issues in my columns. I prefer light-hearted items instead, and besides, I have a weak tolerance for nasty fan letters. Let the other news media handle politics, religion, government, city council meeting and whether or not the school board votes to replace a roof.

I don't have the Des Moines Register's Donald Kaul's style but sometimes I wish I did. But then, I don't have his thick skin either and my little feelings would be hurt if I received some of his critical "fan" mail.

Yet once in a while I get carried away and write something that stirs a few people.

My latest such slip was making the comment that I about fell off my chair when I read the proposed salaries of school administrators and some teachers.

Well, now, you can believe I got a letter on that one. I was relieved that it wasn't a nasty, personal vendetta against me. In fact, I have the feeling it was written by someone (a teacher) who doesn't know me very well ... or how to spell my two names. It was signed Sincerely, X.

Anonymous letters don't deserve printing, but I thought several paragraphs might interest you.

Direct Quote: "Dear Ms. Conville, Some of your items in your column, I thought I would respond to (in which I should respond). You hit pretty hard on salaries, of course, you know ours. Will you please print the W-2 forms for salaries for the Iowegian staff? I have no idea what they make. For instance, your salary (hours, experience, training), Weaver's salary, Beck's salary, etc. While you're at it, see if you can find out what salary the average lawyer, pharmacist, engineer, and even the doctors, make after 15 years. As far as that goes, look into the average dock hand at Hy-Vee in Chariton, the John Deere worker in Ottumwa, etc. I understand that a high school drop out at both can easily make $20,000 a year. I know there are many less paying jobs – someone has to sweep the floors, etc. However, they could go to NMSU and get a high paying teacher's job."

Comment: Now, Mr. or Miss or Mrs. Whoever – you know I can't print Iowegian staff salaries. They're not paid out of your real estate taxes. You also know I can't print an engineer's salary or ask a Hy-Vee dock hand what he makes a year. They're not paid out of your taxes or public assessment funds.

Direct Quote: "Then you talk about discipline. I've had parents tell me if I touch their child they'll take me to court (true

236

– every year). Also I've had just the opposite. Personally, I've had few discipline problems through the years. I can't say that for all my peers. But you're right – they made the same salary. The good teachers left for better pay. But, by the way, who decides who the good teachers are? You? Parents? Who? I can't please parents all the time!!! All I have to do is give good grades (no F's or D's) – require some home work (look good) – don't grade homework too tough (don't want the kids bad-mouthing me) – have a fair amount of discipline – etc. etc. I've seen often teachers like this – they last forever – pillars in the community, even you probably think they are the greatest. However, they haven't taught a decent day of school in years. The principal knows this! So do the teachers! No one else does, however. It would take an act of God to get rid of this teacher."

Comment: I would bet the school youngsters, besides the principal and other teachers, know who the ineffective teachers are. That's my point. Someone should know who these "pillars" of the community are and not include them in the new salary negotiations.

Direct Quote: "But don't give up hope, Majorie, you could always go to NMSU, pick up some education hours, and after 15-18 years with a masters plus, you could get in on this easy money by teaching journalism (possibly English) to 35 teenagers 6 hours a day (each). You'll note that this includes a possible 300 parents to deal with – please them all – good luck. Signed Sincerely, X. Sorry, I have to remain unsigned – I don't need the publicity."

Comment: You're right. With just a high school education, I could use some college hours and a degree or two would be nice. I never ever remarked or wrote that teaching was "easy money," that preaching a sermon was "child's play" or that clerking in a store was a "snap." Even without a masters plus degree, I'm not so stupid as to demean another person's work. Were it possible, I believe we would all "get our eyes opened" and be more tolerant of other jobs if we tried them for awhile.

Since you specifically mentioned the Iowegian and Weaver, may I point out that he not only works his week, but is on call on weekends to cover fires and accidents. His work is down in black and white for thousands to see and evaluate. He can't please everybody either. But then, he doesn't need me to tell about his college, training or experience nor negotiate for him.

Easy money? Who said it?   *March 1980*

&&&

I don't mind facts and figures which are a matter of record, but they said the total visitor count at Lake Rathbun one weekend was 20,000. This figure was derived by counting the cars going over those counter cables laid across the access roads. I am told they count autos back and they count them forth and then what do they do? Well, by golly, I hear they multiply each car count by five on the assumption that each vehicle carries five persons.

Shaky statistics.

&&&

Ah, come on, fellows, enough of the red and yellow blinking

238

lights at Haynes Street and Highway 5. On with the green. Drivers aren't paying the slightest bit of attention to the signs now. The highway cars are still racing right on through, just as before; leaving the drivers from Haynes Street stalled or forced to make daring dashes through four lanes of traffic to get across.

If the blinkin' lights don't function, by golly, then send 'em back where they came from.

&&&

I received several phone calls last week. These were the kind with a bemused caller on the other end of the line. They all started out the same way:

"Thanks a lot."

"For what?" I asked.

"For getting the new stop signs fixed at Haynes and Highway 5."

It's nice to get credit for something good that you've done, but once in awhile you get credit for something you didn't do. Even though I did have the last word, it doesn't mean a thing. Coincidence, mere coincidence.

I don't want to get too persuasive you know, else the next thing they'll have me working on is getting the algae taste out of the Centerville water!

Moral Fiber

Unraveling of the national moral fiber worries me when I have time to think about it.

It's something like ropes whose strands unravel one by one,

239

frayed and weakened, until there is just a pile of hemp which wouldn't be strong enough to support a wet noodle.

I guess I am most disturbed by what seems to be a general lowering of personal standards. There is a marked increase of pilfering in shops, shooting out plate glass windows, false charges in repair bills, car stealing, and "ripping off" in hundreds of other ways.

Was listening to television star Pearl Bailey expound in her own inimitable fashion on a program recently. Pearl didn't mince words about the present situation of cynicism and distrust between people.

Said Pearl in essence: "You know folks, there used to be such things as stealing cars, shoplifting, and billfold stealing in the old days too. But nothing like today.

Why I remember when it was all right for a neighbor to go into your flat and shut down a window if it started to rain, or take down a line full of clothes if a storm came up and the neighbor wasn't home to do it herself.

We shared our beans and cornbread if a neighbor was hungry. We worked hard washing clothes on the washboard and working and cleaning and taking care of the young'uns. But we still took time to help a child or a neighbor who was down on his luck."

Pearl added with a flourish that if asked, she MIGHT consider running for the office of President of the United States. Her campaign theme no doubt would be "Love for your fellowman."

Another television show captured my interest. David Suskind was hosting a group of young inmates of Goshen Correctional Institution in New York. The young folks were masked to protect their identity.

One young red-haired girl, who was serving time for a long list of crimes from mugging, breaking and entering, to beating up other teenage girls, came right out and blamed her parents and society for how she had turned out.

She personally wasn't to blame for anything, you see, because, as she pointed out, her parents were divorced and she wanted to join a gang out of curiosity. Society was at fault because it was so mean to teenagers and wouldn't let them do as they pleased and make their own laws of behavior.

Somehow, though, I didn't feel too guilty as a member of the society she was blaming. I've always believed that somewhere inside a person there is a feeling of what is right or wrong.

August 1975

James Gang

I've never understood the glamour connected with the Jesse James gang of outlaws. Historical heroes, are they? I've seen huge signs at Corydon, Iowa and all through Missouri, even down in Arkansas boasting that the Jesse James' outlaws robbed this or that bank; held up trains here or there and holed up in caves. In one Missouri town the billboard read: "The James gang robbed the rich to give to the poor." Romanticize the James boys for their exploits? I won't.

&&&

I was brought up to look for the good in people and to believe that most people could be trusted.

241

There was a long time there when I'd have been sure that 99 out of any 100 people picked at random in Centerville could be depended on to do the right thing by you.

Well, nobody is sorrier than I am that the percentage has dropped considerably. But I'll probably still go on believing and trusting. I was brought up that way.

&&&

There seems always to be a conflict between youth and age, yet youth and age should temper each other.

Youth shouldn't cast reflection on those whose faces reflect the trials and tribulations of life, for it is that very living that makes their ideas worthy of attention. And age must not cast aspersions on youth as being carefree and rash, for it is that very enthusiasm to attempt gigantic problems that has made this nation one of the doers and not thinkers only. Let age speak out from wisdom and youth uphold ideals.

Maybe youth and age can provide a balance.

&&&

Mrs. Atheist

We have heard the world over from a certain Mrs. Atheist that we are all a bunch of phonies. She points out via the news media that no one knows for sure that the apostles wrote anything down at all or that it was accurate if they did. "You can't believe everything you read," she says.

You made your point, Mrs. Atheist, but then we don't believe everything we hear either. And you may have forgotten,

Madalyn, that human beings can "feel" things deep down in a part of us we can't even see. Call it an awareness.

If radio's slim fingers can pluck a melody from night and toss it over a continent and sea; if songs are culled from thin blue air and television can clutch instant images of faces from out of our space realm and show them to us, then should mortals wonder if God hears prayers? *April 1969*

&&&

Is there really an acceptable excuse for a consistently lousy disposition? Or constant rudeness or curtness?

I've heard this one: "Well, you know how he/she is so you'll have to excuse them."

Don't you often wonder what you should say and how you should act around those persons for whom everybody has to make allowances? You know the type – people who are just plain nasty most of the time and somebody says, "Now just don't pay any attention to the hurtful things they say because THAT'S JUST THEIR WAY, YOU KNOW." I don't buy that.

&&&

Although I'm from the generation that didn't believe in discussing personal business with everybody, I find that I admire First Lady Betty Ford's courageous and honest approach to her medication and alcohol problems.

There are a few people who have such a lineup of pill bottles on their shelves that I wonder how they remember which capsule they are supposed to take when. And they top the day off with sleeping pills.

It isn't just the teenagers who are popping pills. The older folks think they have to take all these prescription drugs for what ails them!

&&&

It is ironic that cigarettes cannot be purchased in the Veteran's Hospital canteen by visitors, and patients must have a doctor's permission slip to buy two packs.

Yet there were cigarettes all over the place in the hands of secretaries, nurses, in the offices, lounges, and dining area. I'd wager that 9 out of 10 patients' wives puffed away. I know I'm old fashioned when I still get a mild shock as a frail little gray-haired lady pulls a pack of long filter cigarettes out of her handbag and lights up, one after the other!

I read the other day about a man who sued a major airline because he was supposed to be seated in the first class "No Smoking" section yet the rows right behind him blew smoke all over him. He won the suit too.

I know what he means. At the hospitals in Iowa City some of the lounges and cafeteria dining areas are designated one side for each. Yet there are no partitions, no special aerating fans. It's the same room for both and I watched smoke wafting from one side to the other. The whole idea seemed pointless and ridiculous. *November 1978*

&&&

244

Mrs. P. Wreck

I read in an advice column one day that the way to cure people who call you late at night is to call them early in the morning. It seems that the night owl callers get the message pretty quick.

Well, a group of us neighborhood women in Charles City several years ago sure cured a chronic complainer amongst us, by reversing the situation.

Every time any of us would get together for coffee or to chat over the wash lines, here would come Mrs. Physical Wreck, sometimes bringing her latest prescriptions so we could admire the blue and gold or pink and purple capsules.

It didn't make any difference what the topic of conversation was; she would manage to change it to her miserable ailments, which included every thing from warts to wind chimes in her ears.

At a baby shower once for a neighborhood girl, we were all treated to the sight of her caesarian section scars plus a 30 minute commentary on the operation. If a neighbor was sick, she was the first to call with advice on how to treat the illness before they died like her uncle did.

And heaven forbid that you would come down with a backache, because she'd develop one too, only hers would be worse than yours.

The pharmacists were happy with her ... we were sick of her and her punies.

One day we got together and decided that Mrs. Wreck would be a great neighbor if she didn't complain incessantly.

245

Besides, we were starting to wonder why we didn't have these ailments too and get out of doing our housework like she did. We agreed that every time she opened her mouth with the news that she felt light-headed that morning or something, we'd all chime in with the same ailment.

It worked! Little by little this physical wreck quit showing us her capsules. The strain of all of us rushing into our houses to bring out even prettier pills got to be too much for her. Her description of a stretched colon got stinted when Mrs. So and So told of a previous operation to remove a portion of hers.

About a week later, we happened to see a friend who lived a block over on 7th avenue. She told us: "You know, Mrs. Wreck said that she has to quit neighboring with you women in her block. You are all such complainers!"

&&&

When I was a little girl I had a pet peeve. It was 'whispering in public'. I still have it. Not low, confidential talking, mind you, but whispering behind shielding hands. The other day I saw a group of kindergarten girls coming home from school. Two of them kept up a whispered conversation, interspersed with giggling. The other two looked hurt and puzzled and left out. I remember how that used to feel and I tried never to do it. Adult women don't look any better whispering than little girls do, and they should know better.

&&&

Merchandising Parties

Since I have never entertained any illusions of being a perfect human being – all sweetness and light, without fault, flaw or foible – I readily admit to a few peculiar aversions or hang-ups.

For instance, I have a "thing" about merchandising parties. I don't go to merchandising parties. You know the kind. A demonstrator comes into someone's home and sells plastic or rubber goods, jewelry, clothing, Christmas toys, or cosmetics.

And I'll tell you why I don't go. But first, let me point out that I don't have a thing against the personable demonstrators nor their merchandise which is usually of excellent quality.

Back in the 1940's we lived in a new housing development of 50 small houses in Charles City, Iowa. In addition to 'coffeying' in the blocks as neighbors became acquainted, it became the rage to have home merchandising parties where a demonstrator sold certain household products like degreasers and mothballs.

The hostess could reap bonus gifts depending on the number of points her party netted, based on: 1) the number present, 2) the total money in orders, 3) how many ladies booked future parties.

I was invited and, loving parties and socializing, I went. The first one started out all fun and games. I won a prize in a guessing contest and enjoyed the conversation. Then an order pad and pencil were placed in my hand and the business of demonstrating products and the soft-sell began. I knew I couldn't just sit there like a dummy and enjoy something for nothing.

I bought products I needed but couldn't afford on my peewee

budget. I also bought a candle dripper cleaner, a cheap item, because who would dare go to a merchandising party and leave an empty list pad on the chair?

I must have been invited to 10 selling parties after that and felt I had to go because I had gone to so-and-so's party and helped her out with her points. Some parties were in homes where I had never shared even a cup of coffee. Others were in homes whose hostesses I had never met and probably would never see again. (People can be very friendly where points are concerned.) After each party I felt more embarrassed and more pressured and guiltier for buying mothballs when I should have bought the kids a pair of socks.

The eleventh products party proved to be my last. When the demonstrator sidled up to me and said, "Now, Mrs. McConnell, you have a party for your good friend and neighbor and that will give her enough points to get the set of matching lamps she wants so badly." Then she added, "I know you just can't let your hostess down!"

I muttered a protest that my 4 ½ room house wasn't big enough to have a party in, when I should have truthfully told her that I wouldn't feel right about asking people into my home to sell them a bill of goods just so I could get a free gift.

I knew I had lost a friend when said hostess met me on the street later and blazed, "You cost me a set of lamps, you know that?" She glared at me and added, "Yeah, you could have booked a party for me and given me all the points I needed, but you didn't."

I haven't been to a merchandising party since, and 30 years is a long time to nurture a hang up.

My friends tell me they love to go to products parties. They have the most wonderful times and get free prizes and refreshments and everything. They think I'm peculiar.

My daughter Nancy had a products party Tuesday night. I didn't go. She knows why, but doesn't understand it. She thinks I am peculiar.

I have some other hang-ups but you surely wouldn't want to hear them all at one sitting. You might begin to think I'm peculiar.

Summer of '61

Some folks remember the Summer of '61 fondly as the time they met that cute girl who they later married. Others recall that summer as the vacation they learned to swim at the ocean beach.

But at our house we remember the Summer of '61 as the three-month period that we were invaded by a thundering horde of visitors – all bent on turning our house into a motel, short-order diner, Laundromat and recreations center - all for free, no charge.

There were three families who traipsed through Centerville that summer, all making stops at our house en route to someplace else. And when you consider that we had a houseful of our own, we were already running a motel, diner, Laundromat and recreation center.

The first batch of visitors came one June afternoon. There was a knock at the door and the man said, "Lady, I'm working my way through college selling magazines." "I don't want any," I said.

"Ha, ha. Don't you recognize me? ha, ha. I worked with your husband for six months at Gambles in Kansas twenty years ago. ha, ha."

I couldn't even remember his name. Then I saw the station wagon in the driveway with wife and six kids leaning out the windows, all grinning like the cat that swallowed the canary.

"We're just passing through on our way to Michigan and thought we'd stay a few days with you folks for old time's sake," he chuckled, obviously pleased with his handling of free stopovers.

I don't know how we lived through that week.

The first order of business was supper for 14, and the next step was to go to the grocery store for supplies. Dear wife appointed herself to go along because then she could point to the items her kids would eat. As it turned out, her kids would eat everything in sight and were only fussy about the size of the helpings and whether or not they could have seconds and thirds. For supper we went through a ham, three fried chickens, mashed and French fried potatoes, three vegetables and strawberry shortcake. Their spoiled daughter cried at the sight of the strawberries so we had to get her ice cream instead.

My grocery budget cried too. Each succeeding meal was like cooking for a regiment at Ft. Leonard Wood.

When bedding-down time came, we had to figure out how to divide 14 people by six beds. We had sleepers on the davenports, in sleeping bags, on rubber-sheet-covered spare mattresses for the bed wetter and in the screened-in front porch swing.

Three more days went by and our company was having such a great time eating, sleeping, playing badminton, going to the Majestic theatre, eating, swimming in the municipal pool, playing croquet and eating, that they stayed an extra day. We should have been flattered, but instead we were flattened.

The night before the Missouri visitors left, I was given instructions to set my alarm for 5 a.m. so I could have breakfast of bacon, sausage, eggs, cereal, juice, milk and coffee on the table by 5:30. (I would have fixed them goat milk cheese had they wanted it, so glad was I that they were finally leaving.)

And as a final, typical gesture, the visiting friend (?) pulled a little notepad out of his pocket. "See here," he chuckled again, very pleased with himself, "see this list? Here are all the other people we're going to surprise on our way to Michigan!"

Batch two of the visitors were relatives, my cousins from Kansas City, who brought their children to Iowa so they could see how backward and quaint the Centerville relatives were. They came for two weeks, but only stayed 10 days because they were so bored.

"What is there to do here?" they'd ask. "We'd just die if we had to live someplace like this." We tried everything to entertain them, but our local swimming pool was a goldfish bowl to them, our theatre played movies they had seen six months ago, and the boys thought our girls were hicks right off a load of pumpkins.

They were miserable and homesick for the lights of the city.

Our egos were shot down and they left us wondering about all the excitement and "life" we were missing.

Years later, we visited the Kansas City cousins and found what we were missing walking around the block - muggings, robberies, and fear of our lives, by living in Centerville. That's why we live here.

The third group of visitors came in August – husband, wife and three children. They hadn't intended to spend the week at our house they said, but the place they came from just didn't work out.

You can't imagine in your wildest dreams what went on that week. Nothing was right. They wouldn't eat the jelly because (dumb me) forgot to put a cover on the jelly dish between meals. They had to rewash the dishes because (dumb me) had left them out in the open in the dish drainer between meals. They turned down my barbecued hamburger grill supper because they weren't used to eating outdoors where the flies were. They wouldn't touch my fruit turnovers because they didn't eat dessert lest they get fat (like some other people).

And didn't I know that each child had to have a separate bedroom because it might "lead to something" if children slept in the same room?

I could write a book! But let me assure you, I quit sending Christmas cards to these people. I want them to think the McConnell motel went out of business. *September 1977*

252

Chapter 13

PEOPLE IN IOWEGIANLAND

It was quite a day – Pancake Day, 1967!

There was something for everyone – cheerful smiles for the lonely at heart, friendly chit-chat for the gregarious, free pancakes for the hungry and girls, girls, girls for the fellows.

My assignment – stay with the queen contestants all day and evening Pancake Day and write a behind-the-scenes story.

In the newspaper field an assignment is an assignment so that you may share the day too with the prettiest, most vibrant girls you're likely to meet in any town on any given day.

If you couldn't care less about girls, then please turn the page to the comic section.

The day for these 15 girls began early. Most of them arose around six o'clock. Dark haired Sheryl Brown said it was five o'clock for her. She had things to do, things to think about, and she had to drive from her home in Albia.

A practice session was called for 10:30 a.m. This would be their first time on the stage itself, the other practice sessions having been at the Community Center.

Wearing shorts or slacks, the contestants were given instructions on pirouetting, stance and position on the stage. The committee stood at street level and the girls picked up helpful pointers.

One girl goofed up a corner turn, smiled in her sweet way, walked on to the center of the stage, and made her turn in front of the empty judges stand like a real trooper.

It was about the only relaxing, informal time of the day.

There was a light lunch, also attended by the three judges, then began preparations for the Big Parade. The girls were to ride in convertibles wearing fall ensembles. Two-piece suits in luscious autumn colors were chosen and there were several long sleeved dresses in orlon and wool.

Peggy Stempel voiced the opinion of all the girls: "I loved riding in the parade. The day was so beautiful and people so nice. It was thrilling."

It was Peggy who hopped out of the convertible on the last turn, clambered into a band uniform and proudly marched with her Pekin High School band twice around the square. That's the caliber of the young ladies vying for the crown.

It was a long parade, but the girls were smiling happily and chattering like chipmunks as they met back at the Continental Hotel, their headquarters for the day.

Following a brief rest, it was interview time for each of the 15 girls. Individual candidates were privately interviewed by the three judges, two men and a woman.

"I thought it would be gruesome," said one contestant to her friend, "but it was wonderful and the judges were so nice and put you at ease."

Small, pert, Linda agreed with a swish of her long blond hair.

It was four o'clock and time to change into swim suits for that portion of the program, following the Johnny Western show.

If you can imagine 15 girls sharing two reasonably small rooms and one bathroom at the hotel, you have some idea of how hectic things were beginning to get about this time of day. Overnight cases lined the floor and beds, and makeup, brushes and coat hangers left scarcely a place to step.

Every girl, without exception, tried to cover up the fact that she was scared silly. "I've never paraded in front of thousands of people in a bathing suit before in my life," said Linda Tuley of Hedrick. Ann Talbot of Centerville, who has been a lifeguard at the local pool for two years and is comfortable wearing a suit, echoed the feeling of all the others when she added that she was all shook up too.

When this portion of the show was over and the cheers and whistles from an admiring crowd died down, they decided it wasn't so bad after all.

Back to the hotel room and to a well-earned hour of leisure. The girls could do as they pleased, just so they were back at the hotel to dress in formals for the 7:30 show. Several Centerville girls went home and took out-of-town girls with them for a brief bite to eat and a short siesta.

The sun had set now, and the stage lights had been turned on. Fresh makeup was put on and finishing touches made to hair-do's. Denise Hayes of Centerville, was heard to remark. "The thing I mind the most is this lighting – makes it hard to put makeup on right."

"It's the Vaseline on the teeth deal I can't stand – yukkk," chimed in Linda Lester of Centerville.

"Did you do your own hair, Denise?" asked Becky McCreary of Centerville, "It looks marvelous."

But the show must go on and it did. Beautifully gowned girls, each carrying a sweetheart rose, were introduced to the large crowd. They never looked better and the judges nodded approval. It was going to be a rough decision. Several ballots might have to be taken to decide the Queen.

The judges went behind locked doors to decide the fates of three girls. Points were given for poise, appearance, personality, results of interviews, and one point for entering the contest.

The time between 7:30 and 9:30 dragged. Linda Van De Pol of Blakesburg thought it was the hardest part of the whole day. Staying dressed up in formals, with white gloves still buttoned on, was not an easy task. They longed to lounge on the floor, drink pop, go out and mingle with the crowd, eat a hamburger and French fries, but could do none of them.

Small talk was engaged in and Diane Craver clowned around with Anne Mart and Peggy Henderson, but still the time dragged. Johnny Western's "Palladan" wafted up from the stage into the hotel room.

Secret votes were cast at this time for Miss Congeniality. Votes were counted by the committee with an impartial observer, but the results were kept secret and the girl who won the coveted award didn't know it until the crowd did.

"In ten minutes we go on stage," announced Mrs. Pauletti at

9:45 p.m., and the air became electric with excitement. Girls, who were tired and drooping before, suddenly came to life. Eyes sparkled, dresses were smoothed, and a "how-do-I-look?" filled the air, as 15 pretty girls went down the steps for their final and best appearance of their career.

All the young ladies were born about 1950. Not very long ago. You saw what that short time can do for a gal.

Everyone was smiling as they took their places flanking the stage. A hush came over the crowd as the announcer opened the envelope. No Oscar night ever held any more suspense, and you could have heard a paper plate drop.

The girls had chosen Joyce Simmons of Ottumwa, as Miss Congeniality. What an honor for Joyce, and how deserved! It was Joyce, they said, who kept calm, cheerful and helpful.

Peggy Henderson was named second runner-up. Peggy, a student at Centerville Community College, is petite and has a million dollar personality. A popular choice, she wore a blue-green ensemble in the parade, a white and black swim suit and a royal blue formal.

First runner-up was Denise Hayes, a striking blonde high school senior who exhibited lots of class throughout the festive day. Denise wore a blue and white checked suit in the parade, a shocking pink color swim suit in competition and a slim black velvet gown that night.

Squeals and applause greeted the choice of Diane Craver for Pageant Queen. She wore a suit in the parade, a white bathing suit and a white formal. Diane's smile is her trademark and she was still smiling as last years queen placed the crown on her

257

head.   She kept right on smiling while tears of happiness streamed down her face.   Diane will wear this crown well.

Another Beauty Pageant ends and so does an assignment. You've followed these lovely young creatures for a day and now you feel 99 years old by comparison, way past the pleasingly plump stage, and so doggone tired you had to change into Kedettes before the day was half over.

Despite all this – it was quite a day, wasn't it – Pancake Day, 1967.   *September 1967*

Speedy

A dapper fellow called "Speedy" Wheeler came by the Iowegian office the other day.

We could tell by the sartorial elegance of his tailored trousers and the natty cut of his checkered coat that here, indeed, was a "big city" spender who hadn't stopped in just to run an ad for a garage sale.   Heads turned in his direction and you could tell he not only expected attention but gloried in it!

But old Speedy was not alone.   A nice looking man by the name of Bob Isaacson stayed close to his side.   He watched his every move and listened to his every word.   In fact, it appeared that if it weren't for Isaacson, Speedy Wheeler wouldn't be what he is today.

For Speedy is a dummy and Isaacson is a ventriloquist (one of the best) and they happened to be in the Iowegian office because Ziggy and Irene Luther remember when Bobby Isaacson was a local boy from the small town of Mystic.

Mrs. Luther called us and put it this way: "There's a

258

ventriloquist in our store. We think he'd make a pretty good story. He'll bring his own dummy!"

We told Mrs. Luther to send him on over and that it was nice he was bringing his own dummy because there might be some confusion if he had to choose one from over here.

Speedy arrived with a flourish and after a few winks at the girls, informed the staff and several paper boys who had gathered around, that he was not a dummy. "You can see I'm no dummy." A ventriloqual figure he called himself. He said he once looked a little like his friend, Charlie McCarthy, but he was keeping up with the modern male trend of growing sideburns.

Mr. Isaacson recalls that he was about 14 when he saw his first life-sized dummy in a store window, and it intrigued him enough to capture his interest in ventriloquism. He studied books on the subject. He practiced "tightening" his throat muscles and learned to emit words and sounds from his belly region. He practiced and practiced.

Isaascon's mouth movements are very slight in contrast with the old master, Edgar Bergen.

Another milestone in his career was the day he met Frank Marshall after the family moved to the Chicago area. Marshall was the acknowledged master of making ventriloqual heads. It was he who originated the original Charley McCarthy and Mortimer Snerd and he made every figure by hand. "Speedy" Wheeler is one of his creations.

From his friendship with Marshall, the Mystic boy picked up the know-how and made his second dummy, Orval Sweet.

"You must have a certain size block of bass wood," Isaacson

told us. "Then you work for hours and hours pounding and chiseling until you have the face you want. Then you have three sections which you put together with glue. You hollow out the head and properly place mechanical devices for movement."

He added, "You know, each dummy is a personality – each has an identity. There are never two puppets exactly alike!

Actually, the hardest thing about ventriloquism is making the dummy's mouth movements synchronize with his words. His mouth has to move once for each syllable. Of course you have to keep your own and the dummy's voices separate." The ventriloquist added that practice and lots of it is the answer.

He has appeared on television and radio programs as well as Shriners Hospitals and before church and school groups. His latest effort was a movie which received the International Service Award titled "Geology and Natural Gas." Ventriloquism is now a hobby, his bread and butter is made at a large Gas Utilities Co. in Illinois.

"I'd like to come back sometime for Pancake Day," Bob said, "Speedy and Orval would like to entertain the folks on the stage but with their big mouths going, they would probably tell quite a bit about the old days in Mystic."

Speedy just grinned and winked.

One of the young Isaacson sons, Andy, a sparkling freckle-faced lad, has show business fever too. Andy gives performances at school with a dummy he made himself. He calls it Freddie or Eddie as the mood of the character happens to strike him.

When Speedy was put away in his carrying case, he sounded

for all the world like he was talking from inside the box. His voice also came from the ceiling and from behind Bill Hayes desk.

Can a ventriloquist really "throw" his voice? Bob says no – it's all an illusion – he tightens his vocal chords and his audience thinks what they want to think and hears what it wants to hear.

The folks in Mystic were glad to see Bobby Isaacson again. People like the Kelly family over there, still remember when he used to attend the old Strand Theater show and run all the way home, a mile and a half because he was scared of spooky shows. His former teacher, Miss Eva Quist recalls that he was a talented and very nice school boy.

This outstanding performer, who made good in show business, still likes Mystic too. He considers his formative years there among his hardest, but happiest.   *July 1970*

Professional Wrestlers

One Society Editor you know bought a ticket to the Monday night professional wrestling matches.

It was not because she was an avid wrestling fan, you understand, but because (1) Henry Little, president of the Big Red Booster Club is a persuasive salesman and (2) The proceeds were to go to the C.H.S. athletic fund.

For someone who doesn't give a doggone for wrestling on TV, this was a major sacrifice of time and money for the good old alma mater. But it was a fine show after all and we didn't mind missing the TV show *Laugh-In* at all. Arriving at 8 p.m. in the wind and icy rain, we found the gym nearly full of impatient youngsters whooping it up and bleachers full of men and women wishing the show would begin.

In the center of the polished gymnasium the ring was all set up and you women will be pleased to know that it was painted right in style with the new Americana colors of red, white and blue.

Henry Little announced the events on the mike but first introduced dapper Coach Paul Unruh who was entrusted with the timekeeper job and dashing Coach Stan Huston whose responsible position was that of 'bell ringer'. Coach proved the faith in him by giving a few practice ding dongs on what sounded like the same old cowbell Bessie once wore around her neck.

Mr. Little announced the first match between Don Kent of Pontiac, Mich., and Guillotine Gordon of Washington, D.C.

Guillotine came out first, a 275 pound giant of a man, topless, his long hair dyed yellow-blonde. We knew he was one of the bad guys even though we had never been to a pro wrestling match before. He strode out giving the crowd an arrogant eye and flexed his muscles. We also knew because the crowd booed and yelled "off with your head, Guillotine!"

His opponent was also big and fairly good looking as wrestlers go. The people clapped. This was the good guy.

The referee gave a rousing performance during the first 15 minutes. He shouted, admonished, jumped up and down, got down on his knees, smacked the wrestlers, got slugged, staged against the ropes, dropped to the floor, and sweat a good bit through his white shirt.

The second pair of wrestlers were Ronnie Etchison of St. Joe and Tornado Murdock. The villain again was very blonde only he had enough sense to get a crew cut because he knows how wrestlers love to pull hair.

The white canvas ring mat resounded with foot stomps and body crashes loud enough to hear up the street to Raymond's Dairy Crème. There were twisted arms, scissor holds, knee locks, head locks and all the vicious-looking things wrestlers like to do. There were grimaces of pain – low groans of agony. Indeed they didn't disappoint the audience when it came to putting on a good show – er wrestling match.

Perhaps the biggest ring attraction was the two midgets, Cowboy Lang and Little Bruiser. They battled it out without much regard for the fundamentals our C.H.S. boys are being taught by their wrestling coach.

The 96 pound bad guy – you guessed it – had peroxide blonde hair and he had eyebrows to match above the fiercest eyes you ever saw. Cowboy Lang smiled a lot and won the hearts of the youngsters. Blondes may have more fun, but Monday night the blondes were getting hissed and trampled.

The big finale was the tag match and what a finale it was!

Kent got his arms caught in the ropes and Tornado took advantage of this to put a foot in his neck, Guillotine was thrown out of the ring, Etchson pounded on Tornado's back. All the while the referee was looking the other way. He should have watched what he was doing however, because the next thing he knew, Guillotine 'mistook' him for Kent and took him to his knees.

A section of the steel ring broke loose and clattered to the gym floor. The wrestling match was over.

Yessiree, we developed a healthy respect for professional wrestling. Despite their clowning and ring antics, they are highly trained mat men. They had to be experts to know exactly when to pull a punch or when to roll with the drop. They also knew how to fall with a crash without getting hurt and how to cup their fingers into the palms of their hands when they appeared to be pulling hair.

It was an especially enjoyable night for the women. They talked it up from the sidelines, giving out expletives like "knock the puddin' out of him" or "pull that old yellow hair right out of his head."

Two women didn't become better friends when one had the audacity to root for the underdog bad guy.

But had the wrestlers listened to the play-by-play advice of one enthusiastic woman fan, me, they would have won more falls.

Wrestling matches are good sport if you can whoop it up with the rest of them.   *March 1969*

At the Lake

I was strolling down Island View beach one Sunday morning, pondering why it was that I got snagged with writing a beach assignment story for the Iowegian's Recreation Edition when I can't even swim.

(When you can't swim, you stroll, and you ponder, and you try not to attract too much attention with all your clothes on.)

So it was that I happened to be on hand at one of the four Rathbun Lake swimming beaches bright and early last Sunday morning, lugging a camera along to snap some great beachy pictures.

Several mothers trotted their tiny tots who were too excited to sleep, from their campers for an early morning swim before the crowd descended to chase them out with their huge rubber ducks.

A few other campers had left their sleeping bags to get washed off in the lake before breakfast. Some young people walked barefoot in the sand.

Out of this bunch of swimmers, I reasoned, would surely emerge a beach story. A child would make a sand castle with his trusty little bucket and shovel; a couple would write love letters in the sand with a stick; a plump, doting father would allow his kiddies to cover him with sand; a beautiful girl would walk by in a yellow polka dot bikini as Beach Boys strummed romantically on guitars.

Island View beach was a perfect setting and its cast of characters were beginning to appear on the sandy stage.

Strolling on down the beach I noticed a little boy with a bright red plastic pail and shovel to match. His smaller sister, toting a bright blue bucket and shovel to match, tagged along behind. They sat down in the sand and started digging with their little red and blue shovels. Great sand castle in a few minutes. Shovels dug, sand flew and two kids went bawling back to their mother rubbing sand from their eyes and shaking grit from their hair.

You can't make a sand castle that way.

Strolling back up the beach, I noted a young couple sitting in the sand. They weren't writing love letters in the sand with a stick. They had apparently gotten up on the wrong side of the camper bunks and were having a few words which didn't faintly resemble "I Love You."

You can't write sweet nothings in the sand that way.

And as for a father who would be willing to lie down and be covered with sand – there weren't any that day at Island View swimming beach. I asked one father if he would pose for such a picture. "Are you kidding?" he bellowed. "Think I want to itch from sand fleas and spoil the rest of the day?"

You can't let the youngsters enjoy the sand that way.

In desperation, and still strolling, I looked about for a comely Peach at the Beach. A group of Beach Boys weren't romantically strumming guitars either. They were ganged around a mobile concession stand devouring food.

You can't get ballads out of mouths filled with food.

There were campers on the other side of the lake and the heavenly smell of bacon frying wafted across the water.

You can't ask for a handout of bacon and eggs over on the other side if you can't swim.

The only thing left to do, obviously, is to stroll down the other three Lake Rathbun beaches someday. There is a beach story around Rathbun somewhere.   *June 1975*

&&&

Out to the lake this weekend to see how the other half (three-fourths) was living over the big 4th of July weekend. Camper to camper, that's how they were living. And I've never seen

266

happier (nor redder) faces or so much downright contentment as around those campers and tents. There wasn't much privacy, maybe, but contentment showed in the face of the old fellow in the hammock.

There were flies and some sand fleas, but the food on the picnic tables looked delicious and the aroma of grilling steak mingled with the smoke of wood campfires. Boy from Fort Dodge met blonde girl from Moravia and contentment showed in their faces as they walked down the beach, arm in arm. Bikinis, fishing poles, water skis … they were all at Lake Rathbun.

Contentment.

Joe the Grocer

Joe opened the front door of his small grocery store in 1933 when he was 37 years old. In 1967, at age 70, his store was still going strong. He claimed the distinction of having been in the grocery business more continuous years in the same location, longer than any other Centerville grocer.

If you were to ask Mr. Zaharris what he liked best about his grocery store he would most likely say – the people. His store is a veritable melting pot despite the advent of the supermarket. His meat business is good and his store is rarely empty. One might say Joe's main claim to fame was his amusing anecdotes. He remembers when he scooped beans, salt, sugar, as well as sticky peanut butter. Now that most every item is packaged, boxed, frozen, bottled or canned, he is glad he doesn't have to funnel coal oil into cans anymore.

Possibly the largest stock of penny candy in town would be

found in his bins. Last week a customer filled a brown paper bag with wrapped goodies – penny jawbreakers, bubble gum, root beer barrels, cinnamon balls, licorice sticks, peppermints and other items so enticing to children and grown-ups alike. These she planned to send to her son in Vietnam who would remember this taste of home.

Joe's hobbies were in gardening – his specialties were tomatoes and black raspberries. Close by and at his home next door, you would find lovely roses and a myriad of flowers. In the fall he would take his dog 'Old Fritz' and go hunting, or take a few days off to fish in the Minnesota lakes.

Yet, it is in his neighborhood grocery store that he was the happiest. He was a confidante, adviser, sympathizer, story teller and mediator of small–boy scuffles. Families remember that Joe, at some time or another, staked them to credit when times were rough.   *1967*

A few years later ...

The small independent neighborhood grocery store has all but vanished from the local scene and the closing of the Zaharris grocery almost makes it complete.

Joe hadn't intended to close his store quite yet, even though he was now 82 years of age and had opened his grocery six days a week for years and years.

But last Friday night two young men came into his store, shoved him down and ran off with his cash box. His leg was broken and his hip injured in the fall.

From his hospital bed, Joe told his daughter Jane to "board up the store."

It's the understatement of the week to say that we've all been pretty mad in our neighborhood that such things can happen to people who mind their own business and never cause trouble for other people, that society is such that a man can be knocked down and robbed.

We're all going to miss running over to the store for a loaf of bread at supper time and the kids will miss standing before the shelves deciding which kind of candy they're going to buy.

I'll miss the man behind the counter who often regaled you with anecdotes of the old days along with selling you tomatoes grown in his own garden behind the store. He's going to miss his customers of several generations.   *1979*

Chapter 14

VACATIONS AND JAUNTS

I know you had your vacation too, enjoyed it and told a few people about it, and your trips may be more interesting than mine, but when you're a columnist, you usually expect your readers to suffer through an account of your trips.

Texas

I've always maintained that we small town greenhorns (if you don't mind me including you) can have ten times more fun on a vacation trip than the "beautiful people" of the Jet Set.

The main reason for this, I think, is that we country folks aren't ashamed to gawk at tall buildings and enjoy sights and sounds we have never seen before. The yawning sophisticate who flits from Paris to London and villa to villa can't conceivably like people as we do.

Anyway, if you can enjoy a vacation trip to Texas in the middle of July – you're no sophisticate.

Actually, the big Texas idea took firm hold at our house last December, along with the ice.

"By golly," I announced, "this summer we'll go down Texas way to see our son David in Dallas and brother-in-law, Robert McConnell and family in Universal City near San Antonio."

And as is so often the case, what was a fine idea in December didn't sound so good come mid-summer. The family hoped I'd forget the whole thing.

We went to Texas; after all, Texas just happens to be one of those 43 states I haven't been to yet.

As official map reader for some unknown reason, I became so proud of getting us through the Kansas City maze without a single wrong exit that I didn't have time to look at all the scenery. Kansas may be a rather nondescript state, but to a native Kansan, those bright orange sunflowers are nodding in the fields just for her.

On into Oklahoma and things began to change. The soil turned to brick red and the exposed red river banks made the sparse water look anemic. And if they haven't picked their corn in Oklahoma yet, it's too late. Farmers were growing something in a good many fields that had reddish tops to match the ground. Everybody but me would know what it was.

Then I saw my first oil well. It was to be only one of the many "firsts" on the trip. Rigs worked at regular intervals day and night, pumping black gold to make somebody rich. It was an odd sight to see the tall structures appear right in the middle of downtown Oklahoma City. There were many refineries dotting the state, their tower-like stacks ablaze to burn off dangerous fumes.

On down the verdant, hilly Arbuckle mountain region in

272

southern Oklahoma to the Texas border. Then you saw it. At the Texas border was a king-sized sign welcoming the traveler to Texas – the state the Texans brag about. I didn't expect to like it, but I did. There seems to be something mysteriously alluring about it. The open expanse of it, perhaps, or the old west charm of it. I half expected to see balls of sagebrush rolling down the interstate and was disappointed that a Texas cowpoke didn't pass us riding his pinto and shouting "Howdy Stranger."

Big Dallas is really a beautiful city at night. Big D gets to you and even though you can see the infamous Book Depository building over your shoulder while riding down the freeway, you are still in awe of the city.

Love Field at Dallas surely must be one of the world's busiest airports and son David, a Field Computer Engineer, happened to live in Love Field Trailer Court. He insisted you do get used to thunderous screeching of the airliners sooner or later.

Then on down deep into the heart of Texas – San Antonio and four memorable days.

Can you imagine Princess Lee Radixwill of the Jet Set leaning out the window and yelling, "Hey, look – there's a real banana tree, or an orange tree, a different Mimosa tree or a heavenly blooming Crepe Myrtle?" Hardly.

And about San Antonio. Here is a sprawling, lazy combination of the old, old west and brave modernity. The big metropolis speaks true Texas as the 103 degree sun beats down on a populace who smile at you in the shops. They are probably smiling because they only use $16 worth of fuel all winter.

Yes, we remembered the Alamo like we are supposed to, but

didn't expect to find it smack in the middle of San Antonio, Fort and all. Picture postcards didn't prepare us for the sight of it.

Big Fort Sam Huston Army Base is there too, plus four or five air bases. One can speculate that if it weren't for the military, San Antonio would be less affluent.

Major Bob *(now a retired Air Force Colonel)* and his wife Pat *(Hedgecock)*, both Centerville natives, showed us all around Randolph Field, where he is stationed.

Yes, I liked Texas – ten gallon hats and all.

One thing I didn't do, though, was call on Lady Bird in Johnson City just north of San Antonio. But maybe I'll stop at the LBJ Ranch for a slab of barbecued beef next time I'm deep in the heart of Texas. *August 1969*

&&&

I promised to tell you of an Indian fight while in South Dakota. Well it wasn't a cowboy and Indian scrap like you see on television – it was a family brawl in a quiet public camping park in Crow Creek reservation country.

The four of us, Mrs. Lila Frogge, Mrs. King, Mrs. Arbogast and me along with our hostess Mrs. Marrone had taken our lawn chairs for a shady, quiet siesta to the park. We were minding our own business when a few carloads of nicely dressed Indian families drove up nearby. Loud talking became louder and finally two Indian women bounded from a car and started slugging it out, and I mean slugging with fists. The males just stood there and the children went on sliding down the slides.

Then the men got into the affray and threw each other over

the ground and across the road. They picked up big rocks and smashed beer bottles to use for weapons. Indians were hurting Indians. I picked up my stuff and said I was getting out of there. The other three ladies were cool as cucumbers. Mrs. Frogge kept right on knitting, Mrs. Arbogast remained stretched out on her lawn chair and Mrs. King thought it was exciting.

A neighboring camper, a woman, sauntered over and said that she had lived around Indians all her life and there was nothing to worry about. If we didn't go over and try to stop them, they probably wouldn't bother us. Indian women, she informed us, usually start all the family brawls and soon everybody is into the melee. Do they get hurt? "Oh, yes, they usually cut each other up or break a few arms, but you just let them go at it because only the Indian police can do anything with them."

By this time I am about to croak, since blood and violence are not my cup of tea. I begged everybody to leave, but nobody was in a hurry. Then a Honda motorcycle raced up to the scene with a young Indian driver and another fellow aboard behind him with a rifle and he started brandishing it around. I was not afraid of being scalped; I was more worried about my head being blown off by a rocketing bullet.

"Wait until I finish this round of knitting and we'll leave," announced Lila, complaining, "Now we'll never know how this Indian fight came out."

Too bad, Lila, too bad!   *July 1973*

&&&

When my husband and I go on a two-week vacation, we try to

275

take off the heavily traveled interstate highway and drive into a little town or two where we've never been before. This year one of them was Ozark, Missouri, a pleasant town built on several hills. It was scenic, had friendly people and some industrial activity.

Another different town was in Arkansas.

We stopped at a motel for the night and were stonily greeted(?) by a heavy-set woman with a heavy southern accent. "How many?" she asked. "Just us," we answered. She gave us a look that made us expect that her next question would be "Where's your marriage license?"

"I'm giving you a room with two single beds in it," she blurted out, "but you're only to use one bed."

After paying the highest motel price on our entire trip, my husband laughingly said, "Only use one bed, eh? Heh, heh."

He thought it was a joke, bless his heart. The Arkansas gal didn't laugh. She didn't even smile.

"That's right!" she snarled, and added, "I'm in a good mood today, but I won't be tomorrow. You can't have two beds to use."

After we left the next morning the maid had to make up two beds. We are expecting a nasty letter from a certain Arkansas motel gal any day now, but my stubborn Iowa husband can answer it!

Bath House Row

Bath House Row in Hot Springs, Arkansas, is the place to go when you want to take relaxing baths in mountain spring water instead of in plain old Iowa water.

Yes sir, Bath House Row is quite a place.

You've heard of Skid Row in New York and John Steinbeck's Cannery Row in California? Well, Bath House Row in Hot Springs bears no resemblance to either of these. It is, instead, a famous spa where hot thermal waters flow from 47 springs on the west side of Hot Springs Mountain, and are piped into seven bathhouses and several hotels. All are operated under Federal regulations and the water and rates are set by the Department of the Interior.

Even the Caddo and Quapaw Indians knew the value of these thermal waters long before 1541, when Hernando Desoto became the first European to discover these steaming springs. This ground was sacred to the Indians of 11 tribes, and here they gathered in peace to bathe their sick and injured.

If you have never been to Hot Springs or bathed away your cares and tensions, then maybe you'd like to hear how it's done – my version anyway. The town itself is beautiful, nestled in the Ozark Mountains and resplendent with dogwood trees in spring, magnolia trees in summer and hedges of holly in colder months.

When you get to Hot Springs, 500 miles away, find a place to stay, which isn't hard. The hard part comes when you try to get up the nerve to go to one of the Bath Houses and take your first bath. Not having had anyone give them a bath in many, many years, one couple we know took two days of their valuable vacation time just to build up the courage.

Finally, I got my tickets for the whole works ... a bath with whirlpool, cabinet vapor bath, hot packs, needle shower and full body massage. I also bought a plastic shower cap and required personal luffa bath mitt with my name on it.

I was shaking like a leaf on a dogwood tree.

Appearing in the doorway on the women's side of the pretty building was a plump black woman we'll call Ruthie, uniformed in white and peering carefully over her glasses. Her greeting was perfunctory. "Take off your clothes and put this sheet around you."

Well, it was either run for the hills or do or die. But since I had already invested money I decided to go through with the whole thing.

I got the clothes off all right, but getting the sheet around me was something else again. I found out later that there is a simple but tricky way of wrapping up so that you are covered in the back and the sheet doesn't slip down around your ankles when you enter the room full of other women.

I was still shaking like a leaf as I nervously remarked to Ruthie that this was my first time in Hot Springs … that this was my first 'public type bath' … that I was scared … that I hoped she had seen fatter women than me. No comment. No comment, I was to learn, was a policy of the place.

Sitz bath

She led me to an 8 x 8 foot cubbyhole which contained three low sink-like white enamel basins, all facing each other. This is the Sitz bath and here you 'sits' for the first 20 minutes of your two-hour stay. The other two women you may have never met before, but after Ruthie whisks your sheet away with the expertise of a matador whisking the red cape past the bull's nose, you have a good start toward friendship.

My favorite Sitz mates during the week were the wives of a Mississippi riverboat captain and a steel company president. Both looked away at the wall when my sheet left me, and both were colorful and interesting talkers.

In the sitz bath your face starts getting red and you start dripping perspiration. They take you to a partitioned room where the oversized white enamel bath tubs are. The room is purposely hot and humid and you step into steamy water about up to your neck. Then you lie back and a wooden contraption is placed over your feet to keep you from floating off. The whirlpool whirls and you drink two cups of thermal water.

Into the vapor cabinet (which clears up your sinuses if you have any) and out into a large room filled with plastic covered cots. Here we have Cleona, who is in charge of the hot packs. She's the friendliest of the black attendants, but only speaks five words at a time or less. "Where do you want packs?"

The first day I started with my weak knees, and the thermal packs felt so good that by the end of the week I looked like a mummy with steam coming off. You lie there 20 minutes, with cold towels around your face. The heat penetrates your muscles and bones. No one talks.

After a great needle spray and another clean sheet, Cleona motions to another room with more cots. That's the "cooling" room and it is only 90 degrees in there. Nobody, but nobody, leaves the establishment without cooling off for 20 minutes.

Most women are so relaxed by this time that they drift off to sleep and have to be wakened for their massage.

Ah, the massage. That's the nice part. My masseuse was a white professional and we'll call her Carma. Now if you think for one minute that these little massage rooms are like the scandalous ones you've been reading about lately, you're one hundred percent wrong. There are no carpets, no soft lights and no sexy music. There are no brocade drapes to separate you from anybody.

Now this Carma is a real honest-to-goodness masseuse. Like the rest, she doesn't comment on anything she sees or anything you say. You could have four legs and she wouldn't bat an eye, but just go on pouring lotion and massaging. If you had a green scar running from your right toe up to your ear, she wouldn't say anything.

But this straight, tall, steel fingered woman had plenty of her own opinions and came out blunt and clear on them. For instance, her opinion of Arkansas Governor Bumpers: "Take the 'pers' off that idiot's name and you'll have what he is ... a BUM."

About Halloween: "The candy manufacturers are pushing Halloween so they can get rich off Tricks or Treats."

She also related with an Arkansas twang, that just that very morning she had thrown a pair of pliers and a hammer out the back door at home because she was tired of her husband leaving his darn tools lying around the kitchen.

You come out of Bath House Row feeling great. Sore muscles are eased and your skin is smooth and shiny. It is suggested that you eat brunch (you only had juice and coffee before bath time) and then rest until 2 p.m. After that, the day and evening are all yours. At the risk of sounding like a walking Hot Springs Chamber of Commerce, I must say that the mountain city certainly knows how to look after the tourists. There are lakes, parks, and lots to see and do. You'll probably succumb to its charm just as many of the people of this area have.

If you think the pounds went rolling off with all that perspiration, forget it. That Arkansas cooking puts them back on.

You won't see very many hillbillies toting whisky jugs and wearing little pointed hats like on *Hee Haw*, and chances are you won't run across many pens of Razorback hogs, but you will be one of the cleanest persons in town.

Bath House Row. It's quite a place.   *October 1973*

&&&

I've been on vacation for two weeks, and after having been back at work for two days, I realize that the two weeks of rest and relaxation have to last me for yet another year. An October R & R is the greatest ... beautiful scenery ... thinned out tourist hordes ... cheaper motel rates.

Of course, along with October's bright blue weather, you tend to miss a few things by a week or even a day. At Branson, Mo. we missed an outdoor performance of Shepherd of the Hills by Ozark country actors. These productions are taken from Harold Bell Wright's famous book of the same name and are highly rated.

281

At Hot Springs, Ark. we missed the massages after the thermal baths because it was convention time in Hot Springs and the masseuses and masseurs were working two or more hours behind time.

We missed seeing Charlie Rich at Hollis, Ark. where he had stopped to have a meal at the famous San Ann's rustic eating place at Hollis. The Silver Fox whose 'Behind Closed Doors' won him a best country-western singer award last year had his picture taken with some of the folks there.

At Montgomery, Alabama we visited in the lovely home of my husband's brother, Air Force Colonel Robert McConnell and wife Pat (Hedgecock) both Centerville natives who previously lived in Universal City, Texas and will be moving back there.

In Kentucky, we didn't go in Mammoth Cave because it was raining and I don't particularly like caves anyway. The 4 ½ mile walk through the underground caverns didn't appeal to me either.

The big disappointment, however, was that we arrived ONE DAY too late for a tour and music session at Opryland, Nashville, Tenn. The tourist season was over.

Despite the 'misses' however, it was a great vacation.

It was my first visit to the Deep South when we drove through Louisiana (as far as Tallulah), across Mississippi, Alabama and Georgia.

It was also my first sight of cotton fields and I looked in vain for cotton pickers going up and down the rows with their burlap sacks, sweat streaming down and their backs bent with toil. Instead, I saw mechanical cotton pickers spewing cotton balls into wire caged trucks and instead of "toting that bale" I saw huge trucks hauling cotton to the nearby gin mill.

I had thoughts while driving by the cotton fields to hop out and pick a cotton plant, but decided that I didn't want buckshot lead in my britches.

As a curious person, I also entertained ideas of marching up to the door of a southern plantation mansion and passing the time of day. A Yankee to Reb conversation could have proven very interesting.

We found everyone we met to be gracious and friendly in the south, although we had been told that it is best to lock up your car doors and don't, under any circumstances, roll your windows down. In Demopolis and Selma Alabama where they gathered to march into Montgomery and riots were rampant, we were treated fine.

En route home through Louisville, Kentucky where the issue of forced busing of pupils is now of national concern because of the riots, we didn't see anything but friendliness and everything was peaceful. We probably weren't in the wrong places at the wrong time. *November 1975*

Elvis in Iowa

I'll probably never live it down in the next 50 years.

I went to see Elvis!

In spite of shudders of disbelief from most of my friends and exclamations like "Are you crazy?" I dared to go to Ames with my two daughters and son David to see the Elvis Presley Show. And for those of you (including my husband) who "wouldn't walk across the street" to either hear him or see him, I want you

283

to know I thought the show was fantastic.

Whether he's at the Hilton Coliseum in Ames or the Conrad Hilton in Las Vegas, he can sing.

I've found out that you either like Elvis or you don't. There's no middle of the road. He's never just OK, he's either lousy or great.

But anybody who can pull in 14,750 fans and sell out tickets in two days can't be all bad.

It was a great show, all three hours of it. Elvis was on stage two hours in a blue suit. There were two bands, The Stamps gospel quartet, an excellent comedian, and a trio of black girls who could really sing.

Is he really fat and forty? Well, he's 41 and not as slim as he was at 21. But when you can sing like that, who cares?

The Ames Hilton crowd wasn't as wild as his Madison Square or Las Vegas groups. And it wasn't drunken.

It was an appreciative Midwestern Iowa audience who came to listen to Elvis. And they didn't get a rip-off performance either.

One amusing incident: Two girls down front caught one of his scarves. One at each end of it. They hung on for dear life. The battle became more intense, with each girl inching her hand closer to the middle. When the number ended, these fans were still tugging and pulling on the same scarf. Then, one of the policemen guarding the stage finally solved the battle with a Solomon-like gesture - he tore the scarf right down the middle. Now each fan has half a scarf that wiped the sweat from Elvis's brow. Fantastic show! *June 1976*

Traffic Court

It would be considered unusual to spend time in a traffic court when you don't even drive a car, but I did recently.

It was like this. My sister-in-law, Rev. Wauneita McConnell was making a trip to St. Joseph, Mo. and asked me and two friends to go along. We were passing through another Missouri town when we had a wreck.

She had stopped at a stop sign, looked in both directions and pulled out onto a thru street. A little past the middle, we were whammed by another car. Luckily, no one was hurt, yet neither car could be driven off from the scene.

The police were called, and after measuring skid marks of the other car, taking down pertinent information and making a drawing of the wreck, the policeman presented Wauneita with a traffic ticket. She protested that the other vehicle had swooped down out of nowhere and hit us. Said the policeman, "I don't know how fast the other driver was going ... he could have been going 100 miles an hour ... but you still get the ticket because you're the one who pulled out from a stop sign."

Then he added that she had better show up at the city hall and post $35 before she left town or there would be a warrant out for her arrest.

At the city hall she paid $35 cash and was told that it probably would be easier for her not to show up at traffic court a month later. Just forfeit the money. Just stay in Iowa.

We proceeded home on the St. Joe route in a borrowed car, and the more we discussed the wreck, the angrier we got at the seeming unfairness of the charge. The street in question was between two hills with no signs of any kind on the thru street except a speed limit. There were skid marks to prove he was coming awfully fast.

The result was we decided to drive back to Missouri on a hot July day (102 degrees) and appear in court that next month and plead not guilty.

When the Judge strode into court that day, he looked as though he could chew up a keg of nails and spit them out all over the courtroom. We happened to be the last case on the docket so had to sit through three hours of varied and sundry cases. It was a learning experience. We heard lawyers argue on a case where a man said he tried to miss a dog and hit a parked car instead.

The other lawyer proved that the man was so loaded that he wouldn't have known a dog if he could have seen one. "Guilty."

In turn, each defendant got the book thrown at him. We saw one fellow thrown out of court because he had come in drunk and disorderly to witness for an OMVUI case. We heard lurid details of a tavern brawl over a girl and the Judge fined a sweet little old guy who had never had a traffic ticket in his life.

So by the time the Judge had fined every person who appeared before him that hot day, my sister-in-law was thoroughly intimidated and scared silly. We, as her witnesses, were also intimidated and scared silly.

When the Judge called her name, she shakily rose to her feet and pleaded not guilty. She asked the Judge to hear her out and she would abide by his decision. The policeman who had given her the ticket was present and showed his sketch of the accident and made mention that the skid marks of the other car were 49 feet. But it was his opinion that the other driver was only going about 30 miles per hour.

The Judge raised his eyebrows. "I'm familiar with that particular intersection," he said, "and I figure that other vehicle was speeding to have caused the damage it did. NOT GUILTY."

Justice was served. The "matter of principle" that had made us drive more than a hundred miles to stand up for was worth it. A fair Judge will listen and pronounce a fair verdict!

August 1977

&&&

Did you ever highly recommend a certain café or a particular place to shop and then go there yourself later and find that it isn't like it used to be? Well, that's the way it was with a certain café at Hollis, Arkansas. We had always found this small, but rather famous eating place to have delicious food in the most beautiful rustic spot in the Ouachita National Park. The scenery outside the spacious windows was spectacular and the food and baked goods were fresh that day.

So we weren't prepared for our recent disappointments. There was one cook and one waitress (?) on duty. We noticed that the other five or six tables were filled with 8 a.m. breakfasters from five or six different states according to their car licenses. But nobody was eating any breakfast. They were sitting there glowering and fidgeting.

The girl finally came over with a menu and gave us time to memorize it backwards and upside down. We ordered a country style breakfast of sausage, eggs, hash browns and hot biscuits with gravy.

The cook began mixing up hot cakes for someone and the batter was so thick she had to cut it out of the pitcher. Then she started frying sausage, pancakes, eggs, hash browns on the same small griddle. Needless to say, the sausage wasn't cooked, but the hotcakes and eggs were scorched.

There was a big pot of white gravy (probably made the night before, which never came in contact with the heat again) slopped on some white stones which the menu said were good old Arkansas country biscuits. A new bride would never live it down if she served biscuits like those. I made a batch just like them once when I forgot the baking powder, but I didn't have a restaurant to serve them in.

In the meantime, two tables of people got up and left, preferring, no doubt, to starve until the next stop. The waitress spilled two glasses of milk trying to carry them with three plates of scorched pancakes to a table five feet away. The cook was overworked, one could excuse, but the waitress…well!

And now I'm almost afraid to recommend the Ozark Mountain Smokehouse at Bear Creek, just a smidgen north of Harrison, Ark., on Highway 65 where you can get the most delectable smoked ham sandwich for 70 cents to eat with free coffee. Here you can sit around a blazing fireplace and talk with the folks from Oklahoma or Mississippi who've also stopped by, or stroll through the oak trees across a log bridge.

Yes sir, I'm almost afraid to mention it.   *November 1977*

&&&

Westward

This was a wonderful vacation, taking me to states I had never seen before. My sister-in-law, Rev. Wauneita McConnell, asked me to go with her and a friend, Josephine Plummer of St. Joseph, Missouri, and another sister-in-law, Miriam Horstman, to Cody, Wyoming to visit a long time friend. We would also go to Yellowstone Park, Laramie, Cheyenne and on down to Denver to visit with niece Elizabeth Hawkins and family.

We did all those things and more, but lest you think you're in for an armchair travelogue complete with statistics on how many sugar beets are grown in Nebraska or how many people live in the Big Horn mountains, let me just give you a few word pictures.

On entering Yellowstone National Park at the east entrance, Park Rangers hand you a pamphlet warning you about grizzly bears. Don't feed the bears, keep foodstuffs under safe cover, don't backpack on wilderness trails, don't ride with your car windows down, and don't trust the grizzly as he will attack man.

At any minute we expected one of the burly brutes to lumber down out of the mountains and tip our car over with one fell swoop of a mighty paw.

We spent the day in Yellowstone, marveling at the thrilling display Old Faithful put on, seeing the thundering spray of Yellowstone Falls, watching the boating on blue Yellowstone Lake and standing in awe before the pulsating earth pits full of bubbling phosphorus liquid.

We searched every lush forest and peered at every mountain stream at feed time, but no bears. "Wait until dark," someone told us. We didn't. Instead we headed out the south entrance down Jackson Hole way.

No room at the Inn

Now Jackson Hole, Wyoming, nestled in the Grand Tetons, is one beautiful place. Here we would spend the night. But the town seemed agog with excitement and all slicked up for company. No vacancy signs on every motel. If we'd had the car radio on, or read newspapers or watched TV we would have known that President Carter and entourage were only a few miles away.

As it was, we motored on south, tired and cranky, 170 miles to Rock Springs, Wyoming. There again, not a single place had lodging. And judging from the exposure of Rock Springs presented on the television *60 Minutes* show last Sunday night, making it the alleged vice and corruption capitol of Wyoming, maybe it was just as well.

Pushing on east in southern Wyoming we reached Rawlins about midnight. Same story, so we pulled into a KOA campground and although cold, hungry and weary, we tried to sleep.

We might have succeeded, too, if it hadn't been for a strange clicking sound that emanated from the back of the car. We were wide awake. "Sounds like the clicks are coming from that sack in the back seat," Miriam announced.

Then I remembered that I had bought two plastic boxes of Mexican Jumping Beans and they were clicking against the sides of the plastic.

So much for those little critters.

Have you ever seen the cosmopolites of Denver and nearby snow covered Rocky Mountain peaks in a light, single engine plane? Have you ever seen the mammoth Coors plant at Golden, Colo. from a bobby plane in a downdraft?

I did. A friend of the family took us up and brought us back down. Say no more. *September 1978*

Montana – Big Sky Country

We took a different kind of vacation this year – to the Big Sky country of Montana.

Usually we head for the Ozark hills of Arkansas (where we know nobody) but this year we choose the foothills of the Rocky Mountains in western Montana (where we know nobody). Mac was stationed at Great Falls during his Air Force service.

We went by bus this time and left the driving to them. They routed us up through Minneapolis, across to Fargo and Bismarck in North Dakota, past the northern Bad Lands and on to Billings and Butte, Montana.

Arriving at our destination of Boulder, Montana, the bus driver let us off, bag and baggage at 4:10 a.m. on Boulder's Main Street in front of a bus station that never opened up for that bus. Not a creature was stirring. Strange mountains loomed darkly in every direction.

We looked up and down the street for the vacation apartments where we had reservations. Nobody told us that it was 1 ½ miles west of the town on the mountainside.

Finding a phone booth I phoned the manager at 4:45 a.m.

"Where are you?" she asked sleepily, "in the Butte bus station?"
"No," I said wearily, "right here in Boulder on Main Street."

She came right down and rescued us and settled us in our three-room unit which oddly seemed to have a faint halo of heaven in it. (When you haven't had your shoes off for two days and two nights then the next bed you see takes on that aura.)

For ten days we breathed mountain air, saw breathtaking sunrises and sunsets, took walks and picked yellow and blue mountain flowers we had never seen before. There were no telephones to answer.

The sky was as blue as Mary Murphy's paint brush except for one wild windstorm night which rolled the dust and the sagebrush. Coyotes howled at daybreak.

Mac had made the chance acquaintance of a young forester who knew the country and about an old ghost mining camp high in the hills near Boulder. He took us there and we bought mining pans and went down in a uranium mine and panned for gold. We hadn't the slightest idea how to swish a pan of rocks and sand around under a clear stream. We spotted bits of gold dust among the sand. Fools gold? Doesn't look like we will be able to retire and live on easy street. But it was fun.

Big Sky country – a different vacation spot. We're glad we went even though we haven't quite gotten over the scare we had when the young forester's old car popped a leak in the gas line and we almost didn't make it back to town. He patched the leak with stickum and put the car in neutral and coasted all the way down miles of mountain curves.

Yes sir, a different vacation.

We got home from our vacation in time to see our prized Silver Lace vine in full bloom. It only blooms once a year, beginning the first week of school, but its late summer show is worth it. The fragrance of it attracted several dozen beautiful Monarch butterflies last Sunday.   *August 1979*

A Memorable Rustic Weekend

Small town hospitality, super good food, the living presence of history, and the beauty of southeastern Van Buren county all combined to make Iowa Press Women's Spring meeting at Hotel Manning in Keosauqua, Iowa a memorable rustic weekend.

But especially for me, going to Keosauqua held a sort of communion in spirit with my grandfather, David McGuire (my father, David Russo, Jr. was named after him,) who was born there in 1843 only six years after Edwin Manning first arrived in Iowa and platted the town on the great bend in the Des Moines river.

I never knew my grandfather McGuire, but I felt closeness anyway, just knowing that he was part of this town when Iowa was still a territory. He was alive to see the first brick courthouse west of the Mississippi.

He knew the first Hotel Manning, a log cabin store, later to be the present Hotel Manning in 1854.

As I stood on the banks of the Des Moines river last weekend, I could envision how side wheelers and steam boats like the Charley Rogers churned up the great river to Des Moines (known then as Raccoon Fork), or downstream into the Mississippi River and on down to New Orleans.

293

I could imagine a steamboat's crew coming down the plank to seek rest and food at this historic hotel. You are catapulted back to the Franklin Pierce administration, when slavery was the burning question of the day and furniture was strong and massive and made to last.

One of the newest attractions was the Sandbar down in the cellar of Hotel Manning. Thousands of tons of dirt were laboriously dug out of the cellar two feet down to make this attractive social place. The original stone cellar walls are still there.

Other highlights of the weekend, beside the journalism workshops, were tours of historic Bentonsport - down river about six miles. Bentonsport is merely a ghost town now, caused by the Iowa legislature putting a stop to navigation of the Des Moines River and the declining railroad services. Bentonsport, however, has managed to retain several of the historic buildings including Mason House, a virtual haven of antiques. Every room held furniture, dishes, pictures and articles of the 1850's. Many tourists stop there each year. The Country Store is worth the time in itself.

You can also see where the author of State Fair "Phil Stong", was born two miles west of Keosauqua, and if you've got a bent for morbidity, you can be at the scene of Iowa's first murder trial right there in Keosauqua and view Hangman's Hollow.

But there's one attraction at Hotel Manning that is only eight years old. He's Charley, the mynah bird from India. Perched in his big cage in the lobby, Charley rules the roost. He lets go with wolf whistles that please the gals who haven't heard a wolf whistle in many a year.

He says "Hi", "Come in Hotel" and other things too numerous to mention. Charley can also cough and laugh. According to some of the press women who stayed at the Hotel, Charley didn't shut his yellow beak all night, even with his cage covered with black cloth, he was so excited about Hotel Manning's first convention!

I learned one thing about Charley. He didn't appreciate your peering into his cage saying "Hi, Charley" or "Come in Hotel." Charley wanted to do his own talking, and coughing, and squawking. If you just stood there for a while, he cocked his black head with the red feathers on the sides, and starts his chatter. Nobody steals his act!

If you yearn for a nice weekend that's different, and you believe in seeing Iowa first, Keosauqua is the place to go. Charley will probably be looking for you to stop by his place in Hotel Manning.

I think my grandfather McGuire would feel pretty good about it if he knew I had been back to his hometown and stood on the banks of the same river where once he watched the steamboats churn. *May 1978*

Chapter 15

PETALS OF POTPOURRI

Centerville policemen patrolling the busy town square round and round never know what will happen next. Take last Saturday afternoon for instance. A pretty dark-haired shopper from out of town waved down a nice red-haired policeman. It seems that the girl had dropped her car keys down the side of the seat between the metal strip and the upholstery. Several people had tried to help fish it out, including this freezing cold columnist, but no luck. The officer came up, calmly viewed the situation, went back to the police car and brought forth a piece of wire which he bent into a hook. With the expertise of a kid clamping onto a prize in one of those glass carnival machines, he came up with the car key in no time. She smiled, he smiled and I smiled. *December 1972*

&&&

During the recent sub-zero days, some people had trouble getting their cars started. Not Mrs. Billy Long.

Some drivers had to call a gas station to send someone out to start their cars. Mrs. Long didn't.

Several people had to call their places of employment and tell them that they would be a trifle late for work because they couldn't get their car engines to turn over. Mrs. Long didn't have this problem. Her car started off like a champion.

But, like most vehicles, Mrs. Long's car did have a problem. When she breezed to work at Union Carbide Plant at 10 below zero, she couldn't get the car stopped. It kept idling away. She drove around and around the plant parking lot. It still wouldn't stop.

We don't know how the situation is now, but we'll bet that there are going to be some raised eyebrows in the Union Carbide office if Mary Long calls in to say that she'll be a little late to work because her car won't stop!!   *January 1976*

&&&

Someone suggested that I try doing another job for a day (just to see how the other half lives)!

I decided that it certainly would not be as a waitress. If Donna Withrow hired me for even one day's work at the Blue Bird Café her business would decline – fast and even one day could be disastrous.

For example, I could never get the food to the table on time. I would probably slide the hot cakes and sausage off into a lap. But the worst would be that I would most likely talk to everyone – or start an interview with the customers.

I probably wouldn't get any tips, and if I did, what would I say? I've already gone on record via my column as opposing leaving tips for inferior service just because it's traditional and expected.

I'd best leave the waitress job to people who are good at it, but I'm surprised I didn't try it for a story.

I wouldn't be a good bookkeeper either (can't figure) – nor teacher (too easy on class discipline) – nor barmaid, cosmetologist, clerk or farmers wife (afraid of pigs).

&&&

An Irish Savings Bank, in order to call attention to excessive absenteeism among its staff, posted the following rules: Sickness – No excuses will be acceptable. We will no longer accept your doctor's statement as proof of illness as we believe that if you are able to go to a doctor's office, you are able to come to work. Death – (your own). This will be accepted as an excuse, but we would like at least two week's notice as we feel it is your duty to teach someone else your job.

&&&

The recent windstorm blew down an old elm tree in the neighborhood and of course it fell across the electric wires.

The Utility crew responded promptly and repaired the line and all went well until the city crew arrived to saw up the hollow tree. Out swarmed hundreds of bees, causing a commotion which quickly dispersed the neighborhood who had congregated to supervise the work crews.

&&&

Well, they got our block on 8th street paved ... in one afternoon last Friday! The capable Jensen Company crew really tied into it and by sundown they were through.

The paving procedure itself was so interesting that it drew a crowd of bystanders from all around – almost as many people visiting in yards as there were after the big April snowstorm and the June wind storm.

Yessir, we watched every move the paving crew made like our lives depended on it. When you calculate mentally how many hard-earned dollar bills are going into each foot of the white concrete ribbon, you take notice.

After the crew covered up the freshest end with burlap and placed the flashing barricades, it wasn't ten minutes until four middle sized youngsters from a few blocks over came gleefully by and walked barefoot across the wet pavement. That was so much fun that they plodded back and forth until they got run off. (If your kid has cement feet and can't wiggle his toes, you'll know where he was that night.)

The young foreman said the road has to "cure" for 14 days and no cars can traverse it. Well, it's getting a tremendously good "cure." So far it has withstood motorcycle spinouts, dirt throwing contests and mini-bike races. We can still expect a roller skating derby and it might be a good idea to have a street dance. Yep, it's getting excellent testing, fellas, and so far no cracks!   *August 1973*

&&&

I recently wrote an item about running a contest to find

300

mushroom spots as suggested by Mrs. Sally Gibson and added that someone might as well tell her where to pan for gold in Appanoose county hills. Well, would you believe I received a letter stating that there is gold to be found hereabouts and he (or) she had some nuggets to prove it? But I guess we'll never know for sure because the letter just said "Unknown Writer."

&&&

I always look forward to receiving my Farmer's Almanac. The one this year offers a tip – set a brick up lengthwise in your toilet tank to save gallons of water. But I knew that years ago.

It also asks you to try this: Stand with your right foot sideways against a wall and put your right cheek against the wall. Then, try to lift your left foot.

You will not have any command of your left foot at all. It is hard to believe, but go ahead and try it for yourself!

It also listed a few ways the government is spending our money. Travelers aid to Los Angeles for migrants lost on their Freeway -$203,000. Study of the Frisbee by the Pentagon - $375,000. Study of Comic Books - $71,000.

&&&

The Lord's Prayer contains 56 words.

Lincoln's Gettysburg address contains 266 words.

The Declaration of Independence contains 3,000 words.

But a government regulation of the sale of cabbage contains 26,911 words.

&&&

It seems to take women my age longer to get used to newfangled inventions for the home. And there are new gadgets every year. For example, there are the new micro-wave ovens that can cook a roast almost before you can set the table; new slow cookers that take 10 hours to serve up ham and beans that used to cook in half the time; the two-hole doughnut bakers and the fondue pots that everybody dips cubes of bread into.

These inventions can get an old-timer homemaker very confused indeed.

&&&

I read where we are going to have to watch out for the new Metric System because it is on its way to the United States.

The Almanac said it may land like a ton (1,016 kilograms) of bricks.

The article pointed out that there are going to be some moans from the shapely damsels who win beauty contests with 36-24-36 figures when they announce over the loud speakers that she measures 90-60-90 centimeters.

And pending the day when we get to "thinking metric", which may take some people a few years and probably never, how are we going to get any inspiration out of the new versions of the old sayings, such as "A miss is as good as 1/61 kilometers", or "The Texan wearing a 37/86 liter hat?" And at the football game will we thrill at "First down, and 9.14 meters to go"?

But seriously America is about the only country left that hasn't gone to the metric system.

So far I've seen two films on the metric system through the

courtesy of the Extension office here. And I've read several pamphlets on the subject and I still can't remember what kilos are and how much a gram is.

I think I'm in deep trouble. *February 1975*

&&&

Hair dryers are exasperating!

You can't hear a doggone thing under them.

While you're in the chair getting your hair on rollers, all the operators and customers will be calm and collected.

Then, like on cue, the minute your ears get under the dryer, funny things start happening in the shop. You know things are funny because everybody starts laughing at one of hairdresser Shirley's hilarious (and true) tales. Everybody's laughing but me, that is. I didn't hear the tale.

Or a customer walks in with a piece of earthshaking news about our town and all faces change expression from funny to shock. I don't know what they're talking about.

I pretend to be interested in a magazine but when I see Linda and Sherry in rapt discussion and everybody laughs, I know I've missed out on something else at Karousel Salon.

Once I stuck my head out from under the dryer so I wouldn't miss out on anything. All eyes turned to me. "You'll never get dry that way," admonished Shirley.

No, and I'll always be wondering what they were laughing at and what the spicy town news was.

&&&

I always like to select my own perfumes, but since most other people don't know that, I gratefully accept what I get.

My first perfume gift, I remember, was Evening in Paris and I thought it had the most beautiful fragrance. I have another favorite currently, but I will never forget that first purple bottle.

I'm sort of fussy about perfume and can almost be run out of a room by what some women wear. Or the amount. Especially the amount. A little dab doesn't do it.

I've taken a real dislike (phobia, if you will) to one particular perfume and I think it should be renamed El Skunko.

&&&

I thought you might like this joke (I swiped it) as a change of pace:

A man visiting a resort met another male guest and asked him if he would like to go for a walk.

"No, I did it once and didn't like it," was the reply.

Finding no one else around, he approached the same man again and asked, "Like to play cards?"

"No thanks, did it once and didn't like it."

"Well, would you like to play a game of billiards, then?"

"No, tried it once and didn't like it, but my son is coming, and he'll join you."

"Your only son, I presume?"

&&&

On *Name That Tune* television show, a man drew his song envelope out of the bunch, but he couldn't name the tune for

$100,000. Thanks to a former Grammar School music teacher, I could have been rich the other night. That is if I had been on the show. I recognized it right away as Mendelssohn's "Spring Song."

Miss Stomberg saw to it that we memorized classics like that. She'd play them on the Victrola and we'd learn them. I probably will never forget "Hall of the Mountain King" nor fail to recognize the part where they rolled the giant down the mountain.

&&&

I need a new pair of glasses, but I'm reluctant to go get 'em. It's the frames that have me stymied.

My old frames are so out of date that I can't think of one other person whose frames remotely resemble mine. But I'm used to them, the way they feel and the way they look.

I've had an easier time picking out wallpaper or naming new babies than I'm going to have choosing new glasses. Frames come in every shape: square, wingspread, oval, granny, and the kind that make you look like a hoot owl and just spotted a field mouse.

You've even got to consider lens tints. There's rosy tint, smoky haze, and the kind that darken like sunglasses outdoors and don't lighten up indoors until you've set a spell.

But since I need stronger lenses to see better, I'll have to go and make a decision. The doctor will probably wish he'd taken up selling shoes instead. *September 1977*

&&&

305

Well, I got my new glasses last week and I can see just great, thank you, but I don't believe I look too great, especially when a friend saw me uptown the other day and asked: "Have you been sick?"

&&&

I can look all over the place for my glasses because I can't remember where I laid them ten minutes ago, yet I can remember in exact detail that wonderful hammock which swung beneath two elm trees in the front yard at my old home place in Centerville.

The trees are gone now and the hammock disintegrated with age, but I can still remember that it was made of woven heavy twine in colors of orange, yellow, brown and tan.

Many of my happiest moments were spent in the deep confines of that hammock. I was great at daydreaming, looking at fluffy white cloud formations, and enjoying the peaceful look of the azure blue sky above. I still am great at doing nothing, but now I have no hammock.

&&&

I got out my old high school yearbook last night to look at the pictures of Centerville High School state champions of 1935-1936

You remember the 1936 Whizzer CHS girls' team? They retained the state crown from 1935.

That was the year the Coach Loren Ewing had six Redettes – almost evenly matched in ability. There were no standout Hot

Shots. Coach Ewing worked them all hard and he insisted they "play as a team" – no vying for grandstanding – no individual records insisted on.

The guards were as good as the forwards. A real knockout team!

Wouldn't it be interesting to see Coach Ewing's 1936 team play against a 1970's girl's team? How would the three super guards handle a 55 point-a-game forward?

And how about Ewing's three great forwards confounding the living daylights out of the 1970's guards who apparently aren't used to forwards who feed the ball to the one who is in a position to make the shot instead of one star performer. Yes sir, they had a terrific team and coach in those days.

&&&

Where was I when the Japs bombed Pearl Harbor December 7, 1941?

I was married, had one child and was living in Chariton but back in Centerville for a pre-holiday visit when the shocking news came over the radio. It took awhile, I admit, for me not to feel anything but bitterness for the Japanese or German people. Time heals the wounds, but I can get stirred up again if I happen to see a German concentration camp movie or a war movie about Pearl Harbor and those planes with the land of the rising sun red circles on them. I don't want to be a bigot, but I still remember Dec. 7, 1941

&&&

Did you see the Northern Lights display a couple of weeks ago?

There were long fingers of ghostly white wavering light emanating from northern skies. It is one of the strange phenomenon's that occur, I've read, when the sun reflects on ice in the Arctic regions.

I remember the first Northern Lights display I ever saw. We were coming home from Bloomfield in my teen years and the sky suddenly became scarlet in the north, with streaks of red moving and changing. It put the fear in me, all right.

October 11, 1978

&&&

In one of my recent columns, I asked for volunteers to write a few columns while I go on vacation in October.

The response wasn't exactly earth-shaking, since only two persons said they'd like to try their hand at it. One was a man. I haven't seen their efforts yet, but can predict that you'll be interested in reading some fresh material. If their columns are too good – well, I can always go back to washing windows at home.

Last call. If you've always hankered to have a by-line on something you've written in print, call me and you can have your chance. Actually – it's kind of fun. Everybody has a story to tell.

Chapter 16

DOES THE PAST
HAVE A PRESENCE?

A friendly woman reader, with perfectly honorable intentions, said to us the other day that a good newspaper prints only news of the present and delves into possibilities for the future.

"News is what is going on right now," she said, and added. "Not many readers know or care what happened years ago."

She questioned that old pictures of pickle plants, street scenes or basketball teams arouse any particular interest in anyone. It was her feeling that people do care about the present age they are living in and what the world forces have in store for us.

This woman's opinion was certainly food for thought and after thinking about it for awhile, we decided that basically, she was mostly right. Any good newspaper worth its salt owes it to you, its readers, to get the news as it happens and to print as much information as it can dish out about what is in the wind for the future.

We pondered, then, over whether or not the past history of a town, its people, its builders and even its failures should be altogether discarded. The past is a closed door and cannot and should not be re-lived lest we dwell too much on it.

Yet, it is our contention that a worthy newspaper deals with the present, the future and a bit of the past if it is helpful to remember or contains nostalgic things that fit into the present. Yesterday is gone, but we certainly can't say it wasn't there at all.

Intrigued with this theory, and in addition to trying to carry news of the present, and a few articles on up-coming trends, we like to bring out a few items gleaned from the past that we hope will give you a chuckle in remembering. We hope there are a few people who will recall the past and not be sorry for it.

Wondrous Wooden Box

I can remember when radio ruled home entertainment, and you can too if you aren't any spring chicken.

Television was as unheard of then as test tube babies and as farfetched as that "giant step for mankind" on the moon.

I don't recall exactly the year we got our first radio, but I remember that it was the day before Christmas. The first words out of that wondrous wooden box with the rounded top were "Merry Christmas to you all!!" We were about the last folks to get a radio in the neighborhood, and it was purchased, cash, after a year of scrimping and whittling the household expenses down to a nubbin.

Those were the days when Fibber McGee and Molly were the friends we never saw. Millions followed their radio antics as we did. Edgar Bergen's voices as Charley McCarthy and Mortimer Snerd were as familiar as your next door neighbor's. (We never

310

knew that ventriloquist Bergen's lips moved.)

Radio voices were everything. We'd sit around the front room heater on week nights and listen to Fred Allen throw his acid barbs at Portland; George Burns make fun of Gracie; Ed Wynn be the clown for Texaco and Jack Benny funning with Rochester. Script writers for these shows were the best, week after week. They had to be, for what you heard was what you got.

One of my favorite radio shows was Amos and Andy.

Here were a couple of actors who parlayed a fifteen minute show into the longest running radio program on the air – 30 years. Remember Madam Queen? The time she sued Andy for breach of promise, audiences sat on the edge of their sofas waiting to know how it was going to come out. It was said that theatre business suffered so much because people didn't want to miss a single episode of Amos and Andy that theatre managers delayed their shows until that popular program signed off.

And if you think Soap Operas are biggies now, consider that you've never sat with your ears glued to the radio waiting to hear Stella Dallas, Ma Perkins or John's Other Wife.

Sound effects men were real heroes of radio too. They had to make the sounds of horse hooves, trains roaring down the track and Fibber McGee's closet stuff falling out. And when Inner Sanctum Mystery came on, the sound of a door squeaking made chills run up your spine.

Then there were the newscasters. You couldn't see them, but you knew Westbrook Pegler, Graham McNamee and good old H.V. Kaltenborn when you heard them. Remember Gabriel

Heatter who always began his newscast during World War II with, "There's good news tonight."

Radio was full of music. There were a lot of big bands in that era: Ted Weems, Wayne King, Ben Bernie, Art Kassel, Henry Bussey, and Bob Crosby. They usually appeared after 10 p.m. playing from such ballrooms as Starlight, Blackhawk, Aragon and Hotel Muehlbach in Kansas City.

My neighborhood friends and I must have memorized the words and music to thousands of songs during those days. One wonderful songsmith was Little Jack Little. Cliff Edwards had a program of the best banjo music you ever heard.

After supper dishes were done, there was Rudy Valle and his Variety Hour. Or Lux Radio Theatre whose dramas were unparalleled.

My Uncle Arthur thought the radio was the greatest invention of all time. He was devoted to it and would sit by the kitchen cookstove late at night coaxing in faraway stations like Del Rio, Texas, where he said he got the most wonderful cowboy music. He didn't care that there was static now and then.

They had spectaculars on radio then, too. One time a hypnotist in Kansas City put a woman into a trance on the stage of the Empire Theatre. It was all given word for word over radio. She was placed in a store window for 24 hours then brought back to the theatre where the hypnotist snapped her out of the trance. I remembered that one for weeks afterward.

The thrill of radio as family home entertainment is probably gone, but radio was and still is a very important part of the communication media.

But will they ever come up with another "Only the Shadow Knows"?

Player Piano Roll Blues

It was back in the days before Instant Entertainment (television) that the strains of "Rose of Washington Square" could be heard coming from a sturdy white frame house on a hill at Unionville, Iowa.

The music was loud and the singing even louder as the W.L. Hull family of eight children took turns pumping the old Artemis player piano. Mrs. Addie Hull remembers these sessions fondly and cherishes the camaraderie these sing-a-longs always brought.

Not every home had a player piano, which was also a combination regular piano that could be played in the conventional way too, as it was felt that Susie or Junior might not ever learn to play it themselves. The tone was also thought to be somewhat inferior in the player type, which was not always the case.

When the little doors in the front were opened, a roll of music could be inserted and when a wide pedal was pumped furiously, the bellows inside would start the roll and perforations on the paper roll would cause the appropriate keys to go up and down, emitting the most toe-tickling tunes, much to the delight of both youngsters and adults.

The nice part about these rolls, were the large printed words that rolled right along with the music. This resulted in professional type music and unprofessional style singing.

Upon inquiring about town, it was found that player pianos

are few and far between and those who do own them say they are inoperable due to holes having formed in the bellows or the deterioration of interior parts.

Looking over an old wooden crate of player rolls, some of the nostalgic ballads were found on Q.R.S., Republic, or Metro-Art rolls. There was "My Wild Irish Rose," "Till We Meet Again," and "Of a Perfect Day," "Daisies Won't Tell" and that good old tune " Three O'Clock In The Morning." These you don't hear often today.

Blues numbers were "IN" back in the 20's with "The Memphis Blues," "Mama's Blues" and "Bluin' the Blues" among the most popular. Oldsters also went for the waltz tunes and you could buy "Cecile Waltz" or a roll of old fashioned waltz medleys.

The children chose ragtime because the keys bounced faster and the tempo was exciting. Favorites were "Raggin' The Scale," Canadian Capers," "Cheese and Crackers" and of course the "Cannon Ball Rag."

You can still hear today, some oldies like "Hindustan," "Auld Lang Syne" and that most beautiful of all Hawaiian melodies "Aloha Oe."

If you yearn for an evening of old time fun, find a home that has a player piano and maybe the owner will let you select a few rolls and give you permission to pump away your tensions. She may even let you sing!   *July 1967*

&&&

Frances (Peterson) Fridley was a neighborhood girlfriend of

314

years ago.   She became an accomplished pianist and organist and I believe to this day that she owes it all to the miniature red toy piano her parents gave her.   While the rest of us girls carried our 10 cent celluloid dolls in cigar boxes, Frances toted her little red piano.

We friends had some good times those summer vacations.

And I wonder if Virginia Carney remembers the times we gathered around the piano at her grandmother's home and while Virginia played Al Jolson's "Sonny Boy" we'd sing along and choke up as we sang "climb upon my knee, Sonny Boy. You are only three, Sonny Boy. There's no way of knowing, there's no way of showing what you mean to me, Sonny Boy."

All those good times without TV.

&&&

So the Rock Island railroad line won't be running down our Appanoose County tracks anymore.

Well, I haven't ridden a train in many, many years, but the passing of the old Rock Island makes me recall the wonderful times when I rode the train to Kansas City when I was a little girl.   Another cousin and I usually went to visit the big city cousins.

I remember planning the trip for weeks; finally going down to the old depot in south Centerville, getting our tickets and waiting for the sound of the train whistle and hearing the smoke-belching locomotive come down the tracks.   It was an earth shaking experience!

When that iron monster screeched to a stop, the conductor

would hop off and put down a metal step.

"All aboard," he'd thunder as we found seats facing each other next to the windows. They were covered with dark green plush. It didn't matter that soot had blown in the windows and splotched the plush. The Queen of England couldn't have felt as elegant and regal on her throne.

By the time we whistled into Seymour, 15 miles away, and it seemed to take an hour, we knew we were truly headed in the right direction and a great adventure.

We marveled that sometimes we went so fast that we couldn't count the telephone poles.

Grandma always packed us a lunch in a shoe box tied with a string.

We were usually a little ashamed of it. When the black man in the starched white uniform came down the aisle announcing, "Dinnah is served in the Dinah," we wished that just once we could march into the Diner with the others and be served a fabulous menu in style. That fantasy was never to be.

As we devoured our food we always wondered why nearby passengers eyed our shoe box filled with homemade bread sandwiches, green peppers and saucer-sized sugar cookies. We were positive that they were feeling sorry for the little girls from the sticks who didn't have money to eat in the Diner. Little did we know.

The biggest thrill was when the train came close enough for us to see the sky-scrapers against the Kansas City skyline. And when it chugged into big Union Station teeming with people, we were speechless. We prayed that our aunt and uncle had met the train. We lugged our own suitcases, having been warned not to let a Red Cap carry them. They cost money.

So the Rock Island line is just a memory. For me, it is an unforgettable memory.   *April 1980*

Coal Mining Days

We saw "The Last Pony Mine" film Monday night at the high school and seeing it brought back mental pictures of the old coal mining days in Appanoose County. The appreciative audience was filled with fellows who had worked in the mines at one time, or with those of us who grew up in a mining community. As Jake Foster said, "I'll bet there'll be many a ton of coal re-dug tonight over a cup of coffee as those miners and their families recall mining days."

Coming over from England my Grandpa Leigh first worked in Kansas mines, then Texas, then Centerville. After my father's death of a heart attack in 1920 when I was 3, my mother, younger sister and myself moved back to Centerville and into my grandparents home and there we were raised. Since my mother had to work, they doubled up on child raising and it didn't hurt us a bit. That's why I know about coal mining from the ground up (or the ground down)!

When I begged to go down into Fairlawn mine he said, "Why not. It doesn't hurt a girl to see what hard work a man does." So he got permission from Mr. Lundgren and I went down in the mine – a number of times, and I'm not sorry. My insatiable curiosity made me want to know about the underground coal and I now know.

317

Fairlawn wasn't a slope (walk-in) mine like the New Gladstone you saw in the film. It was a shaft type and they let you come into the bowels of the earth on a shaky open case elevator affair. The cables in the mine film looked strong compared to the ones I remember looking up and seeing.

Being down in a coal mine is unlike any experience you've ever had. Caverns? Well, they are just different. Northing compares with the sight of layers of coal, glistening moist and blue-black in the lights of miners' carbide lamps. Coal is beautiful, it really is, and I'm glad Mrs. Widmar proved it by using tiny chunks of it for banquet favors at the premier showing.

Coal provided our daily bread and kept us from freezing in the winter so we developed a healthy respect for it.

I helped fill so many carbide lamps that I believe I could detect the smell of carbide any place today. The movie showed one of the miners sloshing water from his pail over the filled lamp. I had almost forgotten that it is this water, dripping drop by drop through a tiny opening in the top of the lamp down onto the carbide lumps, which formed the gas which shot out flames when lighted.

I used to feel sorry for the little Shetland ponies that spent their days in the mine pulling heavy loaded carts. They always looked so wild-eyed when they were exposed to the sunlight again. The miners worked just as hard, digging and lifting chunks of coal onto the rail carts and propping up sides of the coal beds and getting coal dust in their eyes.

My grandpa wouldn't have tolerated pity. He was a proud man – poor but proud he always said – and somehow it never occurred to me to pity him. Coal mining was his way of life, a hard, dirty but honest way of life and I was never ashamed of it. Most miners learned a lot down there in the confines of the low tunnels and I never met one who didn't have a sense of humor.

Appanoose County was suckled on mounds of black coal. It turned into a healthy teenager nurtured chiefly by coal. It reached shaky young adulthood and finally matured in a rich coal field. Appanoose County has turned out pretty well, everything considered.

We don't need it right now, but coal is still down under us, miles and miles of it. We won't forget that it is there and if the time ever comes that we need it again to stay alive, it will be there. Probably long after we are gone.   *November 1972*

Gypsies, Tramps, & Thieves

Each time I hear gaudy Cher of TV sing "Gypsies, Tramps and Thieves" I think back to the days when the sight of two or three big, black, dirty limousines driving into Centerville down Washington Street would drive the neighborhood children into the shelters of their homes.

We had heard so many stories about how gypsy bands would take everything in sight – including any little children who were wandering nearby.   They were said to take washings off clotheslines, produce from gardens and pet dogs.

Those ambulance-appearing black cars were dreaded sights. It was a well known fact that if they were allowed to linger for even a few hours in Centerville, the swarthy Romany women would set up a makeshift booth and tell your fortune. The cost

319

was to cross her palm with silver, but a neighbor woman who did so, always insisted that her diamond ring went with the silver crossing.

How much was true about the wandering gypsies I really don't know for sure. But they looked dark and sinister to a young child.

And as for the 'tramps' of the 1920's and depression '30s, they weren't girls of loose morals. No, they were men, dressed in shreds and soleless shoes who carried bandanna knapsacks over their shoulders on sticks just like you see them characterized now in the movies. Exactly.

We were leery of them too although most of our parents gave them a meal on the back porch. Grandma always fed them homemade bread and butter and a cup of coffee if she had nothing else.

When tramps came in numbers throughout the summer, she still offered food, and some even offered to do a few chores ... but they always sneaked off down the alley.

I could never understand why the tramps never worked, yet got food free and sometimes lodging in someone's smokehouse or barn. I could never understand why such men should eat our homemade bread and butter when we hardly had enough for ourselves, and Grandpa worked so hard in the coal mines and Mom clerked in a store for 40 years.

Mostly, though, bums wanted a dime or quarter in preference to food, and the reason was obvious.

The tramp bonanza was almost washed up one day when grandma saw one fellow throw her bread and bacon sandwich into the back yard before even trying it. That almost did it – but not quite. "Those fellows are down on their luck," she'd always remind us.

Gypsies, tramps and thieves.

Ku Klux Klan

Some say the Ku Klux Klan era in the '20s was horrible and better it should be forgotten. Let sleeping dogs lie or something like that.

It was happening locally, though, and should be noted as such even though it was distasteful. There were such things as robed figures and burning crosses. They actually happened.

My own memories of the Ku Klux Klan era are very unpleasant. Two of my best friends were indirectly brought into the matter and I was in the middle.

One girl's family was anti-Klan and the other's father was a strong supporter of its activities. They were both members of the Christian church whose preacher, J. Roy Wright was a big leader in trying to make Centerville pure and clean.

My family believed that the Klan was out of line in its methods and abhorred the chastisement doled out.

I can still see the huge burning cross in a neighbor's yard and the one at the Catholic Church. I never really knew just what it was the neighbor or the church had done that was so terrible.

County Fair

There are those who say that with the advent of spectacular TV, the rural, homespun type of entertainment has lost much of

321

its appeal.

We speculated about this while taking in the Appanoose County Fair this week and came away knowing that at least some of the magic is still there.

Actually, the appeal of any fair rests in the eyes of the beholder.

The crowds still love the daring of a rodeo clown; the varied exhibits; the livestock shows; the rugged gait of a bronco-buster; the milling around in a carnival atmosphere. The attraction is the "something different" it gives to humdrum lives.

Even with all the work and preparation that goes into modern fairs, some things just aren't there that I'm sure were there years ago. A lot of new things have been added, but there isn't much extravaganza we haven't already seen via the airwaves.

Now you take years ago when the setting for all the big fairs, Chautauqua's, carnivals and "The Big Top" was a large field at the south edge of town. There the lights were brighter, and the rott-ta-toot of a fiesta mingled with the shrill calliope made you know this was where the action was.

True, there were few tractor pulling contests then (who had tractors to punish unduly)? But there were horse-team pulls. I once saw a team-pull contest and it was the last one I ever wanted to see. The beautiful, strong animals were pitted against wooden sled affairs, usually loaded with heavy logs, while their masters (the exhibitionists of yesteryear) stood, feet wide apart with long whips raised, urging their horses to strain their loins to the breaking point. (But then I was never one who enjoyed watching circus elephants being prodded with sharp hooks as they labored in the hot sun, nor ever wished for the return of the Roman arena.)

Neither have I forgotten since those days that I was absolutely fascinated by sword swallowers and fire-eaters. One sword swallower even let a prominent Centerville businessman examine the sword on the stage to see that the sharp blade did not disappear into the handle somewhere. Then he guided it ever so slowly down his esophagus and on down into what must have been his innards. With a flourish, he always seemed to extract it much quicker, to gasps from his audience.

Scoffers in the crowd would loudly announce that there "was a trick to it," but since our big eyes couldn't see it, we always believed it could be done. And the same with the fire-eaters who extinguished flaming torches (the fire was real) with their mouths.

And there was an unexplainable attraction about carnival people. Even though we knew they were unkempt, crooked and disreputable roustabouts, we wondered why they chose to lead the unconventional lives they did. The bally-hoers who hired people inside the tent shows could probably have talked old John D. Rockefeller out of his second dime (he kept the first one, they said).

Now they don't have the dances they once did, either. The go-go girls can't put on the show those grass-wavers did. For packing them in, you couldn't beat that lineup of tough looking dames. And remember Sally Rand and her fans at the State Fair and Little Egypt the 2nd or 3rd at the World's Fair? Many serious, home loving neighborhood fathers were on the very first row.

The dark, grimy Gypsy fortune tellers with their crystal balls are still around, though. They invariably predicted that a dark handsome stranger would soon appear and we would search the crowd until we spotted one. We never failed her.

But the things I can do without to this day are the Freak Shows – Jo Jo the dog faced boy; the man so skinny you could play a tune on his ribs with a spoon and the wild man from Borneo.

The sight of a wretched human being with wild eyes, crouching like an animal in a pit or cage, devouring a live chicken was never my cup of tea. (Such a man was a hopeless alcoholic or dope addict, they said, who would do anything for more of same.) It was as good an explanation as any. You could lose the hamburger you had just eaten while watching the Wild Man show.

We noticed this week that "gimmick" shows and concessions are still around.

There was this duck shoot once where, for a thin dime, you got three shots at moving duck targets. They didn't have to give away many plaster of Paris kewpie dolls at this stand because you had to be quick on the trigger and not let too many ducks go by while you were aiming. It so happened one time that a young fellow from Mystic – redheaded, rawboned and wearing overalls, had practiced and practiced during the winter months and laid in wait for the first big show to hit the county seat. He almost single-handedly wiped out the stand of canes and dolls and when he was shooed off by husky carneys, the large crowd which had gathered booed and booed. The Mystic boy just grinned – he'd had his claim to fame!

As we said, nearly all the magic and thrill of the old days was at our own fair this week – at least for the children. Teenagers still rock the top seats on the Ferris Wheel and three-year-olds still love the merry-go-round and pick cotton candy. And if you want to watch the greatest sucker game of them all, just catch those little fellows manipulating the little shovels for a worthless prize. There are a few big fellows, too, who haven't given up trying to grasp a five dollar bill before the shovel quits working.

The Depression

"The Depression" they're talking a lot about lately is that period of ill repute back in the 1930's. It is getting more re-runs these days than the old *I Love Lucy* shows.

First, I noticed that the state paper asked its readers to send in their memory stories of the Great Depression era, and by golly, they pieced together a heck of an interesting story from the bits and pieces of hardships and woes. We could remember again vividly, the bread lines, banks that went broke, stock markets that fell, men who were out of work, 5 cent corn, and people jumping off buildings. Things like that.

Then the other day I read an article in which the author stated that the food cooked up by "Depression" housewives was so delicious and healthful that we should throw our frying pans and meat out the kitchen door. Said the author cheerfully, "If we would once again live on beans and cornbread; potatoes, macaroni and cheese, pots of cabbage and vegetables, we would be healthier." I think I'll buy that.

Thirdly, a big story again about how great the clothing was and where you could still find some of the pink satin (and silk) slips like Jean Harlow wore, plus tweed skirts and wool coats and things like that. I wouldn't be surprised if those horrible old anklets came back.

Now I happen to remember the Depression about as well as anybody but the reason I didn't get too concerned was because we were mighty poor before it and not in the money bracket after it. It sort of fit in with the way things were anyway.

As for the bread lines, the only ones I saw were past the big, black cookstove in a coal miner's kitchen. The bread may have been made of only flour, salt, water and yeast, but I doubt that my family would have been caught in a bread line as long as there were bread crumbs to spare.

When Wooden's Savings Bank went broke in Centerville we didn't cry all the way to the bank. We didn't have anything in it. Nor when the stock market fell, we didn't hear the thud too well nor leap off the Centerville courthouse clock tower. We didn't even have any 5 cent corn to sell.

About the worst food calamity I can remember was not being able to have butter, peanut butter and jam all at the same time. One or nothing.

You don't know how good a 50 cent beef roast tasted on Sunday. And when you're hungry; soup, macaroni, rice and vegetables in a pie crust taste doggone good.

Why, because of this early "conditioning," there is positively no vegetable I won't eat. Depression food? I grew up on it and

I'm still here to tell about it.

As far as Depression clothing went (and it went quite a ways down a family line) it wasn't so bad. In fact, the crocheted and knit scarves, mittens and tasseled caps looked as good on us as they do on the 1970's gals. The cracker box cardboard shoe soles did get a little soaked sometimes, though.

Once I had a royal blue belted winter coat and matching tam. Bought it myself with my $1 per Saturday earnings at Frankels (from 8 a.m. to 10 p.m.).

No sir, the Depression didn't ruin me. I didn't die of malnutrition; I didn't freeze in my made-over clothes; I didn't acquire any airs from being pampered and spoiled.

We don't need another Depression. I learned many things the first time around and somehow what I learned, I still remember very well, thank you.

&&&

Most people my age have lived through more crisis times than we care to remember and put up with more shortages than you can shake a stick at. Our main shortage was money and that's probably why we had so many crises. Things were a bit different then, though. The fuel and coal was there, the gasoline was there, food was plentiful, clothing was being sold and you could go to the picture show. The shortage was mainly in the green stuff we call money.

And now, just when we were finally getting used to affluences and having the money to buy fuel, gasoline, clothing, food and a side of beef for the freezer maybe, what happens?

Now you can't buy the fuel.

Governor Ray says that we should walk to work and school. We "depressionites" went through that already. It is suggested that we lower the house temperature to 65 degrees. We remember when 65 degrees would have been doggone comfortable.

And what's this about not using unneeded lights? Well, in my time only one hang-down ceiling light was ever on in our house at one time. Nobody could have conserved more on electric energy than we did.

And who do you think will be the ones who will take the energy crisis the hardest? Who will be the last to do without three-way light bulbs, or walk to work or get into a pair of red flannels? Why, the ones who have never been down that road before!

&&&

I remember that I used to earn enough money to buy an Eskimo Pie at the neighborhood grocery by picking potato bugs off the plants and tomato worms off the leaves. We were paid by the tobacco can full.

I also diligently earned a penny a gallon bucket for stemming gooseberries, two cents a gallon for seeding cherries with my thumbs and taking the ends off green beans and breaking them into bite-sized pieces. I got quite adept, too, at flipping peas out of their pods. We got a penny a quart for shelled peas. My grandma used to say, "Marjorie will never die from overwork!" But I got mighty hungry for Eskimo Pies and Red Devil suckers, and I could work when I got the urge.

There was once a time when you could buy a big box of oatmeal for 10 or 15 cents and find a Shirley Temple blue glass mug or cereal bowl inside.

&&&

I never had a doll house, but always thought what great fun they would be for children. I can visualize a replica of the kitchen I grew up in – the big cast iron cookstove with its massive oven and reservoir, the solid oak kitchen table and chairs, the kitchen cupboard with its spice shelves and flour bin and sifter built right in, and the shelf above the table which held the Old Ben alarm clock. There would be grandma's own personal stool made from a highchair with the back and arms cut off. I can see the row of hooks behind the kitchen door where my grandpa hung his work clothes. Sometimes there were frozen one-piece long johns, brought in off the line hanging in the pantry to thaw out.

I wonder how all that would look in a doll house?

&&&

When I was shopping in the Penney store recently I paused to remember the way it once looked many years ago.

Instead of the cash register to record sales, Penney's used to have an overhead cable track which carried the sales slip and the bills and coins over the customers' heads upstairs to the office, where the office girl would make the change and send it back down in the little brown box.

329

Featherbeds

We reminisce sometimes at Sugar Belles Club. That's because we have a lot to remember and most of us can recall about the same topics and the same places and times.

So it wasn't unusual that the subject of featherbeds came up during one evening. The feather bedding we knew about isn't the 'featherbedding' the railroad fellows talk about, either.

Remember those featherbeds in blue and white ticking? Ours were made of as good a grade of feathers as grandma could get together ... usually goose and duck feathers and maybe a few chicken feathers thrown in if she had to. (Those were always the ones that poked out of the ticking.)

And we always had goose feather pillows 'neath our heads if we had to do without something else. We were always used to doing without something else anyway!

Although the "posture" mattress has long replaced the feather bed at our house, I can remember to this day exactly how bedtime was in the old days. You don't forget snuggling down in feathers very easily, and as it turned out, no one at Sugar Belles had forgotten the utter bliss of sinking down into a cloud of feathers when the temperatures dropped to zero.

In the summertime, the feathers surprisingly made a cool pallet – just like insulation.

It was only at bed making time in the morning that the feather mattress became a monster, especially if it was getting old and lumpy. You had to lift it up, shake the wadded feathers up, plump the whole thing around, get each corner straight and then smooth the whole business out so one side wasn't higher than the other. (Grandma wouldn't tolerate a finished bed that looked like craters on the moon.) Then you put the sheet blankets over it and then the sheets and bedspread. The secret of smoothing out the spread laid in the fact that you used a broom or mop handle to leve 'er all out.

By the time I got the beds made I was ready to fall into them again, but then there was the washing to scrub and put on the line and the cooking, ironing and dusting.

I slept on a straw tick one vacation with a friend in the country, and that old feather bed sure felt good when I got back. Somehow the straw lumps wouldn't smooth out with the broom handle. I liked the smell of the fresh straw, though, and I have always managed to sleep on about anything.

Our children all remember sleeping on their grandmother's feather ticking and my daughter Nancy wanted the feathers for a pillow or two.

Someday we'll try the water bed, which some Iowegian co-workers say is positively great. If it's anything like a feather mattress, then I'd like it.

You are pretty ancient, I guess, when your memories include such things as feather beds, coal buckets, fat bacon poultice for bumblebee stings, white cards in the screen door for the iceman to see; jars of Cloverine salve, carpet beaters, ink wells on every desk, Saturday night baths in a No. 10 washtub; cookstoves and 50 cent beef roasts for Sunday dinner, which were enough to slice later for supper and provide small slivers for a delectable meat pie for Tuesday dinner.

&&&

If you remember Centerville's equivalent of the flagpole sitters, you are not very young. Several local residents got into the national craze, and one fellow even built a tree house on Washington Street and proceeded to start what might have been a record stay had not an electrical storm of great magnitude brought him down in a hurry.

&&&

Can you recall that the Ford Garage in town engaged a "human robot" to perform in their showroom? This smartly dressed fellow entranced his audience by moving in completely robot-like manner, and without one visible blink of his eyes, until the populace of a young fry refused to believe that he was real.

&&&

Do you remember the affluent families who let the sons drive the ultimate in class – a rumble seat? That carefree rumble seat – the predecessor of the convertible – that gave the owner the unquestioned distinction of being in the "in" crowd.

Compiler's note: a Sport Coupe or Sport Roadster had a rumble seat which opened out from the rear.

&&&

Remember when Hypnotism was quite the thing in Centerville? The suave professional who hypnotized the young lady into sleeping for many hours in the display window of a local business place as a publicity stunt? A bed was placed in full view behind the plate glass and thousands of Centerville and area residents stopped by to watch the motionless figure. Several self-appointed courthouse park benchwarmers watched the proceedings by the hour to prove the whole business was a fake. They never did.

&&&

Remember the time when our phone numbers had only three digits and used a color with them – red, black, blue and green? I clearly remember that our number was 570 Green. And you always gave the number you were calling to one of the telephone operators who plugged in your call on the big switchboard at Farrington's Telephone Company.

&&&

Wouldn't it be nice if girls still pieced quilts? They're something that last for years.

I remember the first friendship quilt I pieced before I was ten years old. It was a simple four-patch sewed from scraps of material left over from our dresses and grandma's aprons.

Neighborhood girls shared squares and we were thrilled when my mother brought two-inch strips of yard goods home from her store where she worked.

When grandma quilted the hand-sewn creation on the frames and bound it in bias tape, my sense of accomplishment knew no bounds.

Christmas Memory Bank

Everyone should take a little time at Christmas, before

333

another year snows us under and frosts over the past too much, and go back to our beginnings. We might be surprised at what we come up with out of our Christmas memory banks.

Putting yourself back in Christmases Past could be a kind of holiday game you could play with your family the day you all gather around the Christmas turkey.

Taking a mental inventory of our Christmas memories up to now takes more than a few moments of retrospect, and when you've had more than half a century of Christmases Past, as I have, you find that some of them are hazy and some you can't call to mind at all.

It took me a good bit of time and quiet thinking to "put myself back" in time and remember some specific things about my Christmases Past.

I remember that we had an aunt out in California who my mother said was "well-to-do" because she had married well. This aunt sent us a box at Christmas time and we watched for the parcel post truck for weeks. She always sent something expensive and beautiful. One year it was a mama doll apiece, one with a blue dress and one with pink. Mine was named Violet and my sister named hers Rose, and even if someone had changed the dresses I would have known Violet's sweet little face from any other doll in the whole world.

This same aunt once gifted me with a little gold ring which held a genuine (chip) diamond. Nobody but a little tomboy girl would wear it (and lose it) while making a snow fort and snowball ammunition.

&&&

There are so many memories in Christmases Past that only come forth when you start to remember. There was the smell of homemade bread, and the sight of the dough rising in the bread pan. There was the real Christmas tree every year standing in the front room with lighted red candles flickering from green metal holders clipped to the branches. The decorations which stand out best in my memory were the tiny crocheted bells and red stockings my grandma made and popcorn balls made with bacon drippings and sorghum. I didn't think much of them for the same reason I thought that homemade dresses were crude. Such things, I thought then, visually placed us in the lower income bracket where most of we coal miner supported kids seemed to be. Everything seemed to be hand-me-downs or stuff recycled from something else. Now, it's the fad and a preponderance of made-over things and antiques in your home, that just as visible, place you in the nicer financial bracket. We did look forward to the decorations of holly and mistletoe sent by the same relative who always shipped us a box of dates from her own date palms.

&&&

Christmas Eve was a magical night, a still, cold quiet time to treasure the miracle of the birth of the Christ child. When my mother would get home from work we'd have soup and roast pork sandwiches and fruits.

We hung our stockings on the back of a rocking chair because we didn't have a fireplace mantle. Even though I knew that my stocking would have a huge orange in it, plus mixed nuts and a big red delicious apple with a candy cane sticking out, that

335

stocking was a beautiful sight.

I still love Christmas Eve and have vivid memories of how everything was back then even though the gifts were homemade and very humble. I believe my favorite gifts were the new hat, scarf and mitten sets my grandma crocheted for me every year. And the books ... Uncle Wiggly .... Bobbsey Twins... the Marjorie series ...Rebecca of Sunnybrook Farm among many.

I remember reading a new book next to the heating stove in the living room ... noticing that the stars were bigger and brighter and always trying to find the star of Bethlehem ... watching the candles flicker on the tree where they were clamped on the branches ... treasuring a new pair of crocheted mittens and matching cap made by grandma ... the jigsaw puzzle of the map of the United States which proved so educational that I still remember most of the state capitols ... the church Christmas programs in which I was always too bashful to sing and died a thousand deaths before my "reading" was over ... the face of my wonderful mother who taught me that we should do nice things for one another all during the year.

&&&

I was taught not to get disappointed very often, and if I should become disappointed, to get over it fast. This early philosophy has been used a million times since.

But one Christmas when I was about ten years old, I was deeply disappointed over the silliest thing. It has stayed around in my store of Christmas memories, probably as a reminder.

At school, the only pen writing we did then was with a tan

336

wood tapered holder with a "Pen Point" inserted in a groove at the bottom. We dipped the pen point into a glass inkwell in the desk top. The blue ink usually got cruddy, and besides you could only write three words without re-dipping.

I longed for a real Sheaffer or Parker fountain pen which you filled out of an ink bottle by drawing the ink up into a rubber tube inside. Ah, the magic of such a pen! (Who cared that such a fountain pen would drop globs of ink on your Red Chief table paper every time you raised the little lever on the side to see if the pen had run out of ink?)

Anyway, that's what I wanted for Christmas and when a wrapped pen-shaped box with my name on it came from a cousin in Kansas City, I knew that's what was in it. I shook it many times. Yep, that's what it was all right. Only the color I had to guess at and I knew it would be green.

Came Christmas I opened the box first thing. It contained a set of beads for my neck, made of wood and gaudily painted brown and orange. I never wore them. In fact, I still have them in a box which says "A fine Sheaffer fountain pen" on the outside. It keeps me on my toes about disappointments. It should have also taught me not to shake Christmas presents.

An anonymous member of the Sugar Belles Club must read my column from time to time, for I received a gift all wrapped up pretty and I could see through the paper that it was a Sheaffer pen box. Ah ha, I thought. Someone in that ornery group of gals read that I once thought I had a fountain pen for Christmas and was bitterly disappointed when it turned out to be a bead necklace. I shook this box, too. Sure enough, it sounded like a fountain pen inside, but it could be something else. I'll not be fooled again, I thought. No, sir.

I unwrapped the gift and there it was … an old-time Sheaffer fountain pen, side lever and all. Even in this day of ballpoint pens, by golly, that big fountain pen looks mighty efficient. Nostalgia flooded my senses and to the Sugar Belle who sent it – you made my day!!

&&&

The memory of my mother at Christmas especially will never fade. It is too strong to frost over with the years. A widow, she clerked in stores to keep the wolf from the door and she rarely complained. Her greatest gift to her daughters was herself and her almost flawless philosophy of life. No material possession or diamond ring can equal a wonderful mother.

Chapter 17

THATCHER, LEIGH, MCGUIRE

Lettia Thatcher Leigh

Grandma Leigh was a special person. I guess you could say she was kind of a character without meaning to be irreverent. Anyway, she was the only grandmother I ever knew.

She remembered coming to America from England in the mid 1870's when she was eight years old. Her family (*Thatcher*) traveled by boat and covered wagon and settled in Kansas. Here she married my grandfather who had also come over from England with his coal mining family.

She was a coal miner's daughter and married a coal miner and there were never moments of belligerence or regretfulness about this. She knew what it was like to homestead in Kansas and to give birth in a sod house.

There are so many things I remember about her.

She loved nasturtiums. There never was a year, come drought or high water, that there wasn't a whole row of nasturtiums in a certain place back of the garden. And since they had to be picked every day to grow well, all the neighbors got bouquets of nasturtiums whether they wanted them or not.

One of her goals was canning 100 quarts of tomatoes every year. Not 99 quarts. They were put up in shiny new tin cans with the lids sealed with dark red sealing wax. We ate every one, too, usually cold in a bowl or fixed hot with leftover homemade bread, onions, and sugar.

Grandma cleaned house every spring – and I mean the whole house, not room by room, but the whole house in one week. Grandpa helped carry out the heavy things like beds and rugs and then tried to go fishing or someplace. Lace curtains came down, were washed and stretched. Windows were washed and wallpaper was cleaned with pink rubbery stuff. Five rugs were taken out into the yard and beat with wire rug beaters until the clouds of dust subsided. Feather beds were sired and closets cleaned. We were all worn out, but the house shone. In the fall, it got what grandma called a "lick and a promise."

She could make a 50 cent roast beef go further and last better than anybody. She'd brown it in a heavy cast iron Dutch kettle, then put in onions and always a few drops of vinegar which she said tenderized the beef. The first meal would be served with potatoes and carrots roasted around it. Then it was sliced for sandwiches for supper. The scraps left over went into an English Meat Pie with double crust. Her bread was made with just flour, water, salt and yeast – no fancy egg and sugar dough. If it rose too fast and went over the pan behind the old cookstove, it was the yeast's fault. If it wasn't such a good "batch" then it was the flour's fault. All pieces of bread had to be used up before a new loaf was cut. So crusts went into hamburger, into bread pudding, tomatoes and homemade soup.

She was a woman of strong opinions and if I wanted to get into trouble with her, all I had to do was argue. If she said black was white, it didn't do any good to try to convince her. "Hard-headed English woman" my grandpa always used to say.

Grandma believed that her coal mining husband was entitled to the best she could do for him. The choicest food went into his bucket and the reservoir on the back of the stove always held hot water for baths in the galvanized wash tub. She worked hard, and never sat down that she wasn't sewing carpet rags, crocheting mittens or reading the Bible.

Occasionally she would dance a jig through the house and say, "Out of the way for old Dan Quaker." She loved music and picture shows.

As a nurse, she couldn't be beat. She had her own way of making outing flannel poultices for the chest; hot onion pads to hold over aching ears, and fat bacon dressings for cuts and bruises. Many stomach aches felt better after grandma gently rubbed and sang "Round and round daddy's old barn, if it does no good it will do it no harm."

About the only thing that would rile her up real good was if she didn't have her weekly wash out on the line sooner than the neighbor women on Monday morning. She'd heat water on the cook stove, carry it out to the wash house, bucket by bucket, and would use shredded up P & G soap. There were always two rinse tubs. The white clothes got "boiled" and stirred with an old broom handle in the copper boiler. Our washing took a back seat to no ones anywhere around. Grandma would scan the neighbor's clothes lines and come in real pleased with herself.

She always ironed on Tuesday and baked on Wednesday. We cleaned the house thoroughly on Saturday. She'd get us out of bed with a "rise and shine" and I don't think she ever once missed saying that the neighbor girl already had swept her rugs and was practically ready to play outdoors. I always got up too (the mention of the word play, probably).

Yes, I was lucky to have had such a fine grandmother. Some of the good things she taught me are still with me. Other good ideas still should be but some have fallen by the wayside – such as taking the house apart every spring, or getting my washing done first, or rising and shining.

&&&

Grandma always said that you could judge a woman by looking in her pantry. Her lace curtains could be fresh from the wooden stretchers, or her beds always made, but it would be her pantry that could tell what she was and what she could do!

To my grandma, her pantry wasn't a place to throw everything that wouldn't fit into the rest of the house; it was a corner of her heart and she arranged it and fussed over it.

I remember she was a strong woman who not only raised her own seven children but helped raise my sister and me. She did it by stocking her pantry with home canned tomatoes, jars of jelly and pickles, beans, peaches, corn and beets.

In the pantry was a kitchen cupboard/flour hutch which was her pride and joy. Here was her flour bin where she sifted flour into a worn wooden bread bowl. Here she kept her nutmeg and other prized spices and jars of homegrown dill seed, mustard seed, dried parsley, celery and her unforgettable hand picked and dried sage.

We also had a cellar down under the house. Here in the semi-darkness, on the hard packed dirt floor, were apples in wooden crates, hubbard and butternut squash in burlap bags, and potatoes and carrots still holding the fragrance of damp earth in wooden baskets. Yellow onions hung in clusters from the ceiling.

Grandma's pantry and cellar meant a lot to her and was the means of keeping a family from starving. There wasn't any supermarket then. She seemed to have the right measure of fruits, vegetables, meats and sweet things to see us all through the winter.

By the same token, she seemed to have the right measure of the important things of life and the strength that counted to sustain her family.

She kept close to the earth and lived very near a good life.

She was happy.

&&&

Grandma used to make everything from scratch. She made a one-egg cake that was so economical it could turn into dessert for Sunday dinner, a birthday cake or a festive holiday cake. She just made it look different each time by disguising that yellow cake with cocoa frosting, or pink icing for birthdays, or white icing decorated with cinnamon red-hots for Valentines Day.

Sometimes we cut squares of it hot from the cookstove oven with no icing at all. That probably was the best eatin' of all.

She didn't go much for green icing or green gelatin on St. Patrick's Day. Being pure blood English, she was a bit bigoted when it came to the Irish although her only daughter, my mother, married my Irish father.

One year when I was in high school she crocheted a green vest for me to wear over a blouse. I was proud for the wearin' of the green that day!

&&&

Grandma Leigh would have been sad in the passing of Bing Crosby. She thought he had the most beautiful voice in the world. Although she raised a large family on a coal miner's salary, she still managed to bring home one of Bing's records once in awhile to play on our wind-up Victrola. Her house was filled with music, both her own singing and "jigging" and those voices of her favorite stars. For that I will always be grateful. I still remember most of the words to most of the songs of the teens, 20's and 30's.

Someday I'm going to take time to get out all those old records, wind up the old Victrola again, and play "Til the Sands of the Desert Grow Cold" or "Bullfrog Blues", both of which were bought by my dad back in 1917.

&&&

Grandma didn't have a chance to get educated to her highest potential, living in a mining camp in Kansas, but she was full of wisdom. She always told us: "Don't dig ditches for others lest you fall in them yourselves." And she'd admonish my sister and me never to say such things as "hope she gets sick and can't go to the party" or "it would be good enough for her if she broke a leg." Tempting fate, she'd say. I believe it.

&&&

Somehow I can't seem to conjure up a mental picture of my grandma wearing a pantsuit as do many older women these days. (Even if it was a classy double-knit one with a frilly blouse - like mine!)

She was a neat, feminine type woman who wore the prettiest house dresses she could make on her old treadle sewing machine. She could add a touch of lace to printed flour sack material and fashion the nicest dress. I remember she liked Dan River ginghams, crisp and cool, and paisley prints, and wore them with a flourish.

&&&

The work apron was a must in every home. They were made from colorful prints and ginghams or feed sacks. Sunday aprons were a little fancier with maybe a bit of lace trim.

My grandma's aprons were always wide and full with two big pockets and two long strings that tied in the back. She would carry apples and vegetables from the cave. She'd flip it at the kittens to make them behave. She'd stem gooseberries, snap beans, shell peas in her lap and the apron she wore was matched by a cap, but I don't know why, 'cause she only wore it to keep hair from her eyes.

Of course she was known to wipe floured hands down the

sides and unscrew cold-packed tomato jars with it. Sometimes her aprons with their bias tape edge would wipe away my childhood tears. It was comforting to be enfolded in its voluminous width.

When somebody came up the lane she ran to the pantry and back again with a fresh starched apron over her dress. Grandma and her apron were quite a pair and I can see her plainly as though she were there standing erect or in her rocking chair. She was a hardworking soul with a cheery smile.

I guess I inherited her style as a matron, for I'd be completely lost without my apron.

&&&

Fortunate is the child who has a grandmother and happiest is the youngster who is blessed with grandmas on both sides of the family.

Grandmothers are a rare combination of about the best of everything. They are special people. Just ask any grandchild.

Where else can a child find such open, unashamed adoration as in grandmother's eyes? Who else is so indulgent? Where else can he learn right from wrong with such patience and understanding – and the minimum of physical correction?

Fond recollections of my own plump, jolly grandmother include her sparkly blue eyes and her gray hair done up in a bun at the nape of her neck. She looked like a grandma and she acted like one.

Using an old cast iron range, and even later a more up-to-date stove, her sugar cookies made from lard and smelling of vanilla

346

were the fattest, crunchiest creations you ever ate.

She had very little "to do with" during her lifetime, but we never ever went hungry nor without warm home-crocheted scarves and mittens in the wintertime. Her biggest fault, perhaps, was that she shunned better things later when she could have them. The "make-do" theory was too much ingrained.

Without the benefit of much formal schooling, she did know a lot about life not found in books and we were fortunate enough to catch these gems of wisdom during the years we had her with us.

She taught us pride in accomplishment and respect for the rights of others. Through her own life she taught us love. Pettiness, bitterness and meanness were grievances she didn't have time for. She only passed through this life once, but she left her mark.

Grandpa Frederick Abel Leigh

Grandpa Leigh wouldn't have thought much of the Women's Lib movement of today. He firmly believed that a woman's place was in the home. She should have his meals on time, bear his children, supervise and plant the garden, tend to the finances and be able to carry in a bucket of corn cobs to start a fire in the cookstove. He was lucky to have married such a woman.

He did his job in the coal mines, supporting his wife, six sons, and a daughter with a pick and a shovel. When he came home he wanted peace and quiet – or an evening of reading or music on the Victrola. I still remember how he looked coming in from the mine, black with coal dust, wearing his miners cap with the carbide lamp on it and carrying his tin bucket.

He was a proud man and when he changed clothes, he always wore suspenders and long sleeved shirts which were held up above the elbow with elastic bands.

It was always grandpa who delighted us with funny tales of when he was a boy in England, or how he almost died from being stung by a scorpion in Kansas, or helping drive a spike into a railroad in Texas. Some of them weren't true tales, but we could always tell which were which by the twinkle in his blue eyes.

He used to sit near the round heater in the living room and play the Jews Harp. That was before home radio. "Little Brown Jug" and "Casey Jones" were his favorite tunes. He tried his best to teach me the art of Jews Harp playing, but I never did get the twang of it. The metal vibrations against my front teeth were too much.

He showed us how to make music of our own by putting a piece of thin tissue over my mother's ivory comb and humming through it and when all of the neighborhood kids whined into their combs, the adults were sorry they ever contributed to our musical talents.

&&&

Grandpa put great store in Christmas. It was a special time for him and even with his coal miner wages he somehow managed to provide a few extras like big navel oranges for our stockings. We didn't have them very often during the year, but when Christmastime came, we could count on grandpa buying the biggest juiciest ones he could find.

Grandpa loved music and there was always a new record of Christmas carols to be played on the Victrola. His favorite song was Silent Night which he also twanged on his Jews Harp.

One Christmas Grandpa was sent to town to buy staples like flour and sugar and he came back with two real cedar chests (miniatures) filled with the most wonderful candy I ever saw. One for me and one for my sister. He had 'squandered' grandma's meager grocery allowance on these trivials for his granddaughters and he heard about it up into the New Year.

The week before Christmas Day in 1928, when I was eleven years old, grandpa had a paralytic stroke after suffering a fractured skull when a chunk of coal, heavy with slate fell and struck him on the head. He died a few days later and was buried the day before Christmas. We were taught not to blame the mines. Grandma always told us: "It was an accident. He could have been killed any number of ways, like walking across the street or riding on a piece of farm machinery."

I remember that it was the custom then to leave the casket in the home until funeral time, and there it was by the beloved Victrola whose Christmas carol records were stilled this time.

Mother, Pearl Leigh McGuire

M – is for the million things she gave me
O – only means that she's growing old
T – is for the tears she shed to save me
H – is for her heart as pure as gold
E – is for her eyes with love light shining

R – means right, and right she'll always be
Put them all together, they spell Mother, the word that means the
world to me.   *Copyright 1915, Leo Feist, Inc.*

How many years, in May, we sang that song in school. Each of us sang a different letter of the word. I was always a little embarrassed that I got choked up a bit when I sang my part.

There was never any doubt in my mind that I had the most wonderful mother in the world. She was such a pleasant, genteel and uncomplicated sort of person and if anybody ever reaches near perfection as far as motherhood was concerned, she did. As far as I know, everyone who knew her thought she was wonderful too. That's an ultra-high tribute to pay to any mother, but I'm doing it.

Mother never wore the color red, but she liked garnet red carnations, deep crimson peonies, scarlet old-fashioned roses and bright red hollyhocks.

When she was left with the sole care of two small children after my father died suddenly of a heart attack, she moved back to her parent's home in Iowa from Kansas, got a job as a clerk at Frankel's store here and later at Jensen's Clothing store, moving gallantly on, not quitting work until she was past 70. Mr. Jensen was a one-in-a-million boss to my mother and the Jensen family was her idea of wonderful. With no charity, she and my grandparents reared us as best they could.

My sister, Marguerite, died at age 17 after 10 years of suffering with the dread disease, Diabetes. There were no sugarless foods available then, so some cookies were made out of soybean meal and saccharin. I ate them too.

One by one my mother lost most of her family members, but she never once complained that her lot in life was, or should have been, any easier than anyone else. Her philosophy and gentleness, I guess, was the thing that always stayed with me. She taught me many things. I wish I had absorbed more. "Look on the bright side," she'd tell me. She lived this way, or she couldn't have survived the myriad of things that she encountered in life.

She died at the age of 83 still telling us that "things will be better" and with a semblance of a smile on her face.

Father, David Russo McGuire Jr.

Color your life a rosy pink if you and your dad have managed to muddle through the years of the generation gap with such a good rapport that you can truly honor him next Sunday on Father's Day with respect and heartfelt affection.

Consider yourself lucky.

I don't remember my dad. I was about 3 years old and my sister Marguerite only 9 months when he died at the young age of thirty-two and try as I would in the years since, I could never conjure up the faintest recollection of his face. I can't remember standing at the window waiting for him to come home from work, but my mother said I did. I can't recall sitting on his lap or riding in the basket of his bicycle, but I have pictures of these happenings.

He and my mother married in their late twenties, after

meeting in Kansas City, and carrying on a long courtship correspondence for five years while he served in the U.S. Navy until the year 1916. I treasure the pictures of him taken aboard the USS Saratoga and USS Cincinnati and in his Chief Electrician Officer Navy whites in the Philippines, China and Japan. He thought there was a greater future for him in automobiles and the maintenance of them so chose that field in 1916.

It was my father who kept a complete record of my birth and learning progress in a blue satin covered book which I still treasure. He must have been a fine fellow because he married my wonderful mother and because one of my aunts (who didn't like anybody) told me that "Dave McGuire was a prince of a fellow."

Although I don't remember my father's face and I can't recall the sound of his voice nor remember that I was the apple of his eye, somehow I have felt love in my heart for him. I always will.

I'll always remember the look of love in my mother's eyes when she spoke of him. She never remarried. He surely must have been a great fellow.

They say you can't miss what you've never known. I wonder.

May you make someone happy on Father's Day next Sunday.

Compiler's note: David McGuire joined the Navy in 1907 and was with the Great White Fleet on the USS Louisiana (first squadron, first division) that President Theodore Roosevelt sent out to tour the world.

Marjorie and Marguerite McGuire

In my childhood years, my sister, Marguerite, and I always

had something new to wear for Easter. Not because we had to show off at Sunday school on Easter Sunday – we went on the other Sundays too. It was just that a new dress marked the beginning of a new season and the relief from such mundane things as filling the cookstove and living room heater with coal 24 hours a day.

It also meant that, come Easter Sunday we could shed our long underwear like a snake slips off its skin. We couldn't wait to get rid of that beige colored drop seated garment with the stretch ankle-length legs, that had to be folded over in the back so you could pull your lisle stockings up over. It didn't make much difference if it rained or snowed on Easter, it was sort of a promise that was always kept. If we had colds immediately following the long underwear "takeoff" they were always blamed on something else.

My favorite new outfit was a sky blue dress with a wide sash which my grandmother made for me. There was also a lined cape and natural straw hat which had the same color blue ribbon steamers down the back. I called it a new outfit even though most of it came from material that had been in something else. Recycling was nothing new to us.

&&&

I've played a few pranks in my day on April Fools Day. The harmless kind. Grandma always told us never to fool with the kind that frightened people, even momentarily.

We were duly warned after a neighbor girl called everyone to the door by yelling that her dad fell down on the sidewalk and had a broken leg. Her mother was shook up for days and my friend got a shaking even after she shouted "April Fool."

Once my sister and I put sugar in the salt shaker and salt in the sugar bowl and waited at the kitchen table, giggling, while grandma, my mother and an uncle "salted" their coffee and "sugared" their fried eggs.

Once was all we ever pulled that one. Grandma abhorred wasted food. No sense of humor when it came to smart aleck April fool tricks.

&&&

My sister and I got our hair cut at the Continental Barber Shop in those days. We always sat up in the big barber chairs – she in Clarence Gray's chair and I in Mr. Gragg's. Our directions to the barber were always the same: "Please trim my bangs two finger tips above my eyebrows and the sides so the tips of my ears are showing."

The men waiting in the barber chairs for their turns always smiled indulgently, and nodded in agreement when Gray and Gragg deftly shingled the back with the clippers and doused on some 'stuff' from one of the tall colored bottles reflected in the shiny mirrors.

Those were the days when most little girls and boys were getting home haircuts and is probably where the expression "looks like he had his haircut with a bowl over his head" came from.

The reason we were sent to the barber shop was because grandma couldn't make the ornery clippers work without getting all excited; grandpa (whose patience wasn't great) gave up the ordeal; my mother made such a mess of our hair once that we were ashamed to go to school; my two uncles tried their hands at our straight, baby-fine hair with sharp scissors and left to go possum hunting.

Master barbers Gray and Gragg - I will always be grateful to your memories. There were never two nicer men to two little girls.

&&&

I like to think that I don't have an envious, jealous nature … but … I'll have to admit to a twinge or two that my sisters May birthday always sounded better all around than my August month.

For example, my grandma would always say, "Oh, hear the little wrens. They're here for Marguerite's birthday!" Or, "Look at the gorgeous lilacs and tulips and peonies. They're blooming for Marguerite's birthday!"

That was pretty heady stuff for an August person to listen to when all August ever brought to mind was Dog Days, parched grass, temperatures in the 100's and the end of summer vacation. And mosquitoes!

And as for the birthstones! Who wouldn't rather have an elegant emerald than a nondescript brown, cloudy Sardonyx stone?

Hooray for the month of May. We're all enjoying its fabulous beauty.

&&&

There was one neighborhood girl who never wanted anyone else around if she had out-of-town company. My sister and I generally felt very disgruntled if we were sent home and couldn't play our usual games with her 'company'.

We would usually grouch and pout on our front porch steps the rest of the afternoon while friend and company would have a great time. One day my mother said, "Why don't you girls at least pretend you are doing something so interesting that the other girl and her company will feel that they are missing out on something too."

It worked! We got some old quilts, covered the wooden porch chairs with them and made our own tents, laughing loudly enough (of course) so that friend and company would hear us and be intrigued. It wouldn't be long until they couldn't stand the suspense any longer and come over to see what great fun we were having.

So kids, when you are being ignored or left out of the fun across the street, don't sit and fret and look envious. Start doing something interesting, even if it's nothing more than standing out in the yard staring up into a tree. Pretty soon, you'll have company who will wonder what is so interesting up in the tree.

&&&

During my teen years, instead of going to the "Beauty Parlor" to get our hair fixed up, we did it at home. I remember that I used to wash my hair in rain water with a light vinegar rinse, then "put it up" with a solutions of sugar and water to hold the body and give it a slight curl, and then wrap my hair in old bed sheet strips, tied in knots.

&&&

I think I'm the type who likes to be "with it" as I go along. Yet I like to slip into the long ago and be the little girl who hears again the sleigh bells in the snow … builds a snow man … eats apples and popcorn seasoned with bacon drippings … rock a Bye-lo baby doll or a Kewpie doll … and dream by the fire.

OUR SPECIAL CHILDHOOD SHANGRI-LA

It was a wooded serene place of unbelievable beauty.

When my heart is a little tired
And the world seems hard and cool,
My thoughts go back to a quiet hill,
And I remember a small girl's ecstasy.

It is often said that every child needs a secluded spot where he can think his own thoughts, dream his own dreams and commune with God if he wants to. And I believe it.

Three little girls, bosom friends, once knew such a place and still retain the poignant memory of it. These same three friends were together this summer for the first time in many, many years and one of them recalled how we came to find this special place.

Forty years ago it had seemed almost like the legendary

Shangri-la – that wooded place of almost unbelievable beauty nestled in a tiny valley between two steep-sided hills.

We came upon it while exploring an expanse of common pasture land which laid less than a quarter of a mile north of our childhood homes in Centerville. We had crawled under a barbed wire fence and walked through the tall grass. A few cows grazed in the distance and we warily checked them to be sure no bulls were among them.

Suddenly – there it was, our own Brigadoon almost like Hilton's imaginary utopia land in his book, *Lost Horizon*. The sight of it almost took our breath away.

The dry summer pasture seemed to drop away and in its place was an oasis of verdant woods which sloped into a valley of trees and undergrowth. There were hickory nut trees, walnut, weeping willow, poplar, sturdy oaks and the beautiful white birches.

As we made our way down, scratching our bare legs beneath our cotton dresses, we lost complete sight of the noon-day sun and were only aware of the golden shafts of light threaded through the leaves. Faint patches of blue heaven were the only things that looked real and connected us with the world we had just left.

At the very bottom, as though separating the real from the unreal, ran a soundless crystal clear stream. We followed it to a ledge of white, white rock scalloped with velvety moss. We listened to the echoes of the water trickling over the ledge and falling into an opalescent pool. We took off our shoes and let the drops of water fall on our dusty feet. There was no need to communicate with words.

We came there again and again that summer and for a few summers after that. It was our way of leaving the world without dying. It was our refuge from Depression talk among our elders and our respite from the rigors of getting enough to eat and carrying coal for the cook stove.

It was a place of mysterious, compelling beauty and no matter how many times we searched it out, it never lost its magic healing force.

Sometimes we would take thick sandwiches of homemade bread and sit with our backs against a tree and ponder the eternal mysteries of the universe and why wood violets were such a deep purple.

Sometimes we would listen to the songs of birds and the furtive movements of insects and small creatures. We could have been in the jungles of Africa. We could have been in Hawaii or along the Amazon in far off South America. It didn't really matter. We found peace and tranquility briefly, at least, and an indescribable awareness of all things good.

The pungent heady aroma of 'our place' was like ambrosia.

It was not, as some adults might have thought had they known our feelings, an escape from them or from life – a rejection of the everyday world – it was only a place where mortal beings were revived and our faith recharged. It provided the infinite and intangible something we must all find sometime.

We three friends, after many years, got together and visited our Shangri-la again this summer.

The barb wire fence was gone because it wasn't needed to contain cattle grazing on the tall grass. At the right were sheds and machinery used by the Iowa State Highway Commission. A short distance beyond was the tall fence that skirted the little league ball field. To the left were the white buildings marking the county fair grounds. A road cut sharply across the north edge.

We kept on, our middle-aged careful feet finding the way to the green valley almost instinctively. We felt some of the old magic return. Our nostrils quickened to the smell of the woods.

But time, as it has a way of doing, had changed things. The invincible (we thought) elm trees were denuded and without bark and the roots of the mighty oaks were exposed by the ravages of erosion. The winds of forty years had laid other trees willy-nilly across the place where the pool once sparkled.

The white stone of the ledge was broken into jagged pieces and lay discolored in the mud. There was barely a trickle of water to smooth the pebbles.

And the final sacrilege – rusty cans and discarded trash.

We stood in silence. Almost as quickly as it had appeared to us out of nowhere when we were children, it disappeared forever.

We made our way home. The magic was gone, but there are no regrets.   *October 1970*

Chapter 18

MARJORIE'S LITTLE CHERUBS

1974

Several column readers reported that they were disappointed in me last week. They complained that not once did I mention how it felt to be a grandmother for the first time in my whole life. Well, it's like this. I know I am a grandmother and the new grandbaby's name is Marsena. Her mother and Dad – Rosemary and Mike Reed, told me so over the phone. They are in the state of Maine, and I am here in Iowa.

I'm the type who has to hold the baby in her arms, peer down into its tiny face and clasp its little fingers before I'll actually feel like a grandmother. So that's how come!

Wait though, until I receive some pictures. You'll be sorry you happened to run into me in the grocery store when you were in a hurry!

&&&

Since there hasn't been a baby in the family for many a Christmas, I haven't the slightest idea what to buy in the

361

amusement line for a three-month-old. So I read up on it. Apparently, the teddy bears you bought for your own children years ago are still OK. It also appears that rattles would do fine – or mobiles to hang above the crib. It would be a joy to see baby Marsena, but she and her daddy and mother live in Maine, and that's an impossibility this year.

1975

I held my first grandchild for the first time in February. She is little Miss Marsena Reed of Maine.

She was the picture of health with big blue eyes shining. How her mother ever did so well in raising her to five months of age without my counseling I'll never know.

The baby was used to 68 degree room temperature without the warmth of very many outing flannel garments. She slept well in Maine and hadn't even had a cold. That is until she came here where the room temperature was 74 and her grandmother insisted she wear little pajamas with the feet in them.

In Maine she amused herself in her crib when she woke up. Here, her grandmother kept checking to see if she was awake so she could pick her up.

Her throw-away diapers were changed too often by her grandmother (said her mother), who pointed out that the "new type" of diapers would hold a whole glassful of water. (Hadn't I been watching television commercials?)

How Marsena will manage to get raised clear out there on the coast of Maine without me is more than I know!

&&&

362

Our two-story homestead won't be the same after next Friday. Daughter Rosemary and our one-year-old baby granddaughter, Marsena, will be staying here for four months while Mike is deployed to Spain with the Navy.

As I remember 1 year olds, nothing will be left unexamined, or untouched, or probably untasted.

I've had to find a new place for the sprays and insecticides that formerly stayed on shelves under the kitchen sink.

I've had to put the box holding the cat and dog food up higher in the pantry.

I've moved my little china teapot and cups and saucers that I played with a half a century ago up to higher grounds.

We've put a high latch on the kitchen door that leads to a steep flight of stairs to the basement.

I've even vacuumed the living room rug because if she puts everything in her mouth, she'd have a field day on it.

And the head of the house (the baby's grandfather) rescued my old iron baby bed from the garage and sanded off three or four coats of paint and so far has the primer coat on. It's quite a wonderful bed when all is said and done and I wish her sweet dreams in it.

We're also rigging up a "play box" full of odds and ends of toys and stuffed animals that I boxed up years ago. There are tin dishes, blocks, stuffed giraffes, teddy bears and things to make a noise with.

We have also been advised by Marsena's mother that they don't consistently use the word "No" to her. ("No," Rosemary maintains, is a negative word which children react adversely to, then later use against you every chance they get!)

We are supposed to say "Leave it alone."

I hope I'll remember.

Then to make things more interesting here and make the McConnell rafters ring even more, our second daughter Nancy and her husband Dave are expecting a new arrival any day now. This will be their first child also.

&&&

Little Marsena, has now moved with her mother into their own home in Ottumwa. Daddy is scheduled to arrive there the last of this month ending his 4-year Navy stint.

For those of you who may have wondered how the past four months have turned out with the little one around my house, I'll tell you.

I learned a lot. I'm older and somewhat wiser.

Marsena was one year old when she arrived here last September. She was equipped with big blue eyes, sweeping lashes, an infectious smile and a pair of soft little arms. (When you patter about the house getting into mischief, you need all the charms you can get.)

With Marsena came a certain doctor's book which related chapter by chapter how to raise children. I hadn't counted on Dr. Spook (as we came to call him) but we came to know him, if not love him. We heard just about everything he had to say about almost every facet of child-rearing. It's too bad he couldn't hear everything we had to say.

In the first place you don't say "No No" to a child. There is a better way. You say, "This is grandmother's personal wristwatch." Or you say, "This is Marsena's personal teddy bear." This way they learn what is whose and most certainly will NOT grow up saying "No No" to everything you ask them to do.

Then we were given a choice. We could either put everything worth anything up out of reach and tie the cupboard and buffet drawers shut. Or ... we could leave everything where it is and instruct which is personal and which is not.

We chose to move everything from the dresser to higher grounds after a painting foray with the lipstick and tie the cupboard doors shut with a shoestring after a squirting spree with the window washing liquid.

Dr. "Spook" says that it makes a child nervous and frustrated to learn more than one thing at a time. If they learn to stay out of the garbage container in three months time, for instance, then you can't expect them to leave the telephone alone.

Children should have books and magazines that they can tear up into shreds. She never quite distinguished successfully which magazines and papers were which.

However, the good doctor and I agree on one thing. A young child's imagination, inquisitiveness, perseverance and the development of the five senses should be developed.

For example, their sense of touch is important. Touching a lace tablecloth should show them the difference in the feel of lace from the feel of artificial flowers in a $5.50 floral basket. They just don't feel the same, you know, even after the hundredth time.

In a small way, a tiny child can come across the law of gravity when she drops the car keys into the stool. Right there she can see that car keys are heavier and hit the bottom faster than sheets of toilet tissue. We know that, but one year olds have to learn by doing.

Then there's the matter of foods and the eating process. The little person is perched in the highchair, banging the spoon on the tray. Then comes the chopped ham, mashed potatoes and pureed peas. Out spews the peas in a green stream. For someone who just swallowed two chunks of Gravy Train in her mouth minutes before, you find that there is no accounting for taste.

The mashed potatoes are gobbled down.

When she's through, she will throw her spoon down. And when her Pink Panther bowl is empty, she'll throw it down too. Mother explained that this is her way of letting you know that dinner is over. How very clever, I thought, as I wiped up the highchair, the floor and the wall.

&&&

It has been a long time since we've had little people around our Christmas tree and thus the decorations usually stay where they are placed with the exception of the few baubles that bend the bough and break on the floor.

But this year, 15 month old Marsena, will be here for Christmas with us. I can see in my mind's eye what is going to happen to the decorations (and maybe even the tree), but maybe the brightness of her big blue eyes will be worth it. Marsena is a very active, inquisitive child who feels it is necessary to check out everything for herself and the wonder of the Christmas tree

366

with all its glitter will surely "get the works" like everything else does.

The works, where this little darling is concerned, means that it will get the durability test, the taste test and the take-it-apart test. The decorations and the tree itself are predicted to fail the tests. We're betting on Marsena.

Her daddy, who is deployed to Spain with the Navy, will be missing the sight of little Marsena eating a cube or two of dog food, or pulling the books out of the bookcase, or climbing up on her little chair to reach the leaves of the plants; the skinned nose, the head bumps from falling off the couch, or the gleeful look while holding up the cat with two little fists clamped (lovingly) around its neck.

Daddy is also missing his little gal's sugar and spice and everything nice look right after her bath ... running to meet him with a squeal of delight ... sitting primly while a Raggedy Ann book is read ... and seeing a tiny pajama-clad figure asleep in her crib.

Dr. Spock is certainly right about one thing. These tykes are a vision to behold!! The angel on your treetop can't hold a candle to the one under the tree.

Our other grandchild, two-month old Chad will be watching the season's lights from someone's lap this year.

&&&

Marsena's fascination with pocketbooks began early and every visiting lady brought one. Her mother bought her a tiny 'personal' one of her own, but nothing ever stayed in it. Every time little fingers unclasped a visiting lady's purse, I would forget and say "No No" and forget also about my bad knee and race over to unhand the pocketbook. Forgive me, doctor.

Several generations grew up without Sesame Street, but I don't know how. The little tyke's mother watched it with her so she could keep abreast of how much her daughter was learning. So far Marsena has learned to jig to the theme song, sing with Ernie, giggle with the little girl with the yellow braids, watch for the Grouch to pop up out of the trash can and count to three with the Count. (The first time I saw the Count he looked so much like a vampire bat that he scared me.)

But I will say, lest you might think otherwise, that Marsena's mother is a calm, patient person who believes in explaining things to her. Marsena is loved and she knows it. She is outgoing, friendly, happy and not inhibited by too many rules or severe punishment.

About the only time in four months that her mother got upset and delivered a swat to her posterior was the day she pulled herself up to the card table, grabbed a handful of jigsaw puzzle pieces and ran with them to the garbage can where they were mixed well with a coating of bacon grease and coffee grounds.

We miss the flurry of activity at our house now. We miss the welcoming shouts and reading Raggedy Ann over and over. We miss little arms that held tight and goodnight kisses that smeared our faces.

I sort of miss Dr. Spook too. I came to depend on him to know if I was doing the right thing about something ... making the right decision ... taking the right step. It's hard to be left on your own, but I did learn a lot in four months time.

I should phone my granddaughter and tell her how much I miss her, but then, she probably took the phone off the hook.

1976

My sense of timing has never been anything to brag about, and after a day's visit with my oldest daughter, Rosemary, I am convinced that it will never be worth a hoot!

I arrived at her house and expected to be greeted by my little granddaughter, Marsena, waving from the doorway. Instead, I spied six little noses pressed against the glass.

"I'm babysitting today, mom," she explained. "Hope you don't mind." Of course not, I love children.

It seems that Mrs. So and So didn't have anybody to leave B.J. and Suzie Q. with and her mother-in-law wouldn't keep them that day. B.J. is 4 years old and Suzie Q. is 2. And furthermore, she could only afford to pay 50 cents an hour for both, not one. I was sympathetic until I found out later that her husband owns a lucrative business, they have two cars and a pickup camper, a boat, and houseful of new furniture.

Then, as if by instinct, a neighbor asked if she could also bring her two-year-old twins, Bubba and Sissy and 3 year old Mark over from 12 noon until 10:30 p.m. Like Mrs. So and So, Mrs. Such and Such was also poor and couldn't afford more than 25 cents apiece per hour. That included snacks and a meal, of course.

Six little darlings, all under four years old and all under one roof.

Rosemary's house has a playroom with red carpeting, bean bag chair, inflatable couch, and a low play table. There is a chest of toys, games, stuffed animals. Excellent set-up, right? Wrong. That red carpet will last forever. Nobody plays there.

You probably realize that whenever you've got brothers and sisters together, there's bound to be trouble. They fight. B.J. found that by tackling sister Suzie Q around the neck he could make her so mad she'd scream. "I'm just loving her," B.J. told us, his eyes innocently looking skyward. I expected to see a halo and wings sprouting.

Cry me a river

When Bubba cried, his twin sister cried just out of habit and brother Mark joined in. Then granddaughter Marsena cried and B.J. and Suzie Q. cried. Johnny Ray could have used this sextette as background sobbing for his record "Cry".

I even tried the old story book trick by reading Raggedy Ann to the little cherubs. The book never got finished because I only have two legs and one lap and the scramble for priority seating obscured any adventure Raggedy Ann might have been having.

"Why don't I take them out in the backyard and let them play on the swing set?" I ventured in desperation. After ten minutes of refereeing four toddlers all trying to sit in one swing seat and two chasing a cat down the alley, I gave up and ushered them back into the house.

I resisted the urge to lock them all in the playroom.

Don't say "nap"

It finally occurred to Rosemary that a nice little nap before supper would be just the ticket. I said I could sure use one, but unfortunately, she didn't mean me. It is truly amazing how the word 'nap' sent the motley crew into hysterics. Heretofore, they hadn't paid attention to a single word we'd said like "stop that," "don't" and "potty."

Naptime was a fiasco. No one slept. B.J. almost dozed off but sister decided to get even with him by jumping on his stomach. Everybody jumped on B.J. They all cried.

During the afternoon we ran a combination restroom and snack bar. Two boxes of Girl Scout cookies and a large can of fruit punch were consumed. Now it was suppertime. We decided on homemade spaghetti which was not only economical for feeding eight hungry mouths, but temporarily ended chaos as everybody dug in … or shoveled onto the floor. In my ignorance, I hadn't counted on six spaghetti smeared faces, shirts, jeans and a floor to scrub.

Luckily, Rosemary remained her usual calm self and patiently gave each child a bath and put on clean clothing.

Mrs. So and So called with the cheery news that she had to stop at the supermarket and wouldn't be after the kids until about 11 p.m. or so.

The remainder of the evening was a shambles of jigsaw puzzles, television, running through the house, fighting, crying, wetting pants and eating crackers.

At 10 o'clock I locked myself in the playroom. A bean-bag chair never felt so good.

&&&

My little granddaughter had her 2nd birthday Tuesday. She celebrated it at our house and we made homemade ice cream for the occasion and an angelfood cake.

You've read about the little mischief maker in my writings before. She's always on the go and into everything.

Her latest escapade almost ruined her birthday refreshments — she ladled a heaping spoonful of rock salt all over the freshly hand-cranked ice cream when the lid was off and no one was looking. (A two-year-old hand is quicker than the eye every time.)

&&&

And how was your Christmas?

Ours was fine at daughter Rosemary's home.

We chose two-year-old Marsena's toys carefully and for grandson Chad's gifts we also chose one-year-old recommended toys.

And what happened? Marsena found an empty coffee can and pounded on it with a spoon, keeping time to Christmas music on television. Chad found an old pull toy in the play box and even though it was minus one wheel, dragged it around all day, refusing to let go of it.

1977

Had little Marsena with me this past holiday weekend and learned quite a bit about 2 ½ year old minds. I found out that child-proof bottles are only adult-proof after all. (Nothing drastic, just an experiment.)

At our house we keep aspirins in an old-fashioned bottle because we can't readily open those 'push down and twist' creations without sawing off the lid.

During the weekend, I noticed that Marsena could twist a knob off the buffet drawer in nothing flat, put together an intricate Sesame Street Ernie jigsaw puzzle, and take a flashlight apart and put it together.

So, ha ha, I thought, let's see what little twister can do with a child-proof green bottle (empty, of course).

She sat on the floor, cross-legged, and I sat on the couch. She turned the bottle over a few times, noting this and that about it. Ah ha, I thought, childproof is what it is. But here she was, handing me the lid and the bottle, "Here, grandma," she said and scampered off to get the broom handle to lift the lock on the front door that she couldn't reach.

But without Marsena here now, I'll have to resort to the old crowbar to lift the next "push down and twist" childproof lid.

And I'd better start watching Sesame Street this week.

&&&

We had both little grandchildren in our home this past weekend and let me tell you, they are the busiest, most energetic youngsters you ever saw. Marsena will be 3 years old in September and Chad will be 2 in September. One year may not make much difference when you're 50 something, but one year's difference in children just stirs things up.

Every toy that Chad would pick up, Marsena would grab. If

Chad went to sit down in the little chair, his cousin would sprint to it first.

Finally he got the hang of the game and started grabbing, pushing, and outrunning her. "Share," we commanded. "No," they chorused. The day finally ended in fisticuffs, tears and general chaos.

But just about bedtime, when little 'jamies were on, I glanced over at the big chair, and there sat two little cousins, arms entwined, looking at their favorite Uncle Remus story book. The 'togetherness' almost got to me as I wiped the perspiration from my brow. I really love those two grandchildren.

&&&

It was Marsena's 3rd birthday today and among her gifts was a "Play-Doh Beauty Shop" playset. My, it was fun. You stuff play dough into a variety of head shaped people and crank a crank and out comes dough out of little holes all over the heads. With plastic scissors, razors and combs you can trim the "hair" and get it all over the kitchen table. It even has a miniature broom and dustpan to collect the doughy squiggles.

One nice thing about it, it tastes terrible, and you can use it over and over. Another plus – it kept her busy while we mixed up her pink birthday cake.

&&&

Our second grandchild, little Chad Ewing of Unionville, Iowa, turned two years old this September.

He rides horseback with his mother Nancy on her Appaloosa

374

mare, helps feed corn to Grandpa Ewing's hogs, listens and dances to Country Western music, goes to livestock and farm sales and already has two fox hunts (Soap Creek-style) under his belt.

&&&

Instead of staying home this week doing nothing, I'm spending Thanksgiving week in Ottumwa at daughter Rosemary's home doing plenty. One evening I babysat three-year-old Marsena.

Now I know how American tourists feel when they see "Yankee Go Home" signs abroad!

Most of the time Marsena and I have a loving, compatible relationship. (Possibly that's because I don't take over her life very often.) She likes grandmother's cookies and the way I overact when I read her storybooks. I like her young enthusiasm and how quickly she learned to love all kinds of music.

It's only the direct confrontation we had at bedtime that caused the commotion. I tried to get her into sleepy time (her mother has no trouble), but she really did a con job of excuses on me. Three hours later she was still wide-eyed and bushy-tailed. When she finally decided that I meant business and nothing else would work, she quietly marched out of her room, looked me in the eye and gave me an ultimatum: "Grandmother, go home. If you can't be nice, you'll have to go home."

If they ever have another child psychology course at Indian Hills College, I'd better be the first student to enroll.

&&&

I always considered myself a reasonably affectionate person, yet I expect others to sense that I like them without touching or physical contact. I love my children, and they know it, yet perhaps I should have learned to be more demonstrative.

I remember as a child that I used to wince at family reunions when I was grabbed and lifted off the ground by a certain burly, tobacco chewing relative who planted a sickening kiss on my mouth. I didn't like being smothered in Aunt Maggie's ample bosom much better. I usually ran the gauntlet as fast as I could at these family gatherings.

So now, who has two darling little grandchildren whose parents are encouraging them to kiss everybody goodbye? Little arms are raised and encircle necks and little kisses are planted on the cheeks of every aunt, uncle and cousin in the room. So far they are doing it willingly, but one of these days they'll meet up with a certain burly, tobacco chewing relative. I hope they handle the situation with more dignity than I did.

1978

I was going to take a picture of my two young grandchildren this past weekend, but when they came to visit I was astonished to note that both Marsena and Chad had scratched up faces.

It seems that Marsena had tried to stuff their pet cat into a box and the cat didn't cotton to the idea and gave her a scratch on the cheek.

Chad, his mother explained, had somehow gotten hold of daddy's razor and shaved a couple of places on his chin.

No pictures.

&&&

We're getting closer and closer to the birth of a new little grandbaby in our family. June 24th maybe. Daughter Nancy and husband, David Ewing, are taking the whole deal very calmly and attended the four-session Parent Series provided for expectant parents by St. Joseph's hospital. Little Chad, who will be three in September, seems to know that something special is going to happen. Especially when dad and mommy got out his old baby crib, set it up again and scoured up his old high chair.

&&&

Daughter Nancy has passed her due date and even the 4th of July. We'll take care of two-year-old Chad while mommy is in the hospital, and we've been all psyched up to do a good job when the big event occurs. But now we've eaten all the homemade cookies out of the cookie jar, and drank all the Kool-Aid.

Brian Arrives

We have a new grandbaby and he's the cutest little sweetie I ever saw. Well, almost, anyway. (I qualify that statement in deference to my own five babies and the other two grandchildren!)

Baby Brian was born during the night, after a day of buoyant activity for his mother. She had been, as her husband Dave said, "a ball of fire." She cleaned her house, came into Centerville to Shop; washed clothes and hung them on lines to dry, took me uptown shopping, brought in the clothes and helped with supper. In between times, she corralled two-year-old Chad after his numerous friendly excursions to neighborhood yards.

We should have known.

They left for home in Unionville about 7:30 p.m. and I thought, well maybe tomorrow. It wasn't an hour until the phone rang and we were alerted that "the time had come" and to make up a bed for Chad.

It was wise that she followed the Dr. McConville's advice to "get to the hospital when you know for sure" because three hours later he was born.

So you know how it is. We've held him, looked at his tiny fingers and toes, diapered him and pronounced him a doggone cute and very smart baby. (Didn't he smile at me?)

I hear that his other grandparents, Donald and Ruby Ewing of Unionville feel the same way.

And as for brother Chad, he's impressed with the whole thing. So impressed that he wanted to give Brian a swig of his grape Kool-Aid.

&&&

For Christmas my husband bought a Crow Shoot game for Chad and Marsena. I'm sure he remembered how much fun our own children had with the harmless pop guns that shoot little corks (and how much fun HE had).

&&&

'Twas the night after Christmas and all thru the house ... a colorful collage of wrapping paper, silver bows, fruit cake crumbs, scotch tape and corks from the Crow Shoot games.

This year Christmas was at our house. We always think of our house as rather spacious, especially now that there are just the two of us at home. But somehow when everybody is at home for Christmas, the walls shrink and the tall ceilings aren't sound proof.

My part of Christmas was preparing the feast. I planned it carefully knowing each member's special likes and dislikes. (I had cranberry sauce anyway, even if I'm the only one who'll eat it).

I did fine until I tried to put the large beef roast and capon roasters into the oven at the same time. I ended up putting the beef roast and capon side by side into the big turkey roaster.

When it came time to make gravy, I had a weird blend of juices in the roasting pan.

"Which kind of gravy do you want me to make?" I asked the hungry family who didn't suspect that the meats weren't in separate pans.

"Both kinds," they chorused.

Well, that's what they got, capon-beef gravy (which I'd never made before) and it was pronounced great. What they didn't know didn't seem to hurt them.

Gifts were unwrapped, bragged on, and stacked in piles. It was a nice Christmas. Third grandchild, baby Brian, was no trouble at all. He can't crawl yet or lift the baubles off the tree. He can't fight or knock somebody's block castle down.

Next Christmas will come around.

1979

There was a time I could jump rope with the best of them. But the other day I was going to teach Marsena, four years old, how to master the simple art of rope skipping, and fouled up the whole thing as well as my ego.

Confidently, I correctly measured up a length of clothes line rope. No other rope will do. I stood on the middle of it, raising my arms straight ahead at my waist to get the exact amount I'd need. I wrapped the extra rope around my wrists just like we used to do.

With a swing of the rope and a mighty leap (like I used to), my feet didn't clear the rope. In fact, I heard the sickening slap of the rope against the tops of my shoes. My daughter chuckled behind her hand, but my granddaughter spoke the truth. "Grandmother," said the child, "you don't know how to do it either. You're supposed to jump OVER the rope like the bigger kids do."

Well, so much for jumping rope. But I'll bet I can still play a mean game of jacks ... if my fingers aren't too stiff. I intend to practice my ones and twos out on the back porch where no one can see me.

&&&

Grandson, Chad, almost won the foot race for three-year-olds at the Unionville, Iowa, 4th of July celebration. He almost did. There never has been a doubt in my mind since that child was two years old that he is as fast as greased lightning.

So when he began "training" two weeks ago for the Big Race,

380

with his mother as Coach, I felt right then that the other little kids would have to fly low to beat Sir Chad. That boy runs like a Soap Creek hound chasing a coyote!

"Coach" drilled sonny on his ready-set-go starts and cautioned him not to look back over his shoulder to see how the other kids were doing. She even warned him not to go back if he lost a shoe.

Came the big day at Unionville. Chad awoke very excited, not about the race, but because he was going to eat pancakes for breakfast under the big tent. The Coach also awoke exited, but about the race and couldn't eat any pancakes.

As I said at the beginning, grandson ALMOST won the race. As he neared the finish line, friendly little Chad spotted someone he knew and stopped to chat about the big fish he caught.

Oh well, Coach. You forgot to tell the lad about the worst racing pitfall of all … sideline distraction!

&&&

I've noticed in the Indian Hills College brochure of night classes that there is a least one adult night class I should take. The first one is titled "Coping with pre-school children."

Last Sunday afternoon while daughter Nancy and her dad went over to Mystic to play in the cribbage tournament, I babysat with grandsons Chad, 3, and Brian, 7 months. The tournament lasted from 1 p.m. to around 7 p.m. and I was one tired grandmother when they finally pulled in the drive.

I don't know why I think I have to watch them every minute. How their mother ever gets anything done, I wonder. I read books to Chad, over and over, built corrals for horses and went on imaginary coyote hunts with hound dogs. He's eating every five minutes or drinking and probably throws up when he gets home.

Brian is crawling now and picking up everything on the floor and putting it in his mouth. He also wets his diapers and drinks a considerable amount of milk. He can hold his own bottle, but feeding time just gave me another excuse to hold him ... and rock him.

I don't baby-sit very often because they take care of their own children, but when I do I really don't mind at all.

But as Chad told his mother when she stepped in the door last Sunday, "Grandmother is very tired." Yes I was, and all because I don't know hope to cope with preschoolers anymore.

&&&

Grandson Brian sat in his high chair watching the candle glow on his first birthday cake. We, and his other grandparents, Don and Ruby Ewing, wondered if he would reach for the candle. We need not have been concerned. He was too fascinated by the camera flashing.

&&&

Grandson Chad Ewing (no relation to the infamous, rich Dallas Ewing clan on TV) at four years old is showing more and more that he uses his head for more than a place to put his baseball cap.

The other night, while his grandpa Ewing was visiting at his

382

house, Chad's daddy tried repeatedly to put him to bed. He wanted to stay up and visit, being the type who doesn't want to miss out on anything.

Chad used every usual excuse for staying up ... bathroom, drink, starvation, bedtime story, owls hooting. To no avail.

Silence. Then he came racing out of his bedroom and with all the theatrical expertise of a seasoned stage actor announced, "Daddy, I ALMOST saw a mouse!"

The ALMOST was enough for grandpa Ewing, who decreed that such careful honesty out of the mouth of a child deserved to be rewarded. Little Chad got to listen to stories of hunting raccoons and pheasants until he fell asleep on the couch.

1980

As I've said, time and time again, and I know I'm right, running a Pre-school or nursery school won't be a vocation I'll take up. I like youngsters and have a real nice rapport with them, yet somehow I can't get it all together when I'm in charge of even three kiddies.

Take last Sunday's babysitting for instance.

I was to take care of Marsena, 5, Chad, 4, and little Brian, who is a year and a half, while their mothers did a few errands.

The two older ones were told they could play outside on the front porch. Brian was to stay inside with me and amuse himself with the toy box.

Glancing outside, I could hear jubilant laughter and saw two little children with brooms sweeping the front porch. What sweet, darling, industrious grandchildren, I thought, sweeping away the winter's grime for grandmother.

I made the mistake of trying to make coleslaw and set the dining room table for supper.

Of course, husband and son-in-law were supposed to be keeping an eye out too, but that's not easy when you're glued to the kitchen chairs with coffee cups in your hands and deep in men-talk.

As it turned out, Chad and Marsena had emptied the dried dirt that was in all the left over flower pots onto the cement porch floor, mixed it with generous helpings of snow and behold – instant Winter Mud. The gleeful sweeping sent the goop down the steps and half-way down the sidewalk.

Their astonished mothers couldn't understand the situation when they came home. I don't quite understand it myself.

&&&

While spending a week at daughter Rosemary's home in Ottumwa, I attended a summer chorus program presented by children chosen from Ottumwa elementary schools, kindergarten through sixth grade. It is an annual project.

Marsena was one of the kindergartners taking part in the kindergarten-first grade segment directed by Ruth Seim. The stage of Ottumwa Heights auditorium fairly came alive as those little folks sang, danced, played marimbas and "performed" such numbers as "Animal Crackers In My Soup" and "Little White Duck."

Things went along just fine until their last number.

All of a sudden the auditorium fire alarm started clanging.

384

The teacher kept right on playing the piano, louder and louder, and the youngsters kept right on belting out their song, louder and louder.

The audience looked around the auditorium, surprised and very annoyed by the clanging, but nobody left their seats.

By the time the kiddies had filed off the stage, row by row, the clanging stopped.

The announcer came before the microphone.

"Well, folks," he announced, "we checked out the building and there is no fire. We sure teach children how to read in Ottumwa schools! A young lad read the word PULL under the fire alarm and he did!!"

And speaking of Ottumwa summer chorus, it was evident that the older the group, the less animated the singers became. By the time the sixth graders sang their numbers, they were standing stiffly, arms by their sides, and no expression whatsoever on their faces.

The audience sensed the contrast between the tiniest children's excitement and the older group's boredom. The only time the bigger ones livened up was during a disco number which was accompanied by drum playing and marimbas. This they liked. And so did we. There's a lesson for music teachers here somewhere.

&&&

It won't be long now until the grand and glorious Fourth of July. (I'm assuming, of course, that it's still on the 4th and still in July.) Judging from the firecrackers resounding in the night, we're off to a pretty loud start.

Last 4th of July we bought a few silver and gold sparklers for the grandchildren and what do you know? The young ones were afraid of the things that lit up and shot sparks. (These are the same kiddies who watch Star Wars!)

So naturally, not to waste them, we adults ran around the yard waving our arms to show the kiddies what great fun sparklers were.

&&&

Our little grandson, Brian Ewing, had his 2nd birthday July 13th and we were invited to Unionville for cake and ice cream.

Now Brian, unlike his four-year-old brother, Chad, isn't the excitable type. He's patient, deliberate, and takes his time looking people over before he offers them his friendship.

Therefore, it wasn't much of a surprise that when his pile of gifts and cards were placed before him, he was happy, but methodical.

His brother and several of his small cousins clustered around him on the floor for the exciting present opening.

Did Brian rip off paper and ribbons rapid-fire?

Nope, much to the disgust of his young onlookers, Brian proceeded to open each card, ooh and aahed at the pictures on them, and passed them around so each guest could see. He did the same way with his gifts.

By the time he came to his last gift, a toy saxophone, the suspense was maddening to the children and they all dived in to tear the package apart.

And as for the two blue candles on his birthday cake? He blew them out one by one, of course.

&&&

Marsena had a birthday party last Sunday for her 6th birthday.

Fourteen little guests were invited and three "stowaways" also came uninvited but were welcomed. Marsena's Aunt Nancy went to Ottumwa to help with the big event.

According to Nancy, the birthday was a smashing success.

There was shouting, screaming, eating, spilling and crying … all those goodies that make up a successful kid party.

The crying occurred when the game of Musical Chairs was played and someone was always being "left out" with no chair. They also played Pin the Tail on the Donkey.

The Raggedy Ann cake that her friend Shannon's mother made was quite a hit and the Loot Bags they took home soothed excited youngsters.

&&&

Ottumwa just ended its annual Oktoberfest celebration and it was termed a success by the Courier. Oktoberfest is an Ottumwa crowd pleaser and nearly always a financial success as well.

Unlike Centerville's Pancake Day, this event apparently owes its popularity to beer and "brats" (German sausage).

I spent about a week in the Ottumwa home of my daughter Rosemary, and came away coddled and babied to no end!

You can tell I'm not used to being "spoiled" by the number of times I apologized for being waited on.

I didn't even have to cook. Somehow somebody else's meals always taste better. Tacos, for instance, are something we never have at my home.

But you can relax. The babying is over now and I'm back in the old routine. It was kind of neat while it lasted.

&&&

I received a real "brainstorm" the other day. I thought up a pre-Christmas gift I'd like to give my two daughters. It's something I never had years ago.

I'd like for them to have a long weekend away from the mundane responsibilities of motherhood ... washing dishes, fixing meals and wiping little noses. They could go out of town and stay overnight in a snazzy hotel.

It was a great idea. I was proud of myself. When I told the girls about it their eyes brightened. Indeed, they got so carried away with the whole thing that they jumped up and said, "Las Vegas, here we come!"

Well, I didn't exactly have that long a weekend in mind, nor was that much outlay of cash included in my brainstorm.

When they came back to earth I knew they had cooled down when they soberly asked, "Who'd take care of the three kids?"

"I would," I answered confidently although it was beginning to dawn on me that I hadn't delved too deeply into that aspect of the plan.

The girls are going to "talk it over" this week and let me know. In the meantime, I'm assuring myself that surely I can manage three grandchildren, ages 6, 5 and 2 for two days and one night with the assurance that I can give them back and rest for six weeks afterwards.

The daughters had better grab the offer in a hurry. I only get brainstorms like that around Christmastime!

1981

Daughter Rosemary has taken good care of me at her home during my recuperation. She is probably correct when she ascertained that had I gone directly home from the hospital I would not have rested properly.

With six year old Marsena in first grade at Wildwood school, we had time to talk things over again.

But, oh, those Saturday mornings!

Who gets up at the crack of dawn to watch four consecutive hours of Cartoons? Yes, Marsena and every kid she knows.

I'll most likely get clobbered by every mother with young children for daring to be critical of Saturday morning cartoons, which are apparently the ultimate in babysitting for an entire morning. They are also used to elicit good behavior "or else I'll turn off the TV."

After one Saturday morning of Fat Albert, Plastic Man, Scooby Doo, Tarzan, The Flintstones, Bugs Bunny, The Lone Ranger, and one whole hour of Popeye and Bluto trading knockouts, I wished it was summer so I could go out and sit under the apple tree.

They even threw in a violent space cartoon in which the villain used an imitation voice of sinister old Peter Lorre who'd likely be flattered if he hadn't been dead so long.

Ho hum.

Rosemary, on the other hand, ignored the chest pounding shrieks of Tarzan and got her Saturday work done besides putting lunch on the table.

&&&

Marsena confided to me the other day that she and "Jimmie" were going to get married someday.

Last year in kindergarten she liked another little boy and would stand out in the front yard waving coyly as he nonchalantly went by on his bicycle.

Reminds me of her grandmother of yesteryear.

Ah yes, I liked a different boy every year, fickle miss that I was.

I'm planning to be back home after having been in Ottumwa for about a month now.

Marjorie passed away on Mothers Day 1981. Her daughter Nancy bore two more children - Richard Ewing (1981) and Jason Ewing (1984)

Chapter 19

TO MARGE WITH LOVE

Marjorie Louise MConnell, 63, a longtime and well-known resident of Centerville died in Ottumwa Hospital early Sunday, May 10, 1981. Her death was attributed to congestive heart failure.

She became critically ill a few weeks ago, and was hospitalized at University Hospitals in Iowa City. After being released from the hospital there, she went to the home of a daughter, Rosemary, in Ottumwa, and then later was taken to Ottumwa Hospital, where death occurred.

Born in 1917, in Kansas City, Kansas, she was the daughter of David Russo and Martha Pearl Leigh McGuire. She graduated from Centerville High School in 1935, and in 1940 she was married to Ira Lowell McConnell in Centerville.

Before her marriage, she worked for a time as society editor of the Iowegian. In 1968 she returned to the Iowegian as society editor, retiring a few years later to care for her mother. In 1972, she returned to the Iowegian and for several years she had written a popular column, "Talk, Travel and Tidbits".

She had won awards for the column, the most recent one being an honorable mention at the Iowa Press Women's convention in April of this year.

She was a member of First United Methodist Church, the Ruth UMW Circle, the National and Iowa Associations of Press Women, General Federation of Women's Clubs, Alpha Study Club, the American Legion Auxiliary, the National Rural Letter Carriers Auxiliary and the Sugar Belles Club.

Preceding her in death were her parents, one sister and three sons, Chris, Craig, and David.

Excerpts, Centerville Daily Iowegian

Bill Weaver, Columnist

Monday was not a good day, Marjorie McConnell died.

To those of us who worked with her, Marjorie will be remembered as a charming lady who always offered a helping hand, who constantly displayed a smile, who was genuinely concerned about people and who was about as nice a person as you'd ever want to meet.

To you, our readers, she will be remembered as an outstanding writer.

Marjorie developed good new friendships with the men and women in the composition room. Despite her elder-stateswoman status in that department, Marjorie blended in as "one of the gang."

The last column she wrote for us was published this April. Her simple thoughts often were her best. For the record, her last words in the Iowegian said, "Some of us look both ways before crossing a one-way street."

Marjorie encountered more personal tragedy than should be burdened on 100 families, let alone just one. But shouldered it all, best she could, knowing she had many friends to which she could turn to in times of sorrow.

To miss her cheerful attitude and refreshing smile, to never again read her simple, yet lovingly-written comments each week, seems to make my job here somewhat less exciting.

But we go on. As Marjorie knew so well, no matter what happens in a newspaper office – no matter who dies or no matter what machine breaks down – there's always another newspaper waiting to be printed. This newspaper was waiting to be printed when she died on Sunday. It's a shame that this one, or any one, must carry the obituary of such a wonderful person.

Centerville Iowegian

Edwyna Payton Fenton, Columnist

A sad FAREWELL to a blithe spirit in the death of Marjorie ... too young to die ... too capable in adding FEELINGS to Life in general ... We won't see her likes again on the pages of the Iowegian ... So well liked by different types of people ... Maybe that is what being a Success is all About ... Hers was a valiant spirit, which had endured devastating experiences ... but she came back with a quip of humor.

I remember how proud Marjorie and I were of our columnist standing in a survey the Iowegian ran. Now we didn't gloat, because neither of us were gloaters, but we were proud. Wasn't it a pity Marjorie had to go on to her writing in the skies, when she added a lot of happiness to life? She was a really good person to the very core. One could write a book on Marge's virtues and her kindness to others – she will be missed.

Centerville Iowegian

Gladys DePuy, Columnist,

Those of us who were fans of Marjorie McConnell's column, will remember for a long time the poignant stories of by-gone days and the humor of present days that were in each of her columns.

We here at the office were glad that she knew of her recent column award before her passing. Incidentally, the judge's critique of those three columns was this: "Easy reading, good way with words. Subject variety interesting – style fun to read."

I am sure that her many fans would echo that one hundred percent.

It was a shock to learn of Marjorie's death. I just hadn't realized that her illness was so serious. And, as so often happens, the death of someone brings thoughts of opportunities neglected. Marjorie and I had often talked of getting into the little Duster and driving out to spend an afternoon with Theda Long at her lakeside home, but somehow or another, the opportunities to do so were passed by, and now it's too late. How often this happens.

Thursday's Entertainment Page will be empty without the wit and wisdom of Marjorie McConnell and her Talk, Travel and Tidbits.

Centerville Iowegian

Mildred Cathcart, Columnist

How does one express such a loss in words? Marge was a witty columnist, a great lady, and an interesting and loyal friend. As writers, Marge, we write "The End" but to you it is a wonderful new beginning. For us you leave behind, we can only say, "Farewell, God bless you, and we will miss you."

Centerville Iowegian

Robert K. Beck, Editor-Publisher

Marge had her own special way with words. I always told her she had a "personal unique style." That, of course, was a rather broad definition, but the way she expressed things was always homey, down to earth, and just Marge.

I knew her first as Marge McGuire, and later as a pretty high schooler. The next thing I knew, she was working for my father at the society desk at the Iowegian.

She quickly established a reputation as a gifted writer, especially when it came to features. She always found that special something in a story, that little extra dimension that brought a report to life. Her writing had what I call vitality. She would weave the words to vividly portray the event or the setting.

Marge wasn't a good pressure writer. She liked time to assimilate, to gather her thoughts, to devise her approach. Once she had a feel for the story she was a super writer.

Even then she liked the luxury of time so that she could go back and rework, shifting sentences, words, paragraphs … getting the flow and the thrust to her liking.

Her writing had a pleasing frankness. During her most recent health ordeal, she confessed that doctors scared her.

The homey everyday events in Marge's life were approached with a refreshing realism and her pen reflected that realism.

But she didn't like deadlines. Deadlines forced her to write when she wasn't ready to write, or to write things in such a way that she wasn't satisfied with her work.

She wrote an Iowegian column, and intended to crack the writing market – but so many problems came her way that she never really had a chance to devote all her talents and energy.

It was always refreshing to visit with Marge. She had a way of stripping away all the artificial, and despite all the trials and tribulations she faced, to see the humorous, the laughter and to find the joy.

She had an intimate acquaintance with personal tragedy, yet she maintained a spirit of optimism. And her writings reflected her realistic approach to life and despite all the monumental problems of health and family, a certain sunny disposition always seemed to be present.

At the Iowegian we're going to miss Marge – and, for sure, Iowegian readers are going to miss her.

Excerpts, Centerville Iowegian

To Marge – With Love

Quiet, soft-spoken, sweet and serene,
Endowed with charm and held in esteem,
By friend and acquaintances far and near,
One we cherished and held so dear.

She had such deep grief and burdens to bear,
Yet she encouraged others with wisdom to spare.
A lilt to her voice that belied sorrow,
She buried the past and looked toward the morrow.

Knowledgeable, concise and with dignity,
Each duty was performed with clarity.
Conscientiously doing her bit everyday,
We'll miss her presence in every way.

She touched many lives on the path she took,
This friend of ours who dwells with God.
May He grant us peace and serenity,
As we cherish this loved one's memory.
by Mary Robinson Klum, 1981, (Poem to Iowegian)

Ralph Waldo Emerson had this to say about happiness: "To laugh often and much; to win the respect of intelligent people and the affection of children; to find the best in others; to leave the world a little bit better whether by a healthy child, a garden patch, or a redeemed social condition; to know even one life has breathed easier because you have lived."

THE  END